AT
LARGE

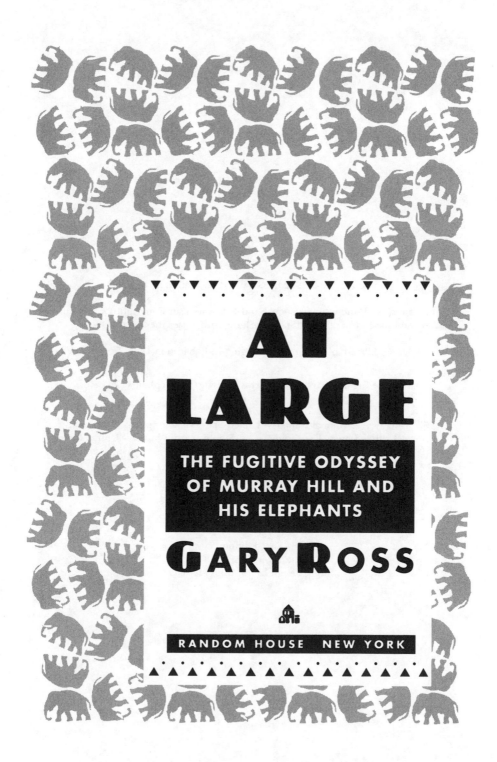

AT LARGE

THE FUGITIVE ODYSSEY OF MURRAY HILL AND HIS ELEPHANTS

GARY ROSS

RANDOM HOUSE   NEW YORK

Library of Congress Cataloging-in-Publication Data

Ross, Gary.
At large: the fugitive odyssey of Murray Hill and his elephants/Gary Ross.
p.   cm.
ISBN 0-679-40937-8
1. Hill, Murray.   2. Animal trainers—United States—Biography.   3. Elephants.
4. Larceny—United States—Case studies.   5. Fugitives from justice—United States—
Biography.   I. Title.
GV1831.E4R66   1992
636.088′8—dc20
[B]   91-53158

Manufactured in the United States of America
9 8 7 6 5 4 3 2
First Edition
Text set in Baskerville
Book design by Jo Anne Metsch

TO WANDA

ACKNOWLEDGMENTS

Without the extensive cooperation of Murray Hill and Dick Drake, their families, and their friends, I would have written a very different account of their obsessive dispute over the elephants Tory and Dutchess. I'm grateful to both men for the endless hours of interviews they granted me, the documentation and photographs they provided, and the calls they made to others to pave the way for me.

In the course of my research I interviewed a couple of hundred people—attorneys, circus folk, government agents, animal trainers, law-enforcement officials—and I thank them one and all. I'm especially grateful to those who took me into their confidence uncertain of my motives and fearing legal exposure if their role in the story were made public. A number of people gave me the benefit of their insights and recollections on condition that I not reveal their identities. Accordingly, although this is a work of nonfiction, I have used a few pseud-onyms and altered some telling details.

Brave and noble elephant! Why should you wish to wander free? Why should you wish to cross the valley and mountains? Look at this delightful place, this heavenly city!

—from an invocation delivered to captured white elephants on their installation in the court of the King of Siam

AT LARGE

PREFACE

I am very sorry to say that as of yesterday morning the girls were removed from my care and put under the control of the U.S. marshals. At this time I do not know what their fate will be. . . .
Murray Hill, in a letter, late 1989

▼ · ▼ · ▼ · ▼ · ▼ · ▼ · ▼ · ▼ · ▼ · ▼ · ▼ · ▼

He was an emaciated little man with dirty white hair to his shoulders and an unkempt beard that made him look nobly eccentric, like a cross between Jesus Christ and Father Christmas. His orange jumpsuit, comically oversized, engulfed him. The other prisoners, killing time at cards, feigning indifference, sneaked glances as the deputy sprung the lock and showed the man to his cell—the last empty cell in the unit.

"You got company," said the deputy, and the little man nodded politely in their direction. Among themselves they made low sounds of amused derision.

Most new prisoners were either nervously worried or else bursting with cocky braggadocio. This coot seemed unconcerned at landing in jail, perhaps even content. He walked with a limp and

▲ · ▲ · ▲ · ▲ · ▲ · ▲ · ▲ · ▲ · ▲ · ▲ · ▲ · ▲

brought to the unit a pungent zoo smell. His manner, as he took in his surroundings, was composed and unhurried, full of heroic implication. He was old enough to be their grandfather. While he set about making up his bunk, the others exchanged looks. Who was this little runt?

Murray, his name was. He hadn't been in the unit an hour when the deputy came back upstairs—"Murray, phone call"—and led him out. A few minutes later he had another call. Before long the sheriff himself was coming up to tell him there was a reporter from New Jersey phoning long distance and a camera crew from Shreveport wanting an interview. The sheriff's hair was neatly combed and he'd put on a clean white shirt.

This Murray was something, but what? Somebody had heard rumors of a serial killer arrested down Dallas way. You think so, man? The idea gave them the shivers. These kids were in for drug possession or car theft; one way or another, they knew, Murray played in a different league. He didn't look like a murderer, but who did? He had a deep, persuasive voice, and the same air of calm disregard you saw on guys who turned up on the newscast, hands cuffed, smirking as the charges against them were read out.

Later, after a supper of TV dinners, the biggest kid in the unit, a black teenager the others called Big Mike, lumbered over to the new man. Big Mike was a giant whose jumpsuit fit him like a sausage skin. Though he was twice Murray's size, Murray didn't seem fazed; he merely nodded as he ran water in the basin.

"Going to make bail?"

"My daughter's trying to sort that out," said Murray.

"Won't make it before Monday, now."

"Don't bother me none, except for the girls. I haven't had it this good in years."

"You been inside?"

"Hell, no. I've been on the road."

Big Mike looked to the others, who gestured subtly and nodded encouragement. Big Mike drew himself up to ask the question that, in jail, many people don't like to be asked.

"Why you here, man?"

"Because the justice system in this country ain't worth a shit," said Murray, washing his face.

"Everybody know that, man. Why'd they pick you up?"

"Grand theft."

"Oh, yeah? What'd you steal?"

"Two elephants," said Murray.

The others laughed and clapped. Big Mike, unsure if he was being made a fool of, said cautioningly, "What you telling me, man?"

"The court ordered me to turn the girls over to people who didn't treat them right, so I took off."

"The girls. You mean the elephants?"

Murray removed his teeth to rinse them. "That was five years ago, in New Jersey."

"You been hiding out with two elephants for five years?"

Murray stuck the bridge back in his mouth, making a face like a woman fixing her lipstick. "If we'd made it to Mexico, they never would have caught us. Somebody must have tipped them off."

"You ain't putting me on?"

Murray dried his hands on his jumpsuit. "What time's lockup?"

"Ten o'clock. Let me get it, man. You spent the last five years hiding out with two elephants?"

"Right," said Murray. "What time do they open the cells in the morning?"

"You ain't jamming us. You been on the run for five years with two elephants?"

"Tory and Dutchess. Female Asians." Murray's voice wavered and his eyes went moist. He turned aside, to collect himself. "Sure wish I knew what was going to happen to them now."

Big Mike shook his head. "I hide a gram of blow and they nail me, man. How do you hide two elephants?"

"Easier'n you think," said Murray, wiping his eyes. "Well,

goodnight, boys," he said to the others in the unit. "See you in the morning."

Big Mike lumbered after him, stopping at Murray's cell door. "Tell me one more thing, man. Why would anybody pull a crazy stunt like that?"

1

ELEPHANT MAN

The training and handling of an elephant are usually entrusted to one man, called the "mahout" in India and the "oozie" in Burma; an elephant and its keeper usually become inseparable and work together for the rest of their lives.
—Encyclopedia Britannica

▼ ▼ ▼ ▼ ▼ ▼ ▼ ▼ ▼ ▼ ▼ ▼ ▼

"Last ride!" Murray called to the few aimless shoppers who, waiting out the rain, had remained in the mall after the last performance of the weekend. Tory rumbled and Dutchess chirped in anticipation as they plodded in a circle back toward the loading platform; Onyx, out in the parking lot, bellered in reply. Murray helped the youngsters out of the howdahs. "See you next year, kids. The elephants figure it's time to go home."

It was a Sunday afternoon in 1980, the end of a four-day date in Illinois. Murray hadn't made much on the ride, but his producer's fee let him pay off the highwire act, the dog act, and the help, with something left over for himself. He and his helper pulled up the flooring and dismantled the ride platform. His helper used the Shop-Vac, emptied the garbage cans, and

▲ ▲ ▲ ▲ ▲ ▲ ▲ ▲ ▲ ▲ ▲ ▲ ▲

stacked the equipment while Murray backed the rig up to the entrance, attached the ramps, and loaded the elephants. It was dark by the time they headed south, toward the Ozarks and home.

Murray was glad to be leaving. Faintly bitter-smelling fluid had begun oozing from the vents above Onyx's eyes. The bull elephant was coming into musth and it was best to get him out of there. Musth was unpredictable. Some years Onyx drained more freely than others, but until recently he had never been unruly or aggressive. The past two musths had brought changes. The draining had grown more profuse. His eyes glazed over, as if he were in a trance. If you came near, to feed or water or shovel up after him, you sensed his altered temperament. With elephants you had to take care at all times, but with males in musth you had to be especially cautious. At the mall, Onyx had begun tracking people with his eyes, and he'd taken a swing at one of the performers. Murray knew of enough people killed by bulls in musth that he was happy to be leaving Illinois without incident. In the past year alone, his friend Eloise Berchtold had been killed in Quebec, and Morgan Berry had been taken by his bull in Oregon.

Kept alert by caffeine and the roaring vibration of the rig, Murray drove into the night. He loved trucking through darkness, snug in the cab, playing the force of the engine against the tremendous shifting load he was pulling. After midnight the oncoming cars thinned out; there was nothing but the yellow tunnel he cut for himself in the darkness. Making money with the elephants was tougher each year, but at least you were your own boss, always on the move, the last of the blacktop Bedouins.

Just before dawn, approaching St. Louis, he got on the CB—"Breaker-breaker one nine, anybody out there?"—and learned that the scale on the interstate was open. Scale men acted as if they earned commissions; on an older rig loaded with eleven tons of elephants they were sure to find some violation to write up. Murray turned onto Route 50. Best avoid the bastards.

Stopping only for gas and tobacco, he made it to his farm,

near Fordland, Missouri, in mid-morning. From the door of the mobile home, Denise greeted him in her slurred, faintly ironic way. It was painful watching the disintegration of someone you loved; it was infuriating, too. How many times had he asked her to get help? Why couldn't she see she had a problem, and do something about it?

Maybe moving down from Wisconsin had been tougher on her than he'd realized. She'd always enjoyed getting out and seeing people. Up there, when he was on the road, she visited her mother or sister to have lunch or play euchre. When he came off the road, ready to sit and do nothing, she didn't go stir-crazy. Now she had nobody to do things with. Robin and Nada were long gone, the twins were busy with school, and Denise didn't go to church, or to work, or anyplace else you make friends. Bored and lonely, she sat in the trailer all day, glass in hand.

But the road was where the money was, and he'd had to go back out when their safari park failed. There hadn't been much choice. Same with the move: economics. Energy costs went up every year. Missouri was central, an easy hop to just about anywhere, and the winter was milder. The twenty acres in Wisconsin wasn't really enough for all the animals, especially after the town had crept right out to their property line. Besides, their mobile home had been falling apart. A grandfather clause allowed them to keep it, but they couldn't put a new one on the property, and Murray sure as hell wasn't going to build a house, even if they could have afforded one. When you figure they got $100,000 for a place that had cost $20,000—well, the time had been right to move on, that's all.

After unloading the elephants, cleaning out the rig, and checking the chimpanzees, mangabey monkeys, dogs, and ponies in the barn, Murray went into the trailer. Denise was watching television. At the sound of the door she set down her glass.

"How much you bring home?"

"Not much. Lousy weather. Where the boys?"

She stubbed out her cigarette. "Where do you think?"

School, of course—summer holidays were over.

Murray thumbed through the mail, which she hadn't opened. Denise lit another cigarette, triggering her hoarse cough. Sometimes he could hardly believe this was the same person he'd married. Of course, she could have said the same thing, remembering the little accordion player who'd been managing the club where she had worked as a dancer. The Cat Girl, she'd called herself. Beautiful woman, and sharp as a tack. He'd liked her at once, but what a young woman baptized in the Evangelical Lutheran Church must have thought of a short, brash Jew from Brooklyn . . .

They were the same age, shared many interests, recognized in each other a certain independence of mind. He knew how to talk and say nothing but she'd have none of it; he found himself telling her things he told nobody else. After she left to play Louisville, they spoke so often that Murray, feeding in handfuls of change, joked about buying stock in AT & T.

Eighteen months after they met he invited her to Connecticut, where his parents had opened an auto-parts store. Denise liked Murray's father, but saw at once the disapproval in his mother's bright eyes. Shirley Seidon was a tiny woman, devoted to her husband, prim and hard to please. Her relationship with Murray, the elder of her two sons, was complex and difficult. She adored him and would go to any length for him despite being highly critical of the life he was leading. Denise longed for acceptance, but even after converting to Judaism she could feel the resentment. When she and Murray drove off, she knew his mother would never forgive her.

Shirley, of course, put on her best face. Arlan—or Murray, as his agent, who had a Murray Hill telephone exchange, had insisted he call himself—was an adult, he could do as he pleased, but who would have thought your firstborn could cause such heartache? Had she and Bernie made a mistake, buying the twelve-base accordion, encouraging his talent, paying for lessons in the Empire State Building? That was fine for a teenager, but a career in show business, with its slippery characters and uncertain air? He could have gone into business like his father, or one of the professions. ("Maybe you can talk sense to him," she told Denise, "make him see there's no security in it." "You've been trying for twenty-four years," said Denise. "Have you had any luck?") And to think that a young man with so much going for him would even look twice at a bleached blonde who took money for waving her fanny at men in bars.

The honeymoon was three days on a vaudeville stage in Baltimore. From there they booked together, playing Minnesota, Montana, and Colorado, often just the two of them, the Cat Girl dancing, Murray doing standup and playing requests on his accordion. For winter they headed south. Back then, Phoenix and Albuquerque were in the middle of nowhere, and the travel added up. Who cared? They were having the time of their lives, seeing all the states, meeting people, you and me against the world. . . .

Could it really have been almost thirty years? In the glow from the television Murray studied his wife's profile, the still-delicate line of her cheekbone and jaw, the fine tendrils of hair, silver now, that defied the elastic band. Overcome by love and longing, he stepped outside.

"Where you going, Murray?"

He was going where he went when he needed to think. To the barn, and the company of the elephants.

Murray was repairing a harness when the twins spilled out of the school bus and came running to greet him. Tory and Dutchess squealed and trumpeted gleefully, extending their trunks to sniff the boys and be petted. Onyx didn't stir, just stared dully.

"He's in musth," said Murray. "Keep your distance."

Funny, they could land people on the moon but they'd never figured out musth. Because it put bull elephants in a state resembling rut in an elk—single-minded and dangerous—some people figured it was connected to the reproductive cycle. Not so, at least not directly. A bull's testosterone level shot up, all right, but he didn't try to breed. Instead he asserted himself, seeking to dominate the herd and run off challengers. Some bulls had their first musth as early as age six, others not until they were fifteen. Onyx was sixteen years old and had started at age eight. One musth might be severe, the next one mild or even more severe—there was no telling. Once a bull reached thirty-five or so, musth started to recede again.

Watching his sons feed the elephants, Murray felt great satisfaction. They were young men now, clear-eyed and broad-shouldered, shaving, tinkering with engines, talking about girls. Soon they'd be out on their own, like their sisters. Once Robin had hit her teens, she couldn't get out fast enough, and Nada had first run away at age twelve. Maybe he had demanded too much of them, making them work the dog act and the trapeze at an age when other girls were playing with dolls. What the hell, everybody has to learn what life is about sooner or later. Even if they had grown up early, they'd had good childhoods. They'd simply decided they didn't want to hang upside down by the knees. Fair enough—just so long as they knew he'd be there if they needed him.

Would Adam and Allan be as eager to leave? Would there just be their mother to come home to?

Denise had managed to get a chicken in the oven, then forgotten it. The trailer filled with smoke. Miracle she'd never burned the place down. Adam and Allan salvaged the supper, and Murray felt such pride he was nearly moved to tears. He'd tried to teach all the kids self-reliance; it was stirring to see their maturity. During supper they wanted to hear all about Onyx's musth and the Illinois date. Afterward they watched *Wheel of Fortune* with their mother while Murray went over the bills. By the time he went to bed, happy for the luxury of sheets, Denise was out cold.

In the morning, when he awoke, there was no need to worry about disturbing her. She was lost to the world. When she did come around, her delirium would be painful to witness, her shakes uncontrollable until she'd quelled them—and begun the next assault—with two inches of vodka from a half-gallon jug. The twins had already made sandwiches and left for school. Murray lit a Camel, poured coffee, and headed out.

In the pungent dimness of the barn, the girls were racking in silent unison, swaying and dipping like backup singers in a Motown band. They greeted him, blowing and squeaking. Onyx fixed Murray with a glazed stare, not moving his massive head. Murray filled the water pails—Tory, as usual, wanted to drink from the hose—then shoveled the night's droppings.

It was a fine September morning, a hint of Ozark autumn in the air. What sense keeping them cooped up? Murray undid their leg chains and led them out. He'd planned on building a corral ever since the move from Wisconsin but had never found time. Instead, he'd strung a forty-foot chain between two oaks and run leads off it. The elephants weren't free, exactly, but it was better than chaining them in the barn. He hitched them up in turn—Onyx, Tory, Dutchess—then fetched a bale of hay. Toting it back down the hill, he realized he should have grabbed his hook. He hadn't used an elephant hook in years, but it was a potent symbol, and with Onyx in musth . . .

Murray split the bale into flakes and tossed one to each elephant. Rather than taking his own, Onyx reached over and snatched Tory's. Every challenge, every little test, had to be met —give a bull an inch and you'll never get it back. "You old son of a bitch," Murray said, patting Onyx's front leg as he reached down to retrieve the hay. Rising, he found himself looking Onyx in the eye, and deep within that dull, glassy saucer, in the instant it happened, he saw his mistake and knew there was nothing he could do—saw the huge head drop but, strangely, didn't feel the ivory, only the sensation of being as high as the fork in the oak tree; he was fifteen feet off the ground, facing the sky, and then he couldn't breathe, he was face down in gravel, manure, and oak leaves, stunned and yet aware of being under Onyx's jaw, between the pillarlike front legs. Numb and disoriented, the wind so violently knocked from him it seemed he'd never breathe again, he registered his predicament not as panic but as simple fact: if you don't get out, you're dead.

Onyx seemed to have lost track of him. The bull raised his trunk, testing the air, before sensing that Murray was beneath him. He backed up, lowered his head, and plunged. Murray felt the good tusk tear into the earth beside him. The other tusk had broken off and been capped. But for that, he would have been impaled.

Get out!

My left side, can't feel a thing. Always knew it was coming, hoped I'd be prepared . . .

Still he hadn't breathed—if the bull didn't get him, he'd die in agonized suffocation. So this was what it was like, the Great White One, and yet, somehow, by the time he became aware of the metallic chink of chains and the swish of Onyx's trunk, he had, using his good elbow, managed to half-roll, half-drag himself just beyond range. The chain was of light gauge and Onyx could have brought it down—hell, he could almost have brought the oak trees down—but elephants don't know their strength. When he ran out of chain, he just glared.

Safe now, unleashing an inward scream, like a diver surfacing, Murray felt piercing pain in his side and chest, and heard a terrible noise, loud and ragged; he wondered what it could be. The pain and the noise were connected. The noise began to take on rhythm, and he realized with surprise that it was his own breathing. He sounded like a straining, amplified, leaky bellows. In shock, adrenaline coursing, he managed to get to his feet and stumble up the hill toward the propane tank. Sensation was returning to his left side, and he was able to pull himself up onto the tank. Then someone who helped out at the farm was hurrying down from his trailer, alarmed, calling, "Hey! You all right? What happened?"

"Onyx," Murray said, and passed out.

Despite the contusions, the bloody ankle and fractured ribs, Murray didn't blame the bull; the attack had been his own fault. Even allowing Onyx out of the barn had been idiocy. How could he have been so dumb? So complacent? He'd known all along Onyx would become a problem. Most elephant men wouldn't go near a bull in musth, not unless they'd hit him with narcotics.

In bed, trying to find a posture that didn't hurt, Murray realized he was not the same man who'd begun importing animals, twenty years earlier, from a dealer in Bangkok. Nor could he help recalling how much simpler life had been back then. That was before Asian elephants had gone on the Endangered Species List, before anyone used the word "exotic" to describe a species, before you had to answer to inspectors who didn't know shit from shinola and monitored your every move. It was before you spent half your time dealing with bureaucracy—Customs and Excise, Fish and Wildlife, Department of the Interior, Department of Agriculture, federal and state departments of transport, on and on. It was before anyone had heard of animal liberation—hell, it was before anyone had heard of women's liberation. Back then you booked as many carnivals and openings and circuses as you could, working like a Trojan but making decent money. Now you had to fill out so many goddamn permits, pay so much duty, and undergo so many tests and inspections you were lucky to juggle half as many dates. It was still a good life if you were young and energetic, but Murray, hurt and cranky, felt every one of his fifty years. His best days were behind him. For months he'd been toying with the idea of getting out; this clinched it.

Denise, bless her, pulled herself together, taking him to the doctor, heating soup, being there when he awoke.

"You were dreaming."

"He wants me real bad."

"You're lucky it wasn't worse."

"Always said, I hope I'm smart enough to know when it's coming. . . ."

"Try to get some rest."

Rest was difficult. Denise was terrified of Onyx, and Murray was uneasy himself. He should have been out there disciplining him. Challenged, a trainer must quickly reestablish supremacy. But how? He was in no shape to take on the bull.

Elephants were like kids—you didn't notice them growing when you were with them every day. When Onyx had come in from Thailand, in 1965, he couldn't have been more than a year old, standing thirty-three inches at the high point of his back. When Murray took him on the road with the girls—the Mitie Mites, "the world's smallest performing elephant act"— the three of them weighed a combined 965 pounds. Onyx was from the Assam Valley, east of Bengal in northern India. He was a handsome little punk; his stocky symmetry made him a Kumariah ("princely and strong-bodied"), the most esteemed build in an Asian elephant. A couple of years later the dealer who'd shipped him from Bangkok visited Murray in Wisconsin. At the time, Murray had a dozen elephants on the line, and Onyx was five times his shipping size, yet Mr. Singh recognized him at once. "My elephant," he said proudly. "Good-looking. I remember."

Onyx's personality, too, was unforgettable. He hated midgets —if one came too near, watch out. If a woman in a dress got too close, his trunk snaked out and went up under the dress—a blast of air, and how that woman jumped! In the ring, when Onyx did a stand-up, he figured the act wasn't complete unless he shot out his penis and got a reaction. Murray would crack his whip, and Onyx would restrain himself for a few shows. Then he'd do it again, and the audience would snicker and laugh.

Onyx also had an uncanny way with electricity. Murray took the chains off whenever he could, keeping the elephants in check with a hot-line. When Onyx wanted out, he simply snapped it. The next-door neighbor had a cornfield, and one day the elephants took out the fence and demolished an acre of corn. Murray tattooed them, and they hurried back through the opening. While he repaired the fence, they protested vigorously. A bonanza over there, and we stay here? Outrageous! Unjust! For half an hour they kept it up, fussing and complaining.

Onyx seemed to have learned his lesson, but the girls couldn't resist temptation. A few days later, alerted by Onyx's bellowing, Murray again found the fence down and the girls in the cornfield. He smacked them and moved them out. Onyx, on the proper side of the fence, interrupted his browsing just long enough to give them the disdainful look an honors student might bestow on truants.

It happened twice in a week. Then it happened twice the same afternoon. The girls always ended up in the corn, and Onyx always ratted on them. Murray couldn't figure it out. Next morning, after fixing the fence, he set off for the far end of the property and doubled back through the woods, downwind. He climbed a cottonwood near the cornfield and waited.

It wasn't long before the puzzle was solved. Onyx glanced about furtively, picked up a branch, dropped it on the line, and stepped on it, breaking the wire. That allowed him to grip the fencepost without getting shocked. Effortlessly he ripped out the section of fence, then stood gallantly aside for the girls, who couldn't resist the corn. Once they'd begun tearing up the patch, Onyx started bellowing. Come quick! Look what the girls are doing! Here am I, blameless as sunshine.

When Murray dropped from the tree, the girls' eyes almost popped. Elephants, unlike horses, have only one gait, a walk, and when the girls headed smartly for the break in the fence their droopy bottoms made them look, from the rear, like comedians in baggy pants. Murray ushered them through and disciplined them, but not before he'd given the bull a piece of his mind. That was Onyx in a nutshell—the instigator feigning innocence.

Wincing, Murray reached for the water glass by his bed. No point dredging up memories. Onyx had to be dealt with. Not yet fully grown—elephants, like people, often live to their seventies—the bull stood nine feet and weighed almost four and a half tons. If he rampaged, the barn wouldn't hold him. Something had to be done, and quick. Maybe fortify the barn with steel?

Who'd do the work? Murray felt as if he'd been hit by a bus. Drawing breath was painful. Even if he'd been in good health, he didn't have time. In a week he was due in Media, Pennsylvania, last date of the season. He couldn't take Onyx, that was certain. Who knew how long the musth would last? Two or three weeks, probably, but there was no fixed time, no fixed length. Sometimes musth came on more than once a year. What right did he have risking other people's lives? Or Onyx's life, for that matter? If the attack had happened in public, the bull would have been destroyed.

No, he couldn't take Onyx, and couldn't leave him at the farm. Who'd handle him? Denise hadn't been able to get around him in years. The twins? They were good boys, steady workers, but only fourteen. Selling Onyx almost guaranteed that he'd sooner or later be destroyed. It was bad timing—who wants a bull in musth?—but he had to find a zoo to take him.

The zoo at Springfield, Missouri, was a decent bet. Springfield was elephant-crazy and Dale Tuttle, the young director, had transformed a formerly dismal place into a respectable facility. A nonprofit society, Friends of the Zoo, was taking over the animal collection, which meant Onyx wouldn't be in the control of city politicians, whom Murray despised on principle.

Murray called Dale to ask for help. Never having had a bull in musth, Dale found Onyx a terrifying sight, and couldn't help noticing his chain. It was worn from being dragged on concrete, and it wasn't made of tensile steel. If Murray got within a hundred feet, Onyx lunged. When Dale went inside for a chat, he suddenly became aware of the flimsiness of a mobile home.

Murray hinted that he'd have to put Onyx down if he couldn't get rid of him. Dale said Dickerson Park wasn't looking to acquire a bull but that he was heading to Chicago for an international zoo conference and would ask around. If Murray would hold off, maybe they could find a taker. When they went back out, the mere sound of Murray's voice brought Onyx charging.

"Lucky he's always been on chains and accepts them."

"You're telling me," said Murray.

At the conference, Dale found that other zoo directors had no interest in a bull in musth, especially one tethered in the woods. At the farm, meanwhile, Onyx was growing even more brazen and bellicose. In desperation, Murray phoned Dale's hotel.

When Dale reported the bad news, Murray said, "All right, look. I'm leaving soon and I got to settle this. When you get back tomorrow, can you bring narcotics?"

"You're going to put him down?"

A bluff, and it worked. Dale asked for a few more days and set about getting the local politicians onside. By mid-week he had municipal approval. McDonald's agreed to put up some money, provided Onyx's name was changed to Big Mac, and Murray arranged to make the donation to Friends of the Zoo. He called Mike Schmidt, an elephant expert at Washington Park Zoo in Portland, Oregon, who suggested the best way of drugging and chaining the bull. Dale brought a crew out to the farm. Using a dart rifle, sticking Onyx where his hide was thinnest—the inside of his front leg—they got enough xylazine hydrochloride into him to knock him out. Everybody felt better when Murray had him securely chained. They waited for Onyx to come out of musth and, while Murray was off playing Pennsylvania with the girls, trucked him away. The twins, who had stayed home from school, cried to see him go.

Onyx would become part of the breeding program at Dickerson Park Zoo, but he'd be owned by a nonprofit organization. The place had proper facilities and he'd have other elephants for company. Murray would get the ivory any time they cut his tusks, and a fee for any calf Onyx sired. Best of all, anytime they wanted to see him, he was only twenty miles away.

At Cape Girardeau, Missouri, across the state from Murray's farm, Dave Hale and his brother, Bob, were planning their second annual exotic-animal auction at their 5-H Ranch. The previous fall, Murray knew, people had come from almost every state and several foreign countries. When he got back from Pennsylvania, he phoned Dave and said he'd decided to sell Tory and Dutchess.

"What are you looking to get for them?"

"Forty thousand each, but I'd rather they stay together. I might take seventy-five for the pair."

Dave said he'd charge a five percent commission. Because he'd had no elephants at the first auction, however, and because Murray's price was the highest ever asked for Asians, he doubted there would be many potential buyers.

"That's all right," said Murray. "It'll help get word out that they're on the market."

The twins loved going on the road with their father. They were at that age when every outing is an adventure, when motels are castles and burgers make a banquet. What was a day or two of school? They helped their Dad ready the rig and load the girls—as well as some turkeys and exotic chickens—and off they went, keeping to back roads to avoid the weigh scale.

The 5-H Ranch was a huge tent, half a dozen buildings, and hundreds of pens on 152 acres. The auction had a partylike atmosphere; owners and dealers and circus people were streaming in from far and wide. The circus is an exclusive club of nomads and misfits with a language and a mythology of their own. You belong or you don't. Murray's sons had seen Disney World from the highway many times, but their father had never taken them in. It would have violated his principles. Only suckers paid admission.

Elephant men are a specialized cell within that subculture, idiosyncratic characters with names like Slim and Mac and Smokey, Bucky and Buckles and Rex. By experience or hearsay they know the personalities of scores of the roughly 350 Asian elephants in North America. From a thriving grapevine they know which ones have recently died or grown unruly or changed hands. Murray was part of this network, but not fully so. No other elephant man was a Jew, for one thing—a Hebe, some called him—and his incarnations as nightclub comic, animal importer, and circus producer diluted his reputation as a trainer. He wore a silver elephant-head belt buckle he'd got from Slim Lewis in return for a piece of Onyx's ivory. Slim, a legendary trainer, had given him the buckle on two conditions: that he never sell it, and that he pass it on to someone else who had worked with bull elephants. Yet when Slim published a photo of the Polack Circus herd in his book, Murray—who'd been in charge of the herd at the time—was cropped out of the picture.

Now, Murray maneuvered the rig into the spot assigned him and checked in. At the registration area, a woman took down particulars of his stock while an officer from the Missouri Department of Conservation looked on. The officer, a craggy-faced man in an open-necked shirt, asked if Murray had a permit for the turkeys. Murray said he did, but not with him. The officer took his name, made a call, and told him he was under arrest: the old permit had expired. The officer rounded up more violators and ran them down to court. They were fined $70 apiece and made to buy $25 permits.

And people asked Murray why he was getting out of the business? Shit. Every time you turned around you got shaken down. Not long before, near the Iowa border, he'd been ambushed at a weigh scale. The federal Department of Transportation had been out that day, and they went over the rig with a fine-tooth comb, looking for any violation—headlights, running lights, clearance lights, pancakes on the brakes, log book, oil pressure, anything.

The DOT inspector was a green kid who politely told Murray to bleed the air out; from zero pressure, you had so many seconds to come up to seventy pounds. Every tractor-trailer has an alarm that goes off when the air pressure drops below sixty pounds, and an automatic brake-locking system that kicks in at thirty pounds. Murray's rig had a visual air-pressure indicator. A little flag dropped from the ceiling of the cab. It had never worked properly, and Murray had bent it to hold it in place. The DOT inspector waited as Murray bled the air out.

"I didn't hear a buzzer."

"It's the little flag here. It don't work right."

"You're red-tagged."

Meaning he couldn't move the rig. Murray, already running late, blew a fuse, calling the inspector every four-, ten-, and twelve-letter name he could think of, shouting in the man's face, aching to slug him but knowing better than to take the first swing. After a while he calmed down.

"I'm red-tagged? Fine. If we're staying here, I'm letting the elephants out for some exercise."

"Elephants? Wait a minute. You can't unload here."

"It's ninety-five degrees and it's even hotter in there. They need to cool off."

"If you want to water them, fine, but you can't let them out of the trailer. Understand? And you're not going anywhere until that indicator's fixed."

Murray adopted a conciliatory tone. "I don't have the right tools, but I'll tell you what. There's a truckstop eleven miles from here, on the Iowa side. I'll get it fixed there. I've got an endangered species and it's goddamn hot. I'm worried about them."

"Can't do it, sir."

"You checked the air—disengaged it, put your own gauge on, pumped it up again. The system itself works fine. It's just the emergency indicator."

"Book says you're red-tagged."

The elephants had started racking, shaking the trailer from side to side. Some of the pancakes were flat, the fifth wheel needed repairs, and now the shocks were going. It never ended.

"Screw the book," said Murray. "I can't get anybody out here right now. You've got forty rigs tied up with Mickey Mouse violations and every mechanic in the area's busy."

"Way it is, sir." The inspector walked away.

Watering the elephants, Murray had an idea. He opened the trailer and began shoveling manure onto the parking lot. By the time somebody came running to give him hell, a big mound was cooking on the hot asphalt. Other drivers gave the rig a wide berth as they walked to and from the booth.

Murray knew that at five o'clock the federal DOT people would be going home; they had to resolve this one way or another. At ten minutes to the hour he went in and explained the problem to the state weighmaster, suggesting the weighmaster call his superior. The weighmaster dialed, spoke in a low voice, and handed the receiver to Murray.

"You the elephant man?"

"That's right."

"You're two miles from the border?"

"That's right."

"Climb into your rig, get those elephants out of here, and don't cross my scales again. Understand?"

"Tell it to them DOT pricks. What do you think I've been trying to do for the last four hours?"

Government jerks. They were all over—on the highways, at the farm, in shopping malls. Here, the auction was crawling with them. Saturday morning, after sleeping in the trailer with the girls, Murray was tinkering with the water system and the twins were shoveling manure when a clean-cut young fellow with a briefcase cleared his throat. Many old cronies had stopped by, but this was no friend. He wore a look of official politeness.

"You in charge of the elephants?"

A question Murray had been asked many times—it usually meant trouble. The curious generally fell into one of four categories: elephant-simple members of the public, looking for a ride or a picture; do-gooders from the local Society for the Prevention of Cruelty to Animals; state agents, from Fish and Wildlife or the Department of Conservation; or federal agents, from the U.S. Department of Agriculture or the U.S. Department of the Interior. From his tone of voice and collegiate look, this kid was a fed.

"Why you asking?" said Murray.

"I'd like to see your papers."

"Who are you?"

The fellow held his wallet so that it fell open. "Department of the Interior."

Murray had even more paperwork on the elephants than on the rig. He kept it in the cab, but damned if he was going to cooperate. These people were in the business of making life difficult; least he could do was return the favor. He scribbled on a piece of paper.

"Here's my name and address."

"What about those papers?"

Tory and Dutchess both chose this moment to empty their bladders and void their bowels. Trying to carry on a conversation was like trying to talk over the roar of Niagara Falls. Murray waited for the deluge to cease. Tory, munching hay, glanced over her shoulder at the inspector and let loose a final, prolonged, flapping cacophony of gas.

"My papers?" said Murray, scratching his chin. "Well, see, I consider my documents so valuable I keep them under lock and key at home."

The young man chose to overlook the ill-concealed sarcasm. "Don't you even carry photostats?"

"Call your office," said Murray, taking up his wrench and resuming work. "They'll have the information."

"You do understand," said the young fellow, "you can't sell those animals unless you produce your papers."

The twins were taking this in, and Murray decided to show them how to deal with government officials. Looking the young fellow in the eye, he slapped the wrench into his open palm— once, twice—and said, "I haven't sold a thing, you jerk. Now what's your problem?"

Later that day a short, dark-haired woman introduced herself: Bunny Brook, from Dawn Animal Agency in New York. She and her sister booked exotic animals for films, television, and commercials, and supplied the animals for the Radio City Music Hall Christmas show. They had an office in Manhattan, and a farm in New Jersey with more than five hundred animals, including camels, bears, monkeys, llamas, zebras, birds, and big cats.

Murray glanced at her as she talked. She wasn't pretty, but close enough to keep you off balance. There was a Middle Eastern quality about her. Though she looked frazzled and tired, with lines beneath her eyes, something strong came through. She was her own person.

He jerked his attention back to what she was saying. Either

she was exaggerating or she had serious money to support such a big operation. As well as the agency, she said, they had a nonprofit foundation that took in abused and neglected animals. Donations helped defray costs.

She said she might be interested in another elephant. She had two: a young female African and a ten-year-old female Asian. The Asian had been wounded in Vietnam; when they got her, she'd been in tough shape, with terrible open wounds. After healing her, they'd been able to work her for a couple of years. Then one day she'd become frightened on a city street and they'd had trouble getting her back in the trailer. She'd become a hay burner, costly and unmanageable, and Bunny got enough calls for elephants that she was looking to buy another.

"Tell me about this one. She's a dear."

"That's Tory. She's the little old lady who worries about everything, especially her next meal. You can trust her with anyone. Dutchess is a big klutz who wants to be a dainty little miss. She'll work her tail off for you, but don't ever turn your back on her."

Tory sniffed Bunny curiously, losing interest when she found nothing to eat. Not many women handled elephants, and Murray was impressed by Bunny's manner. He asked about her facilities; she said she used sea containers to house her elephants. She examined the girls carefully and went through the rig, admiring the way it had been fitted with self-contained water, steel reinforcement, and an electrical system. She had a distracted air but seemed to be serious and to know what she was doing. When she asked how much he wanted for Tory, he said he'd prefer not to split them up.

The girls were scheduled to be auctioned on Sunday morning; the idea was to give them exposure beforehand. All day Saturday, while Dave sold off cougar, deer, camels, llamas, jaguars, eland, elk, and buffalo, people stopped to ask about Tory and Dutchess. On Sunday morning, before putting them up for auction, Dave suggested Murray provide a little history.

Murray took the mike and told the crowd of five hundred that Dutchess was from Thailand and had come into the country in 1964. Back then, she stood thirty inches at the high point of her back, and she'd stayed on the bottle two years. Tory, he figured, was two years older—nineteen. She was from Burma and already off the bottle when they got her. With Onyx, they had formed the Mitie Mites, making their debut at the Shrine Circus in Fort Wayne, Indiana, as the youngest elephants to perform in circus history. . . .

As Murray reeled off this information, his mind wandered back through the years. Tory'd always been sweet and easygoing—he'd never seen an elephant quite like her. All she cared about was food. You never had to worry, she let anybody pet her. She wasn't the best worker—goofed off at every opportunity—but her sweet disposition made up for her laziness.

Dutchess, on the other hand, had a sly, nasty streak. She was a fine worker, though, and she'd saved his bacon more than once. You never know what might spook an elephant; stampedes have been triggered by a scrap of paper. Usually if one elephant goes, they all follow. In Denver, Dutchess had stopped what could have been a disastrous stampede simply by not running with the rest. Mind you, if she didn't want you around she might pop you. Push her too hard and she might take off. Murray smiled at the memory of some drunken Shriners—couldn't have happened to nicer guys. Before the show one afternoon, two fez-headed idiots had spotted the girls, still small, browsing on the back lot. When the Shriners started across the field, Murray, watching from a friend's trailer, went to the door: "Hey! Don't go near them elephants. You might get hurt."

"Those babies?"

"You think I'm kidding? Dutchess'll take you."

Murray went back inside, glancing out just in time to see Dutchess lower her head and butt the fat one, who was trying to pet her; as he staggered backward, the other Shriner, suddenly sober, turned to flee. She caught him with her trunk, square in the face, knocking him on his can. He sat in the dirt, openmouthed, like a kid so shocked he hasn't started to cry. Murray couldn't resist going back to the door, a twinkle in his eye: "Last time I'm going to warn you: don't go near the elephants."

Telling the crowd about the girls, Murray realized he was getting worked up. Sure they were good girls. Sure they'd been his meal ticket and his closest companions for twenty years. Sure they meant more to him than most people he'd come across. He was selling them. He handed the mike to Dave and stepped down.

As expected, interest in the girls was halfhearted. Only four people made bids. Dave explained that the top bid—$21,000 apiece—fell short of the reserve, and he moved on to macaws, cockatoos, pheasants, and peacocks.

The twins were delighted that the girls were going home; Murray was both disappointed and relieved. All in all, the trip had been worthwhile. They'd got a good price for their turkeys and chickens. The industry now knew the girls were for sale, and the twins would be full of stories for their mother.

And maybe this Bunny Brook would prove to be a useful contact. Heading home, bouncing along in the cab while the girls racked in the trailer, Murray found himself thinking of her. Something about her he liked, something good and caring. You could see how deeply she felt for all creatures. The Dawn agency often got calls for elephants, she'd said, and she'd keep him in mind. If you get up New Jersey way, stop in and say hi. Let's keep in touch. . . .

Adam asked what he'd do with Tory and Dutchess if nobody bought them. A zoo, like Onyx? Murray said he wouldn't have put the bull in a zoo if he'd had a choice. "Training may be hard on an animal—maybe the little old ladies in tennis shoes have a point—but it's better than letting them mope around." Without training, he told his sons, wild animals tended to be listless and depressed, zoo idiots. Trained animals that went to zoos often became troublemakers. Suddenly there was no variety in sights and odors. Looking to relieve the monotony, they got into mischief. A zoo was no place for Tory and Dutchess.

"What about a circus?" said Adam.

Most trainers knew what they were doing, but the help was another story. Like the backstretch at a racetrack, the circus drew scarred knuckles and sweaty necks, drifters who worked just long enough to put together a stake. The turnover was constant. Murray didn't want the girls handled by a succession of people who didn't know the first thing about elephants.

"Maybe an animal park?" said Allan.

"I doubt it," said Murray. "They like Africans."

With their greater size, gigantic ears, sloping foreheads, and massive tusks, Africans are most people's image of an elephant. But they're more difficult to train than Asians, high-strung and flighty, like thoroughbreds compared to draft horses. Until a few decades ago, they were thought to be all but untrainable. Animal parks generally kept Africans for show. If they needed trained Asians, for performances or rides, they booked independent owners like himself.

An animal dealer? Never. Having dealt in exotics himself, importing everything from chimpanzees, rhesus monkeys, marmosets, and orangutans to parrots, cheetahs, lions, and llamas —as well as fifty or sixty elephants over the years—Murray knew the economic imperatives. You sold to anybody who could pay. Who could say where the girls might end up?

Which left a private owner, someone who knew elephants, had proper facilities, and wouldn't separate the girls. The way to find such a buyer was to advertise, and the place to advertise was in a little publication based in El Cerrito, California. Don Marcks had started *Circus Report* in 1972 and built it into an indispensable weekly of gossip, information, and advertising: "Auction of the Unusual—10 Juke Boxes, 20 Slots, 60 Genuine Carousel Horses." "The Flying Vasquez—Miguel's impossible quadruple somersault to brother Juan—bookings through Shumaker Artists Talent Agency." "Smuggler Caught—A Japanese businessman has been convicted of attempting to smuggle 283 protected lizards from Thailand to Japan in suitcases." Though slim and cheaply produced, *Circus Report* was the industry bible. Murray had used it to sell exotic stock; they'd always done a good job of laying out the ads. He reached Don and read the wording over the phone.

"Sounds like you're serious about quitting the business."

"Hell, my bull took me and I've been moaning for months. I'm getting old."

"That's a pretty good chunk you want from somebody."

True enough—not many prospective buyers would be able to write a check for $75,000. "Good point, Don. Let's stick this at the end of the ad: 'Will finance right party.'"

2

THE FALL GUY

Dad did what he did because of his feelings for the girls, but there was another emotion behind it as well. Guilt, for selling to the wrong people.
Murray Hill's daughter, Robin

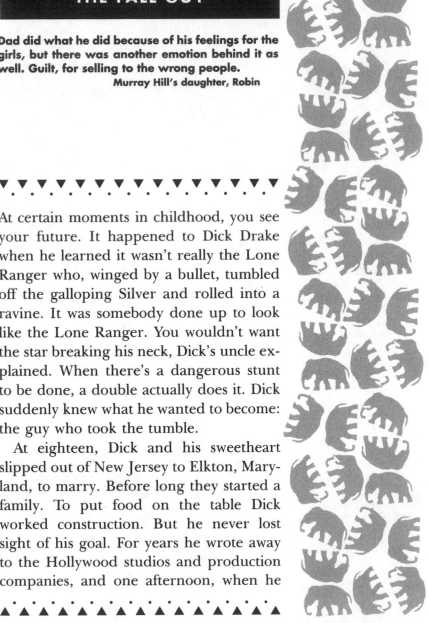

At certain moments in childhood, you see your future. It happened to Dick Drake when he learned it wasn't really the Lone Ranger who, winged by a bullet, tumbled off the galloping Silver and rolled into a ravine. It was somebody done up to look like the Lone Ranger. You wouldn't want the star breaking his neck, Dick's uncle explained. When there's a dangerous stunt to be done, a double actually does it. Dick suddenly knew what he wanted to become: the guy who took the tumble.

At eighteen, Dick and his sweetheart slipped out of New Jersey to Elkton, Maryland, to marry. Before long they started a family. To put food on the table Dick worked construction. But he never lost sight of his goal. For years he wrote away to the Hollywood studios and production companies, and one afternoon, when he got home, he found a reply from a stunt show. He walked into the kitchen beaming from ear to ear.

"Honey, it's the chance we've been waiting for. We're going to California."

It was 1966, the year of Richard Speck's mass murder in Chicago, the first widespread protest over U.S. policies in Vietnam, and John Lennon's remark that the Beatles were more popular than Christ. *Valley of the Dolls* was a best-seller; moviegoers lined up to see *Doctor Zhivago*. In Cleveland, Baltimore, Jersey City, and other American cities, blacks rioted. The Southwest was booming; the Northeast, enfeebled by social and economic problems, continued its decline. Drake's small contracting firm, like many small businesses in New Jersey, had gone belly-up; creditors were breathing down Dick's neck.

Doy, now twenty-six, was pregnant with their sixth child in seven years. The New Jersey winter had been long and severe; for months the kids had passed the flu back and forth. "Fine," she said. "Let's go for it, honey."

"How long will it take to pack?"

They loaded what they could in a U-Haul—card table, baby's crib, pressure cooker—and burned the rest of their stuff in the backyard. They set off from New Jersey at eleven at night and hit Indianapolis in the morning. That afternoon they reached St. Louis, Gateway to the West. They didn't know exactly where they were going, but they were eager to get there. Money was tight: the kids ate baloney sandwiches, or Cheerios out of paper cups. Once a day they stopped for something hot. When Dick got punchy, they pulled off and slept in the car, a Chevy Nova, eight of them. In darkness, in the middle of the Mojave Desert, Doy, amid sleeping children, woke with a start—where was Dick?

"Why you sleeping on the roof?"

"Scorpions," Dick said sheepishly.

Doy had a brother in Paramount, a part of Los Angeles. They stayed with him while they got their bearings. Southern California was wonderfully exotic, with its parched landscape and unpronounceable Spanish names, but they missed the trees back

East. When Dick saw Thousand Oaks on the map, northwest of Los Angeles, he circled it. Turned out to be a pretty spot, nestled among barren hills, rural enough to be rustic but an easy drive to the studios. Heck, it must have been movie and TV country: they were filming *Lassie* there in town. Dick walked into a realtor's and rented an unfurnished house.

Doy tacked a sheet over the front window. Somebody gave them a chair. Doy's brother passed along a fridge, an old couch, and two sets of bunk beds. Dick and Doy slept together on a single cot. Like Blanche DuBois, they relied on the kindness of strangers—the bread man carried them, and the milkman gave them butter and eggs on credit. A neighbor brought over a coffee tin of tomatoes, and the kids ate soup heated in the coffee tin.

No sooner had they got themselves settled than Dick had to hit the road with the stunt show. He asked Doy if she was sure she'd be all right. "Go for it, honey," she said, diapering the baby. "We can manage. Besides, there's always good people who come along and help out." It was an opportunity he couldn't pass up—work he aspired to, on-the-job training, connections, money in escrow. His salary would be deposited directly into the bank.

"We're opening in Paris," Dick wrote to his sister.

In Paris, Indiana, things got off to a rough start. Another stunt man was meant to get hit with an ax handle, but he ducked; the ax handle hit a signpost, the sign fell, and Dick, standing under it, lost a tooth and suffered a concussion. In another Midwestern town, Dick was showing schoolkids how a movie cowboy takes a flaming arrow in the back. The arrow zipped down a wire and thudded into an asbestos pad, or what was supposedly asbestos. Damn thing caught on fire, and by the time they tore it off him, Dick had a pretty good burn. He's got a patch of shiny skin to this day.

Two weeks later—a month ahead of schedule—Dick was on his way back to Thousand Oaks, driving a rig loaded with a soundstage. The money had run out, leaving everybody in the lurch. On the way home, Dick got rid of some tools in return for gas; he pawned costumes and sold off sound equipment. In Denver an old friend loaned him money. In Las Vegas, a stranger gave him twenty bucks for the final jump across the desert. He found Doy and the kids huddled on the floor in front of the fire, trying to keep warm. Dick had a six-pack of Cokes and the shirt on his scarred back. No money had been deposited in his name; there was nothing in escrow.

Welcome to California.

Having grown up on a farm, Dick could do most any work. With mouths to feed, he couldn't be choosy. He mucked stables, fogged mosquitoes at chicken ranches, worked at a place that made monster masks. One day, to amuse the kids, he wore a gorilla suit home. When a dog came tearing after him, he remembered the costume was worth a fortune. There was Dad the gorilla, barrel-assing down the street for all he was worth, barking dog on his tail. Doy and the kids laughed so hard the tears came. They practically lived on potato soup, and Doy missed her relatives back East, but they all stuck together and never regretted the move for a moment.

Dick got work at the big Albertson Ranch near Thousand Oaks. A fine horseman, he'd always had a way with animals. His father had boarded hoof stock, and Dick was always coming home with a hurt raccoon or a baby buffalo he'd won at a rodeo. He had little patience for school, but spent hour after hour training the buffalo. Every year when the circus came to town he got up at five in the morning. He loved watching the elephants do the heavy work, loved their taciturn might and air of noble intelligence.

At the Albertson Ranch he tended cattle, mowed hay, repaired fences. He did what needed doing. Sometimes they filmed at the ranch; now and then cowboy actors like Slim Pickens and Doug McClure came out to work the cattle, branding and bulldogging. Dick made some contacts and started wrangling at the studios. Somebody had to look after the horses you see in Westerns, saddle them and tie them off for the day and then, when shooting ended, unsaddle them, feed them, bed them down, and remember, next morning, that the paint filly had been hitched between the chestnut and the bay.

With his salesman's bluster and ready laugh, Dick made friends easily. He earned a reputation as a hard worker, cheerful and tenacious, driving into Los Angeles when there was studio work, hanging around the ranch when there wasn't. After the ranch changed hands, and the new owners began construction of an equestrian center, Dick asked who was going to run it. "You are," said the boss, and Dick ended up managing the place.

Along the way he'd also done odd jobs at Jungleland, a tourist trap in Thousand Oaks, and got friendly with the owner. Louis Goebel was forty years Dick's senior but had taken an instant liking to him. Louis was a model of the prosperous, respected businessman—pleasant, outgoing, a member of all the civic organizations, careful with money but scrupulously fair. He made deals on a handshake and his word was gold. Born with a bad foot, he wasn't one to let orthopedic shoes slow him down.

Louis was from Buffalo, New York, where his father had owned a slaughterhouse and packing plant. In his early twenties he moved to California. At that time International (now Universal) had its own wild animals for use in pictures, and Louis signed on as a butcher, cutting meat for the cafeteria and the zoo. When the studio disposed of its menagerie, in 1931, Louis purchased the whole collection and moved it to Thousand Oaks, where he had bought land.

An astute businessman, he rented the animals back to the studios, including Universal; with no competition for many years, he built a prosperous business. He started importing stock from Africa, putting exotics on display and opening to the public. MGM used the big holding barn at Jungleland as a soundstage, and many of the old Tarzan pictures were made there. Louis did no training himself, but housed some of the great trainers and their acts. If a movie producer needed lions, he'd call Louis. "That's right," Louis would say, "I have Clyde

Beatty working for me. He performs each day for the public, but I'm sure we can work something out." Any wild animal in a film made between 1930 and the early 1950s—Laurel and Hardy, Cecil B. DeMille, the Marx Brothers—was probably supplied by Louis Goebel.

Louis had it all figured. He picked up dead livestock from local farms, using it to feed his lions. In 1932 he donated the first cats to Griffith Park Zoo in Los Angeles, on condition they buy horsemeat from him. He salted and packed the hides and sold them to tanneries in Italy and Mexico. Bones were turned into meal and used in fertilizer. During the Second World War he rendered animal fat, needed for use in munitions. He imported rhesus monkeys by the thousands for war and medical research. Along the way he also put together a real-estate empire.

Dick modeled himself after the older man. He and Doy had rented a bigger place, with twelve fenced acres; Dick took his first steps into the animal business. He picked up a baby llama here, a buffalo there, and before long had a small menagerie. He idolized Louis and imagined the day when he, too, would have an exotic-animal empire.

As Dick was getting in, however, Louis was getting out. He sold Jungleland, taking it back when the buyers couldn't make the payments. He sold it a second time, in 1968, but not long after that Jayne Mansfield's son got mauled there by a lion. The resulting lawsuit—combined with escalating property taxes—broke the new owners. Bankruptcy proceedings were started, the stock and equipment auctioned off. Dick, who'd been boarding for the new owners, wound up keeping some animals as payment.

Dick was now working at another exotic-animal setup, at Fillmore, an hour away. Africa USA was co-owned by Ivan Tors, a Hungarian-born animal enthusiast who had graduated from screenwriting to producing some of the most popular television series of the day, including *Daktari, Flipper, Cowboy in Africa,* and *Gentle Ben.* Dick shoveled up, transported lions from the quarantine station, operated heavy equipment. And he acquired more stock of his own—trading a llama for a chimp, taking home a sick pony nobody wanted, buying a baby camel.

Ivan Tors spent his time traveling, leaving things in the hands of his partner, Ralph Helfer. A short, bearded man, Helfer had started out with a pet store that specialized in reptiles. He went first-class: champagne, fine suits, big house, maid, and never quite enough money to go around. A devastating flood and escalating costs put Africa USA in jeopardy. Even when the help was going short, though, Ralph seemed to do all right. One day, after everybody had gone without a paycheck for weeks, he showed up in a new Cadillac. He explained that the old one was going to be repossessed; by trading it in, he'd given himself three months' grace in making payments. Came bankruptcy, it was the people working for him who got burned. One, of course, was Dick.

Broke again, with animals as well as family to feed, Dick did whatever came next. Helfer rented an elephant to someone doing rides at the zoo in Salt Lake City, and Bimbo nailed the man against the chain-link fence. The fence gave, enabling the man to get out, but his back looked like a waffle iron and he was lucky not to have been crushed.

"Honey, they need me in Utah. They're having trouble with the elephant ride and want me to straighten things out."

"We'll miss you," said Doy. "Hurry home."

Dick drove to Salt Lake and spent three weeks walking Bimbo in a circle. Word of his reliability got around, and one job led to another. When somebody needed a young gorilla moved, Dick got a call. He stopped in at the Holiday Inn for breakfast and bumped into Ada Smieya, a lion trainer. Dick asked could he use her room to bathe the gorilla. She was ready to check out and gave him the key. He sneaked the gorilla upstairs. When they were done in the tub, he stood the gorilla on the toilet to dry him. The gorilla caught sight of himself in the mirror and threw a fit.

The gorilla wasn't big, but he was unbelievably powerful and agile. As Dick fought to subdue him, the gorilla defecated, grabbing the stool, throwing it, smearing the mirror and the walls, dropping turds in the tub. By the time Dick finally muscled him into submission, the bathroom looked like Freud's worst nightmare. Dick took him out to the van and went back upstairs to clean up.

A maintenance cart had been left outside the door, which was ajar. Dick hurried upstairs, but got there to find the housekeeper on the threshold of the bathroom, aghast. Dick quietly backed out.

The funny part was that Ada was meticulous. He figured she might hold it against him, but next time he saw her he couldn't resist telling the story. "That's great!" she shrieked. "They think I was shitting all over the place! I love it, I love it!"

Dick worked hard but his animal career never got off the ground. He went partners on some stock with a dealer named Tom Hunt, who boarded animals at Dick's place. They bought a little Asian, the only elephant Dick started from scratch. She was just getting off the bottle when, at Hunt's insistence, they sold her to the Albuquerque zoo. Dick wished he'd been able to buy out Hunt's share and keep her. Unfortunately, he never had money. There were ten bills for every check. No matter how tenaciously he worked, he seemed to end up worse off than he'd started. When he went back to New Jersey to run the elephant ride at an animal park, he kept a low profile, staying with his sister and not even looking up old friends. At the time he'd moved his own family to California, he'd left behind some debts. You never knew who had a long memory, and the fewer people who knew he was back, the better.

You may once, briefly, have seen Dick Drake in a movie—doubling the star on a runaway buckboard, on the raft surging through rapids, on the horse going down in the ambush. With his graying blond hair and round, tanned face, he looks like a rough-edged version of an actor whose name is on the tip of your tongue. Over fifteen years he'd built up a list of credits that looked good on paper and would have brought a decent living if he hadn't been subsidizing what he hoped would become a thriving animal business.

He did stunts and wrangling and animal work on such television shows as *Bonanza, Quincy, Charlie's Angels, Gunsmoke, The Rockford Files, Wild Wild West,* and *High Chapparal.* He did commercials for Datsun, Gallo, Kit Kat, and Chiffon Margarine. He worked on such feature films as *March or Die* (of which Leonard Maltin, in his *Movie and Video Guide,* says: "Good cast wages losing battle with static script and walks downheartedly through action scenes. Disappointing epic-that-might-have-been"); *The Good Guys and the Bad Guys* ("Mild Western comedy-drama has aging marshal going after lifelong foe"); *Lock, Stock and Barrel* ("Old West adventure story . . . lumbers along, due to so-so script, sloppy direction"); *Evilspeak* ("Orphan is hassled by fellow students in military academy, seeks revenge with the help of black magic. Haven't we seen all this before?"); *Day of the Animals* ("back packers in the High Sierras at the mercy of hostile creatures crazed by the sun's radiation after the earth's ozone layer has been ecologically destroyed"); and *The Incredible Shrinking Woman* ("worth catching for really peculiar color schemes and an amazing performance by Rick Baker as a gorilla named Sidney").

For one picture, *Hawmps!* ("camels trained as Army mounts in Texas desert. Some comedy results, but how far can you stretch one idea?"), Dick helped break twenty-three camels. He and another fellow were teaching them to turn, Dick on the camel, ten minutes per animal, same way you break a horse. One of the camels, a female, died. An autopsy showed it had been a freak, but there were now people known as animal-rights activists who went out of their way to find things to squawk about, and a story went around about how heavy-handed they'd been. Totally unfair, but the more you deny things, the worse they look.

Dick also worked as a double on the picture, wearing a cavalry outfit and standing in for the actor Jimmy Hampton. Dick looked good in uniform and was the best camel rider on the set. In all the establishing shots he rode the camel nearest the camera. When they cut the film, they ended up with so much footage of Dick in the foreground they had to give him fourth billing. It was the peak of his movie career.

By then Dick had moved his family to Tehachapi. In the desert between Mojave and Bakersfield, Tehachapi was a sleepy little place that drew workers and tourists from Edwards Air Force Base twenty miles away. It's a town where Louis L'Amour outsells Danielle Steel, the AM radio in every café is tuned to the country station owned by Buck Owens, and you can buy a bowl of takeout chicken gizzards at the Texaco station. FIRST PUMP, THEN PAY, says a sign at the Union 76 station. THIS IS TEHACHAPI, NOT L.A.

Still, it's only two hours from Los Angeles, and smart money had been buying up Tehachapi for years. Louis Goebel owned a forty-five-acre ranch near town, where he boarded camels and other stock. His son had been living at the Camel Farm, but when the son's marriage ended Louis needed someone to look after the place.

Thousand Oaks had changed in the time Dick and Doy had been there. Property values had risen steadily. Dean Martin had moved into the area. Alan Ladd had a big ranch. Richard Widmark moved out from Los Angeles. Carlo Ponti and Sophia Loren purchased the old Eve Arden estate and did it over. The Albertson Ranch, meanwhile, had been turned into Westlake Village, complete with a lake, a marina, and exclusive homes.

The part of Thousand Oaks where Dick and Doy lived wasn't zoned for exotics. There was a new church next door, a school across the way. The place was getting crowded. In the old days you'd turn your exotics loose. Now the bylaws about what animals could be where, and what permits and facilities you needed, were enforced. Dick was told he was operating illegally. Before the municipality would consider a conditional use permit, they wanted an environmental-impact study, which would have cost $20,000.

Louis's place in Tehachapi was running down and he figured

Dick was the fellow to whip it into shape. Dick asked about buying, or at least having an option to buy. Louis made a splendid offer—six months free, then $1,000 a month, applied toward a very modest purchase price of $125,000. Dick moved his family and his animals into the high desert.

Louis had another reason for wanting Dick in Tehachapi. He had been importing animals—as many as fifty camels or a dozen cats or a thousand monkeys at once—through the quarantine station at Long Beach. The cages were hoisted out of the ship's hull and lowered into the dip tank, immersing the animals in disinfecting solution; after a quarantine period ranging from 30 to 120 days, depending on species, they could be moved out. When other importers began playing fast and loose, moving animals too quickly, the U.S. Department of Agriculture cracked down. Louis, sensing what was coming, sought to get Tehachapi registered as the quarantine station. Louis did the politicking while Dick worked long and hard to ready the property.

In the end, the quarantine station became one more thing that didn't quite pan out. Tehachapi was judged to be too far inland; thereafter, all exotic stock coming into the U.S. went through Clifton, New Jersey. Dick boarded stock at Tehachapi, did studio work, and traded animals when he got the chance; but he was no longer looking to become another Louis Goebel. Louis's timing had been perfect. He'd got in ahead of everybody and, after the Animal Welfare Act went through, in 1966, he'd seen the future. He told Dick flat out, "This business is almost done. Regulations get tighter. More animals go on the list. Anybody dealing in exotic animals today is living on borrowed time."

Dick also knew he didn't have Louis's head for business— patience for budgets, finesse in negotiating, knack of seeing three moves ahead. Louis had untold wealth, and Ralph Helfer kept landing on his feet, and Tom Hunt must have been a millionaire many times over. Dick had worked for, and with, some wealthy people, but he did the work while they filled their pockets. Louis had put it delicately, but he was hinting that

Dick would never make it big in the animal business and should maybe try something else.

What really decided it was the incident with Zamba at the Camel Farm. A crew had come in to shoot a movie, and friends of the Drakes had brought their trailer down from Red Rock Canyon. The parents started drinking. Their boy went out to play with his paper plane, seeing how far it would fly. Among the stock Dick was boarding at the time was a lion, and the boy ended up by its cage. Doy's nephew Bobby fetched him, gave him hell, and took him back to the parents. They stopped partying long enough to tell him not to do it again. Bobby brought him back three times, but the boy's plane finally ended up in Zamba's cage.

The boy was in a bind. He couldn't ask his parents for help, since he wasn't supposed to be down there. He couldn't climb over the chain-link fence. Beneath the fence, though, was a gap big enough to put his arm through.

The boy got down on one knee, reached under, and nearly got a finger on the plane. He flattened himself, but no matter how hard he tried, squishing his face into the mesh, he couldn't reach it. He got up, dusted himself off, and looked around for a stick. Then he had a better idea. His leg was longer than his arm. He sat down, facing the fence, and worked one leg under, trying to reach the plane with his toe.

Dick's son Kenny saw what was about to happen and ran down the hill, hollering, and got there in time to grab the boy and pull one way while Zamba pulled the other, but Kenny was only thirteen at the time and a lion can drag a full-grown wildebeest uphill.

Talk about sad—the shock and grief, the guilt and remorse. The investigation, the depositions, the autopsy. There was a five-inch opening between the fence and the ground; the boy's skull had been crushed. A ghastly time for everyone, right through to the insurance claim. Here the boy was dead and buried and the parents were looking for money. Not that it was unfriendly—they stayed with the Drakes while the whole thing got sorted out. If you've got coverage, we may as well sue and see if the company coughs up, right? The lawyer said look, you understand that at best they'll find the owner of the property, Mr. Goebel, perhaps ten percent liable, the Drakes another ten percent, and yourselves eighty percent responsible. Ready to deal with that? They took it before a judge. Devastating enough to lose a child—a soul-searing thing, impossible to imagine— but then to be told flat-out it was your fault?

And the sadness of dealing with Zamba. You could walk him down the street, through a crowd, anywhere, and he behaved like a charm. For the Dreyfus Fund commercial he'd sauntered into the bank like an old pro, then done the subway segment in one take. Somebody joked that the lion took direction better than the actors. In *The Gang That Couldn't Shoot Straight* he went through a car wash. Everybody worried he'd go wild, but Zamba acted like he'd been going through a car wash all his life. Seemed a waste to destroy such a beautiful animal. Who'd have thought a simple act like pulling the trigger could be so hard?

That was the last straw for Dick. He'd never get away from exotics entirely, not with kids who worked circus and so many friends in the industry. He and Doy would keep horses and anything else. People would lay over with their acts. Dick would look after Louis's camels, and he'd get called when somebody needed to move a rhino. But he put his dreams of an animal kingdom behind him.

Dick was in Saskatchewan, driving diesel and handling hoof stock, when a Royal Canadian Mounted Police officer came out to see him. On circus lots, cops aren't ordinarily bearing messages of congratulation. Circus Vargas was touring Canada; they'd gone to some trouble to find him. Dick tried to think. Had he forgotten to write a check to cover the postdated check he'd written to cover the insurance check Doy said had bounced?

When the Mountie told him his son had been in an accident —a bad accident—Dick had a pretty good idea which son. Some kids sailed through life without grief, and others . . . well, they were the ones somebody slammed the brakes on in front of, the ones loudmouths in bars looked at the wrong way. Fistfights broke out on the main streets of towns they were passing through. Beer cans flew out the driver's window. Borrowed vans hit slick patches and rolled over. They were the ones state troopers made walk a straight line, heel to toe. Tattoos appeared on their upper arms. They stumbled in horny at four in the morning, and their girlfriends wound up with black eyes and chipped teeth. They were the ones who could get dope anywhere in the country. The ones trouble seemed to find, or vice versa.

Eddie Drake, Dick's and Doy's eldest, was a spirited, muscular kid who knew how to pull engines out of cars, break camels, and process phenomenal amounts of beer. Like Dick, he had a quality that made women look twice. Maybe he was raw and foul-mouthed, turning "fuck" into three different parts of speech in a single sentence. Maybe he did party hard, the good times coming close to self-destruction. Didn't matter, when he smiled. He was invincible. Like his dad, he was full of bluster that hid something sweet. Eddie took scar tissue in stride and wore T-shirts that said things like "Kill 'em all, let God sort 'em out." That didn't mean he lacked a sensitive side.

Who'd guess he could be so tender? He'd take a book and sit on a rock in the sun, perfectly content, or spend hours playing with his chimp. There was a childlike quality to his fun and you couldn't help getting caught up in it. Come on, he'd say, let's go up to the snow, and three of his sisters would pile in, everybody laughing. He always took a sister with him no matter where he was going. He'd do anything for family, couldn't understand people who wouldn't, even gave his parents hell—"What are you doing home? Don't you know your daughter's in the school play?"

The night of the accident, he'd been going to see his sister in San Francisco. He'd been working on the *Grizzly Adams* television series; Cheryl, like her parents an expert rider, was performing with the Equinettes at the Cow Palace. Eddie wanted to catch her show. On Highway 12 his truck went off the road; he

▲ 43

came to on a gurney. Doy went up and spent a week at the hospital. Eddie's pancreas, his spleen, and his liver were sliced up, and they had to pin his femur together and put him in traction for a month. That could have been it right there, but he was made of the same resilient stuff as his father.

Eddie took after his dad in other ways, too—same hands, same teeth, same mischievous glint. He had the same easygoing manner and, when things didn't go his way, the same sudden, violent temper. From an early age he'd gone wrangling with Dick and seen how movies got made and animals were handled. During the filming of *The Guns of Will Sonnet*, Walter Brennan liked to play with him between takes. On the set of *Big Valley*, Barbara Stanwyck used to invite him into her trailer and give him lunch.

As Eddie got older he developed the same practical skills Dick used to earn a living. Over the years father and son worked together on many projects. For *Honky Tonk Freeway* they went to Florida with Hubert Wells, perhaps the most respected trainer in the country. Eddie was in charge of the rhinoceros; Dick was supposed to teach an elephant named Katie to water-ski. Time was tight, and Hubert, realizing that Dick had limited experience, phoned a more seasoned elephant man back in California, Wally Ross. Hubert asked Wally if he thought Dick could get the job done in three weeks. Wally had known Dick for years and spoke highly of him, but he told Hubert candidly that Dick was better at handling animals than training them. Hubert wound up hiring Wally as well. Working long days together, Wally and Dick managed, just before the shoot, to get Katie up on skis.

Then the studio called to say they weren't going to go as scheduled. They'd do the bank-robbery scenes in New York first. A couple of weeks later the studio called again. We're going to Los Angeles to shoot interiors—can you hang in there a bit longer? Dick figured there were worse things than getting paid to read magazines and go fishing while a three-week job turned into four months of paychecks.

Eddie, with nothing to do but yank pull-tabs, ran amok. Dick knew the kind of hell-bent reputation he'd earned, and one day they had it out. Eddie was full of beer, he'd wrecked the rental car, he was treating his girl disgracefully—bouncing her around the motel room, waking people in the middle of the night. Dick confronted him, knocked him down, threatened to kick his guts out. That's it, he told Eddie, you're going home. Of course, Dick had had some escapades in his day. Next morning, when Eddie showed up sober and chastened, it was like the whole thing had never happened.

The producer, meanwhile, worried that when they finally did the shoot Katie might jump off her skis. He wanted a mechanical elephant built, life size. The prop department came in with an estimate of $255,000, and the poor producer, already over budget, started coming unglued. Dick was the only one who thought to ask the obvious—why do we need a mechanical elephant? Because, said the producer, we're afraid the helicopter will spook her—what if she freaks? She won't, said Dick, I know it. Can't take the chance, said the producer, you know what a screw-up will cost? Look, said Dick, it costs four hundred an hour to rent a helicopter. We'll rent one, tow Katie around the lake, buzz her a few times, and you'll have your answer.

Dick was right, Katie didn't care one way or the other. He'd saved somebody a quarter-million dollars and didn't get so much as a thank-you, the story of his life. The picture, budgeted for $15 million, came in at $25 million. It bombed at the box office. As for the scene with Katie on water skis—the high point of Dick's animal-training career—well, if you happened to scratch your foot at the wrong time in the theater, you missed it.

Eddie had quit school in eleventh grade, preferring stock chutes and holding pens to classrooms. When he wasn't off earning a buck, he pieced together a circus act from the stock at the Camel Farm in Tehachapi. He trained a llama that had broken somebody's ribs, a yak born at the ranch, a little African elephant Dick had got from Tom Hunt, an Australian sheepdog, and a chimp. Every day for months he put tricks on them, training them individually and then teaching them to work together. Though he sometimes had trouble keeping his animals in the ring, he ended up with a mixed act good enough to get some dates.

Eddie thrived on circus, the long hauls and sleepless nights, the good times that rolled through one day and into the next. He enjoyed the nomadic life and easy camaraderie of circus people. He loved the spotlight, the parties, the pretty girls who admired him in his white sequined costume and then looked away, embarrassed. After a couple of seasons, though, he saw he needed a more mature act to get the bookings that made it worthwhile to travel. He was twenty, and he'd been taking the same act out since he was seventeen. Time to make a move. When he saw a little display ad in *Circus Report*—"Two female Asians for sale, Tory and Dutchess, will finance right party"—he got to thinking.

Murray Hill? Hey, I remember the little guy, met him on the Gatti show a couple of years back. Murray had visited the show just before Eddie got fired for rowdiness. Nada, Murray's daughter, had worked the same show with a dog act. Murray was said to have nice tricks on his elephants and they had a reputation as good show animals. Eddie showed the ad to his father.

"What about going after them?"

Dick wanted out, not deeper in. When one of the kids showed an interest, though, he and Doy liked to be encouraging. Dick himself had nothing set aside—it was all he could do to keep the household going—but Eddie had some shares in a waste-treatment company, his savings. He could sell them to get a down payment, then work the elephants to pay off the balance. Tory and Dutchess were already trained; working them into his own act would be simple enough.

"Well," said Dick, "maybe we could go partners."

He tried to remember what Murray was like. They'd met a year earlier. Dick had made a run east with people going to a convention in Chicago; they'd hired him to drive their motor home and stopped in to see Murray on their way back to California.

The motor home belonged to Margaret Houlter, who knew both Dick and Murray. Some years earlier she and her husband had contracted to supply ride animals in New Jersey. Gene had died just before the date, and among the many things she'd had to do in that trying time was scramble to get someone to replace him. She needed somebody who could get around elephants, looked presentable, and could deal with the public. Dick was perfect.

"Hang on now, here we go, off into the jungle." Walking the elephant in a big circle, Dick warned the children to watch out for lions. "They're right behind that bush. They might jump out at us." It scared them so much they wanted to go around again. The park got fifty cents of every dollar; Margaret got a quarter and Dick a quarter.

Margaret and Gene had also known Murray for years. When they did the Schlitz parade in Milwaukee, they always stopped in at the farm near Burlington. Murray and Denise were unfailingly hospitable but Denise had a real problem even then. Margaret knew the unseen side of the business, knew Denise wasn't taking care of phone calls and paperwork. Each year Murray's fuse got shorter; he was grinding it out, trying to keep his family and his animals fed. Often there were also down-on-their-luck circus people—out of work, separated, recovering from an injury. Poor Denise, trying to put food out for everybody. And poor Murray, having to cope with her drinking on top of everything else. He and his sons went around to the grocery stores, collecting trimmings and old fruit for the animals.

No matter how tight things were, Murray's stock was fed and cared for. The animals came first: that was his credo. He drummed it into his family, chastising Denise for getting her hair done when they needed monkey cages, letting the kids know they were expected to contribute. Unlike many in the industry, he was utterly reliable. One morning when Margaret and Gene pulled into the farm, Murray looked like death warmed over. He'd been up two days straight with a sick chimp.

▲ 47

Margaret had introduced Dick to Murray. Dick was surprised at how little Murray was, no bigger than Napoleon, which maybe explained his cockiness. His wife was friendly but in such tough shape he insisted on serving, so you wouldn't notice her shakes. You could feel the strain in the mobile home, see it in the kids.

Dick struck Murray as somebody who used nervous laughter and bullshit charm to cover up weakness—the kind of man whose wife always answers the phone. Sociable and outgoing, Dick was a born storyteller. Denise made omelettes, and Dick and Murray exchanged industry gossip.

When Dick phoned, a year later, Murray greeted him warmly and asked after Eddie, whom he vaguely recalled from the Gatti show. "Ed's fine," said Dick. "He's young, he needs guidance. But he's willing and he's a fast learner. I've taught him what I can and now it's time for him to learn from other people. Reason I'm calling, we seen that ad in *Circus Report* and wanted to ask about your elephants. What are they like?"

Dutchess was in excellent shape but Tory needed careful handling. She had a rupture, which meant she couldn't do certain tricks. One night in Cleveland, after Murray had mixed his elephants into the Polack Circus herd, they were doing a standing line when Murray noticed the rupture bulging out of Tory's anus. He never made her do a hind-leg trick again. She became the front animal in the line—the only one that stayed on all four feet.

The two men chatted for half an hour. A few nights later Dick phoned again. In the following weeks he and Murray spoke often, and things started coming together. Dick asked about Murray's rig—was it for sale as well?

"It's an International Harvester pulling an American trailer. Most tractors that age burn a gallon of oil every eight hundred miles or so. This one gets eleven hundred miles out of a gallon. The trailer's ten years old, and it's fitted out with hay decks, ramps, and steel bracing on the floor and walls. I put in a self-contained water system and a four-kilowatt generator."

Dick said they might be interested. He had the idea of putting $20,000 down against a purchase price of $100,000 for the girls and the tractor-trailer. The other $80,000 would be a loan, secured by the elephants. The interest rate would be ten percent annually—banks wanted almost twenty at the time—and the full $80,000 would be repayable over five years.

Once negotiations got serious, Murray did some asking around. He called Hubert Wells, the California trainer, who had put exotics in dozens of films, from *Dr. Dolittle* and *Ring of Bright Water* to *Born Free* and *Never Cry Wolf*. Yes, he said, Dick had done a good job on *Honky Tonk Freeway*.

Murray called Tom Hunt, the animal importer, who lived in Michigan. Hunt also gave Dick a good recommendation but for one thing. "He's not great on the paperwork, and sometimes he's slow on the money, but it eventually comes." What about taking care of the elephants? "I never had problems with him that way. He always looked after the stock."

Murray called Margaret Houlter in California. "I've known Dick for years," she said, "and I like him very much. He does a great job."

Murray's family had raised the girls, made a living from them, and now wanted out of circus. Here was a family wanting into circus in a bigger way. The arrangement would work nicely at both ends. Murray would get a guaranteed income while he built a new career. The Drakes would get reliable elephants with a good reputation, a tractor-trailer rigged for them, and a year's bookings. Best of all, Tory and Dutchess would stay together.

"We got a deal," Murray told Dick. "Long as I know the money will come in every month, and the girls will be properly taken care of."

3

GOOD-BYE GIRLS

Listen, boy. The elephants come first. Don't ever forget that.

—Murray Hill, 1981

Tory and Dutchess were booked to tour the Pacific Northwest with a small circus based in Oregon, a month-long run that Murray had first made the previous spring. His contract with Reid Brothers gave him $14,000 for the month plus a piece of ride proceeds. Eddie Drake, as it happened, was booked on the same circus. He could take over the girls as the circus moved through Oregon, Idaho, and Montana; along the way, they could put the deal on paper.

Eddie drove his pickup from Tehachapi, towing his little African elephant, his chimp, and some rented dogs and ponies. Dick showed up at the wheel of a red sports car with one of his daughters. When Murray learned that they still didn't have the down payment, he was skeptical. Eddie had earlier promised to send $5,000 to hold the elephants and hadn't come through.

"You people sure as hell talk a good game."

"Couple of days," said Dick. "Just waiting for the broker to sell Eddie's stocks."

"No twenty thousand, no deal."

"Hey," Dick said with his nervous laugh, "we'll buy those elephants, Murray. We'll definitely take the rig, too. I've already got dates booked."

"You said you'd take my dates. I've got signed contracts."

Dick shrugged. "We'll get somebody to fill in."

"These people have used me year after year. They're expecting my animals and that's what they're going to get."

As Murray had brought no help, Eddie agreed to work for him. That way he would learn to handle Tory and Dutchess; he and his girlfriend would also get the proceeds from the elephant ride. Dick traveled with the circus, continuing the negotiation. He tried to keep the mood light but his efforts sometimes backfired. At one point, he joked about what a tough negotiator Murray was, almost as bad as a "Russian kike" he'd once come across. Cut you down every which way, said Dick, squeezing out the last nickel.

"You don't like Jews?"

"I got nothing against them myself," Dick said affably. "Hell, I deal with them all the time. You see how they operate in the motion-picture industry. Only ones I don't like are the kikes."

"What's wrong with kikes?"

Dick, twigging, backpedaled fast: "Hey, I'm just talking about the ones you meet in New York sometimes. You know what kind of guys I'm talking about."

"What's the matter with New York?" said Murray. "I'm a Jew, know that? Born in Brooklyn."

Dick smoothed it over, but relations were strained after that. A couple of days later, setting up at a fairground, one of the help did something backwards. The kid was from San Francisco and Murray started carrying on about Californians. There were morons in every state, he said, but the biggest morons he'd come across were in California. Before heading home, Dick told Eddie they'd better wrap things up quick, before the whole deal fell apart.

The circus moved on to The Dalles, Pendleton, and Hermiston before crossing the Idaho line. Murray was sore but he didn't want the deal to collapse. Eddie had started practicing with the girls and was doing an excellent job. Confident and handsome in the ring, eager to learn, he saw Murray as a mentor, asking questions and heeding the answers. His only problem, so far as Murray could tell, was that he liked his pot and his beer. Every night was party night, and some mornings he had a hard time crawling out of bed. Murray warned him and then, one morning, decided to teach him a lesson. It was a pullout day, and they had a long jump to make. Eddie and his girlfriend had taken their sleeping bags into the grandstand of the fairgrounds. When they didn't appear at sunup, Murray started to leave without them.

Wakened by the noise of the diesel, Eddie and his girlfriend came running across the field, half-dressed, to flag down the rig. Murray pretended not to notice, finally stopping outside the gate.

"Jesus," Eddie gasped, hopping up to the cab, "you almost forgot us."

"Forgot, huh?"

"You mean you were going to leave me? The next date's three hundred miles."

"The animals come first. If you can't drag your ass out of bed to feed them . . ."

After that Eddie was up every morning. He was learning by the day. "You find out more at the rear end of an elephant than the front end," Murray told him. "You have to shovel up anyway, so pay attention while you're doing it." When there's mucus in the manure, he said, it's probably a stomach cold, though it may also be caused by a change of water. The manure tips you off to internal problems. If you notice fresh blood, it may mean a scratched intestinal lining. Dutchess sometimes passed blood from hay that was too coarse. Put her on softer hay. If it doesn't clear up in a few days, get concerned. If you ever see dried blood in the stool, get concerned right away. Dried blood could mean any of half a dozen problems. Call a vet immediately.

The girls had different appetites, Murray said, and their eating habits changed with the seasons. Between them they generally ate about six or seven bales of hay a day and maybe twelve pounds of grain. If it's decent hay, said Murray, figure on about 125 pounds per day per animal, more if you're not graining them. The hotter varieties of hay, though good for cattle, tended to cause diarrhea in single-stomached animals like elephants. Lespedeza was good for the girls, so were Johnsongrass and timothy hay, but a good oat hay was best of all. You can use the prepared horse feeds, he said, but don't overdo it. Some manufacturers use too much molasses to hold the feed together. The sugar base doesn't cause worms, but it increases the manifestation in animals that already have them. Molasses keeps prepared feeds from spoiling, which is useful in winter; in warm weather, though, best not to use it at all. "The girls are outside more, and the hay is fresher. Don't give them prepared stuff in summer."

"Sure thing."

"The longer you keep any feed, even packaged, the less nutrition it has."

"Come on, Murray, I've been around animals my whole life."

"Listen, boy. The elephants come first. Don't ever forget that. Make goddamn sure you look after them properly."

The circus moved into Montana to play Kalispell, Helena, and Butte, then came back through Idaho. Dick drove up again. He'd sent a certified check to the farm in Missouri, but it was for only $10,000 rather than $20,000. Murray had told Denise not to cash it because the deal might fall apart.

Over breakfast, Dick pushed an idea he'd suggested earlier. What about taking $10,000 from the $14,000 Reid contract to make up the difference? The sale was originally to have taken place at the start of the Reid run, in which case Eddie would have been entitled to the $14,000. Things had taken longer than expected, but Eddie had begun working the act just the same. Make the effective date of the deal the beginning of the Reid run.

"Like hell," said Murray. "Our deal was that you ain't bought a thing until I get twenty thousand. I'll return your ten—the check ain't even cashed—we'll shake hands, and that's that."

"Wait a minute," said Dick. "It's too late. We've got to have those elephants."

"Ain't my problem if you booked them before you bought them."

"I've put my son in a fix," said Dick. "Let's work this out."

Murray didn't like the way the deal was unfolding, but for months he'd looked forward to being rid of the burden of handling the girls. His leg was bothering him; he needed teeth pulled; he was too old to be grinding it out on the road. He'd sold off a colony of chimps, the last of his stock. Besides, he'd had it out with Denise before leaving for Oregon, throwing out every bottle he could find and getting her into an alcoholism clinic in Springfield. The treatment program lasted a month; the twins were by themselves in the trailer. He needed to help them and to be there when she got out. She was bound to be frail, needing all the support she could get.

Still, he wasn't sure about the Drakes. Dick had bragged about "straightening out Dutchess" and Murray was starting to have his doubts about him. On the other hand, Eddie was doing fine with the girls. The men had already had an attorney draw up an agreement of sale. Eager to conclude things, Murray, like Dick, had got ahead of himself. He'd already put this part of his life behind him.

Tell you what, he told the Drakes. Make all your payments on time. Once you've paid off eighty thousand, we'll say the other ten came off the Reid show. They shook hands, found a notary, and executed the agreement. It outlined the terms of the sale and of Murray's security. The elephants served as collateral—Dick had insisted the tractor-trailer not be encumbered, in case they decided to sell it or trade it. The Drakes agreed to insure the life of each elephant for $40,000, naming Murray as beneficiary, and to maintain public liability insurance in the amount of not less than $500,000. They agreed to keep the elephants "in a fit and healthy condition" and not to "mistreat, neglect, or in any other manner harm, damage, or injure" them. The Drakes agreed to reduce their indebtedness by roughly $1,700 a month. If they were ninety days late in making a payment, they would be deemed to be in default, and Murray would have the right to repossess the elephants.

The Drakes also signed an addendum in which they agreed to accept the dates Murray had already contracted, paying him a ten percent commission. The first date was an elephant ride in Lincoln, Nebraska, the following week. Over the winter they'd do the Florida run that Murray had done the previous year.

The deal finally done, Dick went home. Murray and Eddie headed to Lincoln, where Murray said a brief, wet-eyed farewell to Tory and Dutchess. Despite his mixed feelings about the Drakes, the difficulty of giving up the girls, and the touchy prospect of dealing with a newly sober Denise, he headed back to Missouri in high spirits. For the first time in almost twenty years his life would not revolve continuously around the girls. He was free.

A couple of years before selling the girls, Murray, like everyone else in the animal business in the United States, had felt the squeeze of increased liability rates. The country had grown lawsuit-happy; every year, it seemed, the premium got jacked up another ten or fifteen percent. What could you do? Only a few firms indemnified animal acts and, if you wanted to leave Lloyd's and move over to Great Southwest, guess what? Just so happened their rates had gone up as well.

Figuring there must be cheaper coverage, Murray had called every outfit in the Springfield book. A few weeks later a genial, middle-aged fellow had come out to the farm and introduced himself as Jim Greenstreet of All-Risk Insurance. The premium he quoted was half what Murray had been paying, and Murray had started buying coverage from All-Risk. Though he'd never filed a claim, he'd liked Greenstreet and been happy with the service.

When Murray sold the girls to the Drakes, he didn't know what he'd do next. He didn't want to sit around the mobile home indefinitely with Denise, who was showing great character in battling her demons but whose unhappiness seemed compounded rather than eased by his full-time presence. For years he had wanted out. First the kids had been too young— "What'll happen to us?" Nada had asked in tears—and then Denise had been too sick. He couldn't just walk out while she was insensible. Now that she had a grip on sobriety, however, his thoughts again turned to divorce. He wanted the freedom to travel, and he was looking to find less demanding ways to turn a dollar. Maybe he'd call Bunny Brook, whom he'd told of the deal with the Drakes. He'd keep booking for the Drakes and producing a mini-mall circus, and he'd see what came along.

Recalling that Jim Greenstreet had once expressed interest in getting into show-business insurance, Murray called him. Insurance, Murray figured, was a matter of contacts, and he'd met hundreds of people in the animal business. If I steer clients to All-Risk, he asked Greenstreet, will you pay a commission? Greenstreet said he was prohibited by law from compensating anyone who wasn't a certified agent or broker. But it was simple enough to get certified. Matter of fact, he said, a training seminar's coming up next month in Kansas City. Why not take the course, write the exam, and get yourself licensed? On any business you bring to the agency, we'll split the commission fifty-fifty.

The course lasted three days and cost $300. Basically, they gave you questions from the test and helped you memorize answers. You could get licensed either as an agent (a salesman for one company) or as a broker (who can deal with different companies). The broker's license was more complicated but seemed the better deal. Murray hated questionnaires and applications, and failed the test. He took the course again and finally got himself licensed as a broker. Greenstreet welcomed him to the agency, and Murray started placing ads in the trade papers. In a few months he had a couple of dozen clients. Greenstreet handled the books, and his secretary sent off a statement each month. All-Risk was simply using Murray's name to attract business.

Many clients were old cronies who phoned Murray at the farm. Someone who knew the Drakes asked why he'd sold the girls to somebody who was rough with them. Murray shrugged it off: people who'd never worked elephants didn't realize you had to use a firm hand at times. Through the grapevine he also heard that Dutchess had taken a swing at a girl in Montana, sending her to hospital. He phoned Eddie and asked if it was true. Eddie implied that the story had been exaggerated. Somebody else asked Murray if he regretted having sold Tory and Dutchess.

"Hell, no," he said. "You kidding? First time in my life I've had a chance to put my feet up. You know how much work they are?"

In truth, there were moments—saying good-bye to the twins as they left for school in the morning, or hanging up after talking to somebody's answering machine—when he couldn't help recalling the girls' pungent warmth. Lying in bed, unable to sleep, he'd remember their nightly rituals of snuffling and settling. In the barn, he'd hear the swish of their trunks sweeping hay into neat little mouthfuls. During a rainstorm one day he could have sworn he heard the sudden torrents of urine, the thudding loaves of manure. Felling a tree, he recalled their effortless strength, the hundred ways in which they were useful. Driving to the office in Springfield, he'd find himself thinking of the pleasure they took in coating themselves in mud, the way they sometimes froze at the same instant to listen, their gleeful exchange when they'd been apart. "Move up, Dutchess," he said aloud at the wheel of his truck, smiling at the way they played dumb if they didn't want to work. Who, me? You hear anything, Tory? Tory was so goddamn sweet, always on the mooch, you couldn't help but like her, and even a miserable sourpuss like Dutchess, after you'd spent twenty years with her . . .

In circus, there's no warning. Things go fine, then hell breaks loose—the tiger leaps, the elephant swats the trainer, the tight-rope walker slips. It happened that suddenly at Toms River, New Jersey, where Murray had put a mini-circus into a mall—high-wire act, cradle act, unsupported ladder, dog act, and Rola Bola. In the Saturday afternoon show, the Portuguese fellow who did Rola Bola—juggling on a board atop a rolling cylinder—missed his backflip. You could hear the sickening crunch when he landed on his neck; he lay immobile, awkwardly heaped on the floor, and everybody had the same awful thought. Murray—producer of the show—accompanied him to hospital. Mercifully, though the fellow had knocked himself cold, he suffered no serious injury. But the accident shook everyone and it had, for Murray, a quality of foreboding.

Murray was scheduled to hook up with Eddie and the girls for dates in Missouri in late September and Pennsylvania in early October. He phoned Eddie to confirm the dates. Eddie said he'd be there with Tory and Dutchess, no problem. The trailer needed work so he'd go to Montana, where he had a line on another. Then he'd head to Missouri. Murray went ahead and signed the contracts.

Ten days before the date, Eddie called to say the Montana trailer had fallen through. He was back in California. Murray told him there was another trailer at the farm he could use. Eddie told him not to worry, he'd make the date. There were trailers for sale in California and he'd work around the clock rigging one out.

When Murray called again a few days later, Eddie wasn't home. Dick said he was working in Los Angeles. No, they still hadn't found a trailer.

"How the hell you plan to make Springfield next week?"

"Next week?" said Dick. "Eddie thought Springfield was the first week in October."

Was this faulty communication, or was Dick lying through his teeth? Murray called again the next day—he needed a definite answer in case he had to make other plans. Doy said Eddie's truck had broken down and Dick had gone to get him. Murray told her to have Eddie call back. It was urgent. Eddie phoned two days later and said he was flat broke, couldn't make Springfield after all. As for the Pennsylvania date, could Murray maybe loan him $2,000 so he could make that?

Eddie had screwed up, but Murray was the one with egg on his face. On short notice he couldn't find elephants to substitute. He showed up at the mall in Springfield himself, with nothing but his balloon bounce and a big papier-mâché elephant he'd borrowed. It was the first time he'd ever failed to deliver—sorry, folks, no rides, I can't fulfil the contract. He felt so bad he did the moonwalk for free, losing his shirt, to say nothing of what he'd spent on long-distance, pinning down the Drakes and then trying to replace Eddie. For the Pennsylvania date, he was able to get somebody to pinch-hit, but he was still sore. He returned home fuming.

When Murray was in foul humor, his kids found it best to steer clear—play in the barn when he was inside, go off in the woods while he worked in the barn. They'd heard him tell people: "If you want a Cadillac, you pay for a Cadillac. This is a dependable operation. You don't have to worry about a thing." They understood why he was upset and they admired his principles, but you didn't want to aggravate him. He was liable to chew your head off.

Murray's black mood persisted. Nothing seemed to be going right. He'd told Denise the marriage was over. It wasn't an easy thing to do after twenty-eight years, and he worried about driving her back to the bottle, but it seemed right: "Look, we're going to get divorced, okay? Whatever you want the papers to say, that's fine with me." Her response threw him for a loop. She stood up, forgot where she was going, and sat down again. Her eyes brimmed with tears. She said, "If anything happens to you, how am I going to get Social Security?" Man, that bothered him. How long would she have stayed in the marriage just to get his Social Security? How long had she already?

Things were tight financially as well. The commissions on liability insurance, it turned out, weren't so hot. The idea was to keep at it, adding new clients while collecting premiums from old ones, building year by year. Selling insurance had potential but wasn't something that happened overnight. Murray had hoped to earn income from All-Risk; he was barely covering his own premiums. Meanwhile, the $1,700 check from the Drakes was what he and Denise and the twins lived on. At one time, seventeen hundred had been decent money. Nowadays it was amazing how fast it went. Murray had enough in the bank to get by the first time the check didn't arrive, but once the Drakes were two months past due he wasted no time getting on the phone.

Hey, Murray, where you at? Pretty good, thanks, how about yourself? Good, and the family? That's good. Sure is, starting to get cold at night, but still nice during the day. Dad's fine, yeah. Tell you what, man, it's funny you should call, I was going to phone you. Probably wondering about that payment . . .

Amid the chaos in the house in Cameron Canyon, just outside Tehachapi—where Dick had moved his family after Louis Goebel's death—Eddie told his father that old Murray Hill must be losing his marbles. When Eddie had said things were slow in California, Murray had suggested coming East, putting the elephants on the road for the winter. Murray knew the animal business had slow times; that was why they'd written the ninety-day grace period into their contract. Did he really expect Eddie to truck the elephants clear across the continent, from California to Florida, to give rides at second-rate shopping malls, where you were lucky to make feed money? It might have been in Murray's interest to get ten percent for booking the dates, but he'd have to be crazy to think it would be worthwhile for Eddie to accept them.

Not that Eddie didn't have every intention of making good

the late payment—and, when another month slipped by, payments—as soon as they had some money. It's not like they were sitting idle. Dick was taking any work he could find—hauling produce, running a bulldozer, transporting stock. On weekends, Eddie and his friend Frank Matejka trucked the elephants into the high desert, setting up the elephant ride on streetcorners in Lake Los Angeles, Bakersfield, and Ridgecrest. Even on good days, however, the ride barely paid for diesel, oil, and hay, never mind the mortgage and groceries and phone and heat in a busy house.

Finally, in late November, Eddie scraped together a payment. Then it was Christmas, things stopped dead, and they were late again. Animal work is scarce in winter and the four elephants—the Drakes also had a young African and a male Asian, Butch—did little more than haul firewood and eat up what little money was left. When one month turned into two, then into three, and there was still no money to bring the payments up to date, Murray started sending nasty letters. He was hot. He'd learned that the rig still hadn't been put in the Drakes' name, which meant he was liable for any traffic violations or accidents. He'd learned that the check for mortality insurance on the elephants had bounced, which meant that if anything happened to the girls his note wouldn't mean much. And he'd learned that Eddie, despite agreeing to use Murray as his agent, was booking Murray's old dates himself.

Murray sent a registered letter, which the Drakes never picked up. When he phoned to give them an earful, Eddie figured he'd had just about enough of this shit. Eddie and his girlfriend were living at Cameron Canyon with Dick and Doy and assorted other kids and grandkids, tripping over each other in the little house. There was a cold snap; it was all they could do to keep their animals warm and fed. Dick and Doy had applied for a second mortgage, Eddie's little African elephant had taken sick, and Murray was ranting that he was tired of being screwed around and wanted another payment right away or else. Where did the little son of a bitch get off?

Did he think they liked being broke? Did he figure they had

money and were stiffing him out of spite? The contract said they could fall ninety days behind, they were within their rights. He sounded like a school principal, mixing his lecture with cusses and threats: "I want a reinstatement of the mortality insurance on the elephants. I want a legitimate financial statement. I want more security. I want liens on the tractor and trailer. I'm sending this letter registered so there's no excuse that you did not receive it." When, in February, Dick got a letter demanding that an enclosed additional collateral agreement be signed, notarized, and returned, he went to an attorney in Bakersfield.

As both creditor and agent to the Drakes, Murray was in an odd spot. At the same time that he was harassing them for money, he was negotiating with Eddie to do a job in New York. Murray had stayed in touch with Bunny Brook, and she had invited him to supply two elephants for an American Express commercial to be shot in Manhattan. Eager to get the agent's commission, Murray had offered the job to Eddie.

Eddie talked it over with Dick. It would mean trucking to Missouri, picking up Murray, then going to New York. Travel was expensive, but the date would pay $4,500 (less Murray's cut) and the Drakes desperately needed money. But Dick was antsy about sending the elephants back East, and he asked the attorney what he and Eddie should do. After speaking to Murray, the attorney told Dick it didn't sound like Murray was planning to repossess—he just wanted extra security and a thousand dollars against the past-due payments. The attorney wrote to Murray:

This will confirm our telephone conversation of March 12, 1982, wherein you stated that you were not at this time interested in accepting additional security tendered by Mr. Drake, that being the buffalo and trained horse, in exchange for a waiver of default up to this time and an extension of the 90-day grace period to 120 days. You further indicated that it was not your desire to declare a breach and execute on the security at this time or in the foreseeable future; but rather it was your desire that the security agreement as it currently exists be fulfilled by both parties. . . .

Eddie decided to repair Murray's old rig and take the elephants East to do the commercial, then work a carnival in Alabama and do elephant rides in Greenville, South Carolina, before moving on to the Indianapolis zoo, where he was booked to give rides all summer. He'd take his friend Frank Matejka, his chimp, and a camel that Dick had borrowed. On the way, they'd stop in at Fordland and pick up Murray, who'd accompany them to New York. Eddie promised to bring the thousand dollars and the second collateral agreement.

It was noon when they pulled into Murray's farm. Eddie and Frank unloaded the animals, then went over to the mobile home for coffee. Murray greeted them warmly. When he found out Eddie didn't have the money or the additional security agreement, though, he got worked up. Eddie assured him everything was coming in the mail.

That afternoon, Eddie backed up to the manure pile to clean out the trailer. The rig got stuck. Murray offered to pull it out with his pickup but Eddie, proud of himself, said he'd trained Dutchess to pull. While he broke out the harness and hooked her up, Murray kept busy in the barn. He didn't want to confuse the girls about who was handling them now.

Dutchess refused to pull, and Eddie took her around back to discipline her. He wound up on the ground, gasping for air. Dutchess had run, and it had taken him half an hour to get her back. Later, when he was tying off the camel, he again grew frustrated. He wanted her to stand still but she was nervous. He grabbed a fence post and smashed her in the mouth. "Stay still, goddamn it!"

One of the twins, Adam, was watching from the barn. He knew enough about training to see Eddie was going at it backward—first you give the command, then you reward or discipline the animal. It shook him to see blood spilling from her mouth, shook him even more when he got a closer look. Eddie had knocked out some teeth. Adam didn't tell his father until much later—it was nobody's business how you treated your animals—but the incident disturbed him.

When the money and the collateral agreement didn't turn up in the next day's mail, Eddie called home. His mother told him it would probably arrive the following day. Meantime, Eddie handed over the health certificates for the two elephants, the chimp, and the camel. Murray needed them to obtain a New York State health permit.

Next morning Murray told Eddie, "If I don't get that agreement today, you're going to sign a copy of it right here. We ain't leaving without it signed."

Nothing came in the mail, and Murray took Eddie to the bank in Fordland. Eddie complained all the way—call California, he kept saying, call my dad. "Goddamn right I will," said Murray, "soon as I get back. In the meantime, you're signing." Eddie didn't like it, but he signed the second agreement, giving Murray a security interest in the tractor, the trailer, the chimpanzee, and the camel, which he assumed the Drakes owned.

When they got back to the farm, Murray called Tehachapi. Dick was out, or so Doy said. Murray told her it was urgent. A few hours later he got a call from Dick's attorney, who said the additional collateral agreement hadn't gone out yet. Matter of fact, he was waiting for Dick to come in and sign it. Furious, Murray confronted Eddie: "Listen up, boy. Tell your father, unless I get the money and the signed agreement in twenty-four hours, everything stops right here." Eddie went in to phone, and a few minutes later Dick himself was on the line. Genial as ever, he started a song and dance about how he and the attorney kept missing each other.

"I'm tired of your bullshit. I want the agreement and the thousand dollars tomorrow."

"That might be a problem," said Dick. "It's five o'clock our time and the post office is closed."

"Send it to my insurance office, so they don't have to deliver out here. And no more goddamn excuses."

"I'll get it to you, Murray, don't worry."

"I don't want one of your phony checks. I want a money order."

"I won't be able to get anything off till tomorrow."

"If I don't get the agreement and the thousand, this is the end of the line. Understand?"

That evening, Thursday, they had to leave for New York to make the shoot, scheduled for Monday. They drove through the night and all next day, stopping only for food and fuel, and for a trooper who fined Murray for not having state fuel permits. Murray called Denise, who said nothing had arrived; and he called Bunny Brook, who said the shoot had been postponed until Wednesday.

In the middle of the second night, Murray pulled in for coffee and a sandwich while Eddie and Frank were sleeping. The truckstop happened to sell keys, and Murray had a duplicate cut for the ignition.

Any trucker in the northeastern United States can tell you stories about New York. Parts of the Bronx? Every time you stop, guys are on your windshield. They've got two spray bottles, one with soapy water. Pay, you get a clean windshield. Don't pay, you get the other bottle—if you're lucky, it's only urine. Or the Holland Tunnel, trying to get out at night? Traffic's at a standstill and they're all over, shaking down motorists. Think the cops give a damn? Or you get off at Hunt's Point Avenue, stop for a light, a black kid appears out of nowhere and, before you can react, yanks the Escort radar detector off the visor. Or you pay the toll on the George Washington Bridge, hand the girl a twenty, she gives you change and suddenly there's a hand on your hand, some acrobat is up on the running board. You're rolling with, say, eighty thousand pounds of sulphuric acid, fighting over a five-dollar bill. Kid grabs the money, he's gone. You pull over, hurry back to the toll booth, say to the girl, "You see that?" She shrugs: "I ain't seen nothing, mister." Now, unless that kid jumped down a thirty-foot embankment, she saw him all right, it must have been her little brother, by now you're so mad you're about ready . . .

Then you remember. You think of the night your buddy lost a trailer loaded with cigarettes on Ninth Avenue. No inkling, just a red light, the icy ring of a .38 Special against his temple, and somebody saying, "Mind if I drive, mutha?"

Or the time another buddy, asleep in his cab in the Bronx, got wakened by vibrations at four in the morning. Somebody was under the trailer, stealing the spare. Your buddy, adrenaline surging, took off after him—almost caught him, too—at the last instant he slipped away. Though your buddy hadn't been gone five minutes, he found his rig vanished, along with fifteen tons of dressed beef.

You see a black face and think, "Them." You're tempted to arm yourself, but in New York they'll jail you for an unregistered weapon. So you settle for a can of ether, use it once or twice, and hope word gets around. You keep your eyes open. You trust nobody. You never leave your rig where you can't see it, and you time your drop for daylight. You stay the hell out of New York at night.

Which is why the Pocono Truck Plaza, on the Pennsylvania–New Jersey border, does a brisk business. For many truckers coming east on Interstate 80, it's the last stop before New York. In mid-afternoon they start pulling in to wait for morning. The stop has a reputation, and on the CB you might run across somebody who has marijuana, or happens to know a very nice young lady. It's a spacious layout, with floodlit, blacktop parking, Union 76 fuel, restaurant, and truck facilities ("service—electronics—permits—showers—soft drinks—snacks —garage—scales"). There are motels nearby; across the street is a wash, down the road a Peterbilt dealer, next door an adult boutique ("XXX video booths—lingerie—novelties—videos— mags"), open twenty-four hours. The Pocono Truck Plaza has just about anything the weary trucker might need before venturing on.

Late Saturday afternoon, Murray Hill turned in to the truck stop. He'd told Eddie and Frank the bank commercial had been postponed—they'd lay over for the night, then stay at a friend's farm in New Jersey before heading into the city. Eddie opened the trailer to clean out manure while Murray went to find a phone.

"Soon as I'm done," Eddie said, "me and Frank are going for a beer. See you later."

The phone call was to Denise in Missouri. She attended her meetings faithfully, trying to keep up her spirits, but had that air of mournful concentration to which the recovering alcoholic is susceptible. She told Murray the second agreement and the thousand dollars still hadn't arrived.

"Check with the office, too?"

"Nothing came, here or there. I checked."

"That lying son of a bitch."

"What are you going to do, Murray? Don't do anything stupid."

Murray called the Pennsylvania State Police. That same night, he said, a tractor-trailer was going to be reported stolen, along with two elephants, a camel, a chimpanzee, and assorted equipment. "I'm the legal owner. I'm repossessing. Is there anything you need to look at? I'd be glad to show you the paperwork."

"Have you consulted an attorney, sir?"

Murray had been told by both an attorney in Missouri, and the original attorney in Oregon, that he was on solid ground so long as the agreement spelled out that he could repossess without legal recourse. The only proviso was that he couldn't create a civil disturbance. And what exactly was a civil disturbance? Well, said the attorney, if you knocked on the man's door and announced, "I'm taking back my property," and he picked up his shotgun and said, "Hell you are," you'd have the makings of a civil disturbance. Why do you think cars get repossessed in the middle of the night? If nobody's around to object, you're in the clear.

When Murray returned to the rig, Frank and Eddie had left. The keys, normally in the ignition, were gone. The temperature was dropping and a light rain had started to fall. Murray went around back and opened up the trailer to check the animals. Tory and Dutchess, racking in their chains, grew animated. The camel, hitched up behind them, spat and strained against her chains. The chimp screamed and rattled his cage.

Murray closed up the trailer and took Eddie's and Frank's sleeping bags into the motel. A few minutes later he came back out, crossed the asphalt, and climbed into the cab. He had to fiddle with the new key before it finally turned the ignition.

It was after ten o'clock when Eddie and Frank returned to the truckstop. Scores of rigs were aligned in rows under the blurred floodlights. Passing cars made a wet, hissing noise; the drizzle was turning to sleet. Eddie, full of beer, rubbing his arms to keep warm, figured he must have got confused.

"We left it right here, didn't we, Frank? Down at this end? You don't think—"

"It's gone," said Frank.

Eddie, stunned, then furious, hurried into the motel. Murray had left their sleeping bags and stuck a note under the door of their room. It said he was repossessing the elephants in accordance with the terms of the contract and would return any personal property in the rig. Along with the note was a hundred dollars.

"You believe this shit, Frank? All my stuff's in that truck— clothes, tools, everything."

"Mine, too."

"He's got my chimp."

"And the camel."

"My new tape player. Man, and right after I fill up the tank." He slammed his fist on the registration desk. "Three hundred and forty bucks' worth of diesel."

"Smiling the whole time, too."

"That little motherfucker," said Eddie, crumpling the note. "He's going to pay."

4

MEADOW GATE FARM

Both elephants extremely nervous and frightened. Holes and boils from misuse and abuse of hook. Hook wounds and lacerations ranging in age from 7 to about 180 days.
—Dr. Michael Milts, D.V.M., 1982

▼·▼·▼·▼·▼·▼·▼·▼·▼·▼·▼·▼·▼·▼·▼

Early next morning, Murray was awakened in the sleeper by the racking of Tory and Dutchess. At Bunny Brook's instruction, he had parked near the front gate of her farm. In the chilly dawn, he ran rope lines from the truck to the fence, creating an enclosure, then opened the trailer doors. He unloaded the camel and tied her off to the back of the truck. Then he went inside for the girls. In the smelly dark, they stirred in anticipation.

"Foot," said Murray.

Tory raised her foot, but when he reached for her front chain she shied, pulling her head back. Strange; she usually leaned toward him so he could scratch her. He undid her chain and said, "Foot," to Dutchess. She too pulled back, extending her chained foot rather than lifting it. When he undid their back chains, Tory

▲·▲·▲·▲·▲·▲·▲·▲·▲·▲·▲·▲·▲·▲·▲

started toward the open doors of the trailer. Murray steadied her and passed between the elephants. He hopped down and said, "Come ahead."

Tory came first, hesitantly, shying badly as she came out, staying as far from him as she could. She seemed to have developed a limp in her hindquarters. When Dutchess came out, she, too, balked, keeping her head pulled back and her body angled away from him. Murray felt something in the pit of his stomach.

Bunny and her husband, Leonard, had come from the barn; some horses, camels, zebras, and donkeys had also wandered over to watch. Bunny's air of pleased anticipation turned to puzzlement as the girls emerged. She was surprised by their skittish agitation. They seemed to her different elephants than those she'd seen at the auction in Cape Girardeau. She glanced questioningly at Murray, but he kept busy, avoiding her eye.

The girls had been taught to carry their chains so that he didn't have to bend down. He took the chain from Tory's trunk and, securing her hind leg to the truck, saw that her nails were long and deeply ridged. They couldn't have been trimmed since the Drakes bought her—they were turning to claws—and her foot pads needed work as well. He stepped toward Dutchess; again she shied, holding the chain in her curled trunk and pulling her head back. "Give me your foot, damn it! What's the matter with you?" He ducked under her massive head and, with the heel of his hand, whacked her jaw. "Get over!" She moved, and he took the chain from her trunk. "Now give me your foot." Wild-eyed, like a horse about to bolt, she lifted her foot. Chaining her, Murray saw that her feet and nails were as bad as Tory's.

Only when she dropped her trunk did he see the hook boil on her forehead. It was a few days old, raw and swollen, the size of an orange.

Damn that kid! There'd been no need to use a hook. Murray ran a hand down the inside of each of her legs. They were riddled with dried-up hook boils. He checked her back legs and found them scarred as well. Tory, too, had scars on all four legs.

Murray wished Bunny and Leonard weren't there—this was humiliating. All the same, he needed to see it through.

"All right," he said, "stretch out."

Ordinarily the girls went into the stretch position on command, sinking awkwardly to their rear knees and then extending their front legs. They refused to go down. Murray had the same awful, helpless feeling as when Denise had told him on the phone, years earlier, that Allan had had an accident. He commanded the girls again and they only looked about anxiously. To get them down he had to brandish his hook. Even so it took a few minutes.

"Now lay down."

Both girls were on the verge of panic. Neither rolled over on her side.

"Lay down, damn it! What's wrong with you?"

He knew what was wrong. To discipline an elephant, some trainers stretch it, lay it down, then beat it in the area of the kidneys. The girls were scared.

Bunny's look had turned from puzzlement to horror. She ran a dirty hand through her hair. People's animals were their own business, but she felt so deeply about every creature it was all she could do not to—

"Need help?" said Leonard, to ease the tension.

"No, I don't need help."

Goddamn people. What did they know? Murray wished nobody else was there. He wished he didn't feel embarrassed and ashamed. He wished he'd never sold the girls in the first place. Again he commanded them; they refused to lie down.

"Up," he said, "get up," and clumsily, from the stretch position, fighting their own tremendous weight, they regained their feet.

"Stand outside the fence," he told Bunny and Leonard. They moved back, and he unchained the girls, who shied again. "Move up," he said. He'd taught them to circle even when they weren't in a ring, and they began moving around the enclosure, Tory favoring one hind leg, squeaking anxiously. She had always been a poor herd animal; she wouldn't take another tail for long. Dutchess, though, would stay tailed up come hell or high water. Now, no matter how firmly Murray commanded her, she wouldn't take Tory's tail. She looked frantically about, as if to see where she was going to get hit from. Those bastards!

To avoid mishaps in the ring, Murray had trained the girls to defecate on command. He tickled Tory and said, "Dump it. Get it out." She strained; her intestine bulged out below her anus, but nothing came.

"Poor thing," said Bunny. "What's the matter with her?"

"They must have had her doing hind-leg stands," said Murray. "She used to do a beautiful standup. Her back was straight as a board and she held her feet out like two mirrors. But all that weight drops straight down. I warned them about it."

Bunny fixed him with a baleful look. "How could you sell to them?"

"Hell, I told them about Tory's rupture."

"Didn't you even check them out?"

He felt bad enough without questions meant to make him feel worse. "How stupid you think I am? Where's some water around here?"

"They've been mistreated," she said with contempt.

His anger at the Drakes he directed at Bunny: "I've had these girls twenty years, for chrissake!"

"Spigot's over here," said Leonard, genially interposing himself. He showed Murray to the water and helped with the hose. "Guess you got problems," he said quietly.

"Damn right I got problems."

Bunny, not about to let him off the hook, called after him, "You sold them to people who abused them." It sounded like an accusation of murder.

Man, this woman didn't know when to back off. If he weren't on their property he just might have given her a piece of his mind. He shrugged—"I put a clause in the contract. What else could I do?"—and went inside the trailer to fetch some feed and compose himself. He sure hadn't counted on this. Under stress, Dutchess was a runner—he'd have to watch her closely on the American Express shoot. It would take weeks to regain her trust. When he came back out and threw the girls some grain, Bunny glared at him and started for the house.

"I can't believe you'd sell to those people."

"Don't get all bent out of shape," said Murray. "It ain't your problem."

"The first thing we have to do is get the vet down here."

She and Leonard had owned Meadow Gate Farm for ten years and knew many veterinarians in the area. Though it was Sunday, she got one out to Colts Neck that afternoon and another the next morning. Doug Bowman lived nearby. A farm vet, he was good at intuiting the similarities between cows and camels, and between elephants and horses. The second vet, Dr. Michael Milts, who lived in New York, did a lot of work for the Bronx Zoo. He drove down from the city to examine the camel and the girls. His report was terse:

> Camel (small female dark brown). Two left front teeth knocked out within 3 to 4 days. Animal extremely nervous and head shy. Has been abused.
>
> Dutchess (larger elephant). Hook boils on inside of both front and hind legs. Very large hook boil center of head.
>
> Tory (smaller elephant). Numerous hook boils on inside of left front leg. Large rectal hernia. Toe nails overgrown and twisted. Pads of feet in very poor condition—foot rot. Severe limp high in left hind leg.
>
> Both elephants extremely nervous and frightened. Holes and boils from misuse and abuse of hook. Hook wounds and lacerations ranging in age from 7 to about 180 days.

Angry and confused, Murray walked the property to do some thinking. The Brooks had a fine farm, forty-two acres with good pasture, a creek, a pond, and lovely shade trees, but their animal operation had long since outgrown it. Like a junkyard, the place had an air of useless profusion—everywhere you looked there were broken wagons, horse trailers, pails, rusted bed frames, ducks, geese, swans, old mattresses, warped doors, buckets, ostriches, spare tires, chickens, goats, gas cans, pigs, monkeys, garbage, camels, zebras, wagon wheels, stripped appliances, feed, fencing, caged lions, manure, chains, lumber, and farm implements.

Leonard told him that animals showed up mysteriously—abandoned kittens, deformed birds, limping dogs. Everyone in the area knew that no creature would be turned away from Meadow Gate Farm. The Brooks took broken-down thoroughbreds from the racetrack, camels with leukemia, pet-store primates their owners no longer wanted. In all they had close to six hundred animals, which they supported with public donations and with their income from renting out stock for movies and commercials.

The barn was chaotic and foul; the house was a continuation of the barn. Everything was mixed together—books, cats, empty cages, spoiled food, art objects, sour milk, animal feces, parrots, antique furniture. The plumbing didn't work, and the bathroom made the public facilities in Calcutta look hygienic. Bunny cleared a space on the couch and made coffee. When Murray offered to help, she told him there was a vicious dog in the kitchen—he wasn't to come in. Leonard, meanwhile, gathered the soiled newspaper that covered the floors, and laid down fresh sheets. The place reeked. It sounded like a zoo at feeding time.

Were these people crackers? Their notion of training certainly struck Murray as bizarre. There was no order, no system. Many of their animals were uncontrollable. Small wonder Bunny had been interested in Tory—her own elephants were so undisciplined you risked getting your head knocked off. No way you could safely work them. Even with help—Murray had noticed a couple of farmhands—simply maintaining that much stock couldn't have left time for anything else. When he'd wakened that morning, before six, they'd already done a feeding.

Over coffee, shooing a baby donkey determined to urinate on his boots, Murray explained why he'd repossessed the rig and the girls. Leonard rubbed his beard skeptically—"How do we know this is the case?"—but was persuaded by the paperwork. The tractor-trailer was still registered in Murray's name, and the purchase agreement spelled out his right to repossess on financial and humanitarian grounds.

"What's the next step?" said Leonard.

"He needs a lawyer," said Bunny.

Bunny got hold of a local attorney she and Leonard had used, Peter Sachs, who told Murray there was nothing to worry about unless the Drakes filed a complaint.

Murray thanked him and, raising his voice above the squawking of cockatoos, told Bunny and Leonard he needed to see the police. "I already spoke to the Pennsylvania cops last night, before I took off. I'll show the Jersey police the paperwork so they know I repossessed fair and square."

"There's a barracks in Colts Neck," said Leonard. "I'll run you over right now."

Dick Drake had grown up in the part of New Jersey that's midway between the Pocono Truck Plaza to the west and Meadow Gate Farm to the east. His father had farmed near Scotch Plains, boarding hoof stock and selling lumber off the property to make ends meet. When the farmhouse burned down, Fayette moved his wife and children to a property near Far Hills. Water came from a big gravity-fed cistern. On winter mornings you could see your breath; everybody hurried down to get near the old coal stove, which also heated the water. There was no telephone. Dick was eight before they got electricity.

North Jersey was where Dick had met Doy Matheson and fallen in love with her kind heart. It was where they'd gone to school—both graduated from Morristown High—and square-danced on horseback, and ridden with the Trail Pals. They entered all the local competitions and shows, and if Dick finished second it was usually because Doy had finished first. Together they won the matrimonial race, galloping side by side the length of the arena while holding hands.

North Jersey was where Dick and his construction partner had got their picture in the paper by wiring elk horns on a deer they'd shot in a hunting contest. It was where he'd met Richie

Novack, fighting over the last barrel in a horseback game of musical chairs and winding up best friends. It was where he'd buried his parents, and it was where his sister still lived, with her husband and two sons.

Dot Wilkie, three years Dick's senior, worked at the municipal hall in Bedminster; her husband, Bill, was an appliance repairman and volunteer fireman who monitored the world on his CB radio. Their son Billy was a carpenter; his older brother, Alex, worked construction, taught martial arts, and maintained an arsenal that filled a bedroom and seemed adequate to outfit a small army.

The Wilkies had built a house on twelve acres of what had once been the family farm near Far Hills. The house itself was modest, but the land had become extremely valuable. Far Hills is the sort of place where the road signs showing rampant stags are unmarked by bullets, and deer really do bound across the highway. Many of the Wilkies' neighbors were millionaires. Mike Tyson owned an estate near Bedminster and was often seen tooling around in his white Rolls-Royce; Douglas Dillon, the former U.S. ambassador to France, sometimes took guests fox-hunting; the Malcolm Forbes mansion was a local landmark.

In the fifteen years since Dick's move to California the Drakes and Wilkies had seen little of each other, but their ties remained strong. When Dot Wilkie received a distraught call from Doy Drake in California, telling them Eddie's rig had been stolen from a truckstop on the Pennsylvania border, the Wilkies swung into action. Bill went to pick up Eddie and Frank, while Alex and a couple of friends, the Meyer twins, sped up to the interstate. They went as far as the tunnels into Manhattan, checking every rest area for manure, but found no trace of the rig.

Dick knew Murray would do the American Express commercial, and that he'd need health permits to take the elephants into Manhattan. He called the city health authorities to say that Murray had stolen the rig and shouldn't be granted the permits. Leonard, who dealt with the city officials frequently, assured them Murray was the legitimate owner.

American Express was doing a series of lighthearted spots. The idea was that life would have been simpler for historical characters—Columbus, George Washington, Hannibal—with a credit card. Murray trucked into Manhattan and spent an apprehensive day in the studio. Tory stayed in the background while Dutchess carried an actor, dressed as Hannibal, on her neck; she seemed anxious and uneasy, but Murray stuck tight to her and she didn't misbehave. He was paid a much needed $4,500 for his work.

Dick, meanwhile, got the address at Colts Neck. It was his friend Richie Novack, a trucker, who spotted the rig in the field at Meadow Gate Farm. He called Dick in California. Dick phoned Eddie, telling him to notify police and make sure Murray didn't go anywhere while they were figuring out how to get the rig and their own animals back. Richie Novack drove Eddie and his friend Frank down to Colts Neck. At the barracks, told by the duty officer that Murray had already been in, they realized that the police had no intention of helping other than to accompany them to Meadow Gate Farm so Eddie and Frank could pick up their personal effects.

On the drive out, Eddie seethed. He'd had the chimp for years and loved him the way kids love a dog. Buddy was his pal, his pet, and his meal ticket. At Bunny's front gate, he asked a farmhand if Murray Hill was there. When Murray came down from the house, Eddie wanted to throttle him.

"Give me my stuff."

"Your clothes are ready for you," said Murray.

"What about my tools?" said Frank.

"Tools are up there. Everything except the bolt cutters that disappeared out of my barn. You can back the pickup onto the property and load up."

"What about the camel and chimp?" said Eddie.

"I don't see any trailer."

Eddie glanced at Richie, a curly-haired giant with hands the size of biscuit tins and a deceptive air of lethargy. Richie seemed amused that a little runt like Murray could cause all this fuss.

"You're here to pick up your things," said the trooper. He'd unfastened the snap on his holster.

"Look, man," said Eddie, "what do you want for a buyout? We'll pay off the rest of the contract."

"Wouldn't pay your goddamn bills and all of a sudden you got money for a buyout?"

"How much?"

"Think I'd sell after the way you treated them? How'd I get involved with you people? Take your shit and get out of here."

"This is the last time I'm going to ask."

"That sounds like a threat," the trooper warned Eddie.

Eddie would have straightened Murray out then and there if the cop hadn't been around. As it was, they could only load their things and head back to Dot's place. When Eddie reported what had happened, Dick told him to go back. Now that Murray knew they were on to him, he'd probably make a run for it.

Later that day Eddie, Frank, and Richie returned to Meadow Gate Farm, along with Eddie's cousin Alex. They staked out the place and waited. "I'll tell you," said Eddie, "the minute that little mother steps off private property . . ." It wasn't until they'd spent a fruitless afternoon that they realized nobody had money. They'd have to pool their meager resources to get dinner.

Richie Novack was built like a defensive tackle gone to seed, six three and more like three hundred pounds than two hundred. Alex Wilkie was an imposing six-foot two-hundred-pounder. Frank was a decent size, and Eddie, though shorter, was solid and muscular. Leaving Frank in the woods to keep an eye out, the others found a bar that served hors d'oeuvres and gobbled them. Back at Meadow Gate Farm, it was starting to look like Murray would spend the night. They ended up trying to sleep in Alex's Cougar, all four of them. Mostly they squirmed and farted and bumped each other.

By sunup, Eddie was ready to invade the place. But it was

well fenced, and there were guard dogs. They distracted the dogs long enough for Frank to slip into the cab to retrieve the paperwork, but Murray had removed it. More sitting around. Eddie entertained the others with descriptions of what he was going to do once he got his hands on Murray. More listening to the radio, as the hours dragged by and tempers started fraying. For lunch they split a sandwich and ate some wild onions. At the bar they nursed a beer and wolfed peanuts and pretzels.

The second night was sheer torture, and by the third morning everybody was exhausted and half starved, with stiff backs and sore necks. Richie had kicked out the speaker, they were flat broke, and the Cougar was getting ripe. Alex, having missed two days' work, wondered aloud why they were leaving the ball in Murray's court. Why not go in and take care of business?

Now, Eddie Drake was no slouch in a dustup, but his cousin, he knew, was in a different league. All that ninja shit? His own survival course, complete with sharpened bamboo stakes? Anti-tank weapons in the basement? Backyard firing range? Man, Alex was from a different planet. This was a guy who bagged deer with a bow and arrow—try it sometime. Eddie had watched his cousin's transformation over the years. At an age when most kids were reading *Mad* magazine, Alex—the ninety-eight-pound weakling—had sent away for *Soldier of Fortune*. After the testosterone kicked in and other kids were swapping centerfolds, Alex had a stash of grainy black-and-whites of gooks with their brainpans blown open. While his classmates shot baskets, he was mastering in succession each of the martial arts.

Alex was now a quietly intense, brutally fit black belt who ran his own word-of-mouth training school ("teaching Special Forces guys serious shit, man," Eddie told Frank, "shit the Special Forces don't even teach them"). He was a piece of work, all right. With his Filipino butterfly knives and Indonesian ground-fighting techniques, with his crossbows and AK-47s and Klan literature and Rambo posters and customized slam-fire weapons and .308 heavy-barrel assault rifles, why, if truth be known, he even scared Eddie a little. Turn him loose on Murray, the sorry little son of a bitch? No way. The cops already knew of the dispute, for one thing, and Dick had said let's go by the book, and—much as Eddie longed to wipe out not just Murray Hill but his entire bloodline—when you came right down to it who wanted to pull seven years for manslaughter?

In Dick's day you rolled up your sleeves to settle things. That's how Eddie had been brought up, as several unfortunates could attest. But the world had changed, and the Drakes, keeping pace with the times, made like any other modern, law-abiding citizen who wanted to cripple somebody.

They got a lawyer.

Murray needed money but had nothing until the Greenville, South Carolina, date in late April. He could have hooked up with Pat Guthrie's carnival in Alabama to earn a few bucks; but he'd given up life on the road, his back was bothering him, and he was unsure of the girls. All of which meant he had little choice but to return to the farm in Missouri and the wife he planned to divorce.

When Bunny invited him to stay on at Meadow Gate Farm, he accepted gratefully. The weather was gorgeous—New Jersey was in bloom—and he'd always felt at home with animal people. He also needed time to get the girls in trim and win back their trust. Each day he worked on them, helped with chores, and got friendlier with Bunny and Leonard.

Talk about an odd couple. Leonard was a middle-aged New York Jew, ten years younger than Murray, a kind man with a frequently depressed manner and shit on his shoes. His father had owned a clothing store in Times Square; he'd been an artist when he met Bunny. His conversion to animal keeper had begun innocently enough: they'd both been fond of dogs. Twenty years of living with Bunny showed in his hunched posture and air of ironic resignation, like that of someone who offers to carry your bags and finds they're full of books.

Bunny was a manic dynamo. Arab blood ran through her

veins; she was a woman of volatile opinions and abrupt passions. She'd spot some horribly overpriced piece of artistic junk
at the flea market and—though the truck needed new brakes—
buy it, make a place for it in the jumbled living room, and never
look at it again. A strict vegetarian, she seemed to eat nothing
but eggs and pills. She'd been married previously—so, Murray
gathered, had Leonard—and had three grown daughters. Two
of them lived at the farm; the other lived in Manhattan and
wanted nothing to do with the animal business. Bunny's sister
ran the New York office of Dawn Animal Agency; apparently
they had a brother who lived in Michigan.

Murray overheard Leonard on the phone, referring to
Bunny as "my wife," and Bunny used Leonard's last name,
Brook; yet at the auction in Cape Girardeau she had introduced a much younger man as her husband, and one of the
older farmhands also seemed to feel for her in a way that sur-
passed the professional. Fascinated by her frenetic zeal, Murray
felt a growing attraction. At times she seemed to acknowledge
it; at other times he might have been a fence post. It was hard
to chat with her for more than two minutes. Distractible as a
child, with a manner that suggested she had more important
things to do, she was maddeningly vague and elusive. Murray
had gleaned what little he could from an irritated remark here,
a terse instruction there. No point asking anything directly; if
you pried, she'd tell you to fuck yourself.

No mention had been made of room or board, electricity, or
feed costs. To repay the Brooks' generosity, Murray asked
Bunny if she'd like to do a camel ride at the Greenville zoo
while he was there. She said sure, and he made the arrangements.

A few days later, he was checking the ride equipment—ticket
stand, howdahs, loading platform—when fat snowflakes came
swirling out of the afternoon sky. The storm caught everyone
by surprise. It began as a freak deluge of wet snow; then the
wind rose and the temperature fell. Bunny had heated quarters
for her elephants but there was no place for the girls, and Murray had no way of keeping them warm. He loaded them as the

blizzard gained force, and was ready to pull out when Bunny got back from town. She checked the barn, then hurried down to the rig. By now the ground was covered with snow. You couldn't see fifty feet.

"Got to get the girls out of here," he yelled over the bitter wind. "Can't believe how fast the temperature's dropping. My trailer ain't set for this weather."

"How long will you be gone?" she shouted.

"I'll stay down South until the Greenville date. Can you take care of the camel and chimp for me?"

"No problem."

"Meet you at the Greenville zoo," he said, climbing into the cab. "Sure hope you can make it down—I'm looking forward to seeing you. Say good-bye to Len and everybody."

Murray's two daughters were living on a farm in North Carolina; Robin had said he could lay over there. Once he got a couple of hundred miles south of Meadow Gate Farm the girls would be fine. Meanwhile, he crawled along Highway 33, which was almost deserted, peering through the driven snow and thinking about Bunny. What a contradictory woman. Did she feel anything for him? He'd never met anyone so hard to read, warmly expressive one minute, cool and clipped the next. He was about to pick up the southbound interstate when a vehicle appeared behind him, lights flashing off and on. A trooper? On a night like this? He pulled off and waited.

To his amazement, it was Bunny who, with an air of urgency, opened the door of the cab. The wind howled and snow blew in as she climbed into the seat beside him.

"What are you doing here?"

She rubbed her hands, warming them. "Is Greenville all set?"

"Course it is," he said, wondering why she'd go to such lengths to ask a stupid question.

"You're sure they can use the camel ride?"

"I already told you. Is that why you followed me out here?"

The girls started racking in their chains, shaking the semi from side to side. Bunny sat there, jolted by the motion of the trailer, watching snowflakes pelt the windshield. She turned and smiled at him in a way she never had before.

"That's one reason," she said.

The Drakes had emptied their wallets to put the elephants on the road for the spring and summer. Expecting their first decent pay in months from the American Express commercial, they'd been living on promises. The house at Cameron Canyon was the usual maelstrom of family and friends expecting food on the table. Suddenly the postdated checks written to cover bounced checks were coming back NSF; men with deep voices were calling for Richard E. Drake. To top it off, they were burning up the line between California and New Jersey. In the month after the repossession they ran up long-distance charges of $1,600.

Doy thanked her lucky stars they'd been in Tehachapi long enough that people knew them. The merchants were understanding, which solved the immediate problem. But there was nothing coming in, and who could say how much Eddie would earn once he started substituting Butch for the two females at his ride bookings in Michigan and Indiana, or how long Dick would be tied up getting the tractor-trailer back.

Doy was a woman of bounteous energy, happily juggling the roles of wife, mother, and grandmother with baseball, team penning, and volunteer work. In twenty-five years of marriage she had not held a paying job, but money had to come from somewhere. Besides, she enjoyed mornings in the high desert, liked getting up at four and driving out to Clear Lake, where she had landed a job waiting tables. It was something new, an adventure, and it wouldn't be the first time she'd bought groceries with crumpled dollar bills.

Dick, meanwhile, had driven nonstop to New Jersey to see the lawyer Eddie had lined up. Bunce Atkinson turned out to be a balding fellow in his mid-thirties who'd only just set up shop in Colts Neck. He'd attended Rutgers at a time when graduation meant military service. A few years earlier, in high school, he wouldn't have given the prospect of serving in Vietnam a second thought. Everybody had had parents in the Second World War and uncles in Korea; ducking the service would have been unpatriotic. But the war had made its way into the living room. Kent State had etched itself in people's minds, and so-called peace with honor was in the offing. Why fight for something nobody believed in? He joined the reserves instead. After basic training he was assigned to small-arms repair in Fort Lee, Virginia.

It was there that Atkinson decided to take the Law School Admissions Test. New Jersey was turning into one big toxic-dump site; something had to be done. He planned to work for either the federal Environmental Protection Agency or the New Jersey Department of Environmental Protection. After finishing law school and clerking for a Superior Court judge in Bergen County, however, he joined a firm that specialized in commercial collections. He acted for title companies and helped banks in their loan workouts when corporate borrowers ran into problems. It was a far cry from the EPA, perhaps, but along the way he'd realized he preferred the courtroom to the office. Litigation was what he excelled in and enjoyed.

After four years, Atkinson and a partner went out on their own. Besides banks and title companies, he wanted to represent developers, and Colts Neck looked promising. The two men had recently opened an office when Eddie Drake found Atkinson's name in the phone book. Eddie wasn't the type of client Atkinson imagined he'd attract, but half the fun was seeing who'd walk in the door. Dick turned out to be a buffed and polished version of Eddie, a genial mesomorph with the carnival midway in his soul.

Atkinson told the Drakes that the first step in recovering the disputed property was to enjoin it. He obtained a court order compelling Murray Hill not to remove the tractor-trailer or the animals from Meadow Gate Farm and giving him three weeks to show cause why the court should not grant the Drakes return of all property, plus damages and costs.

When a state trooper drove through the slush to serve the

order, however, Bunny Brook said Murray was no longer there. She wasn't sure where he'd gone, she said, and nobody else could accept responsibility for any legal papers. The trooper served her nonetheless. Having no way of contacting Murray before meeting up with him, she took the papers to Peter Sachs, her attorney, and asked him to return them to the court.

Dick had a good idea where Murray had gone, or at least where he'd show up: the elephant-ride date was a paycheck waiting to be cashed. He and Eddie headed south the next wcck, hitting Greenville on a rainy Sunday afternoon.

Unknown to Murray, Peter Sachs had appeared in court on his behalf. The court thus assumed Murray knew he had been served. It issued a new order, which Dick took with him to Greenville. He tried to enlist the help of Lee Sims, the zoo director. Sims said that the zoo had contracted for elephant rides and Murray was fulfilling the contract—that was all he cared about. Meantime, he wanted no negative publicity. Dick tried to enlist the cooperation of the police, but was told no judge would be available to look at the legal papers until Monday morning.

Bunny had returned to Meadow Gate Farm after overtaking Murray in the snowstorm; she had made her way to Greenville with the camels two weeks later. When they weren't giving rides at the zoo, she and Murray were happily sharing a motel room. Once the Drakes started sniffing around, she and Murray agreed there was no point in his staying. While the Drakes were busy elsewhere, he loaded the girls and followed a cruiser out to the highway. "I'll escort you to the city line," the cop had said. "After that, you're on your own. Just don't turn around."

Bunny had to stay in the area an extra couple of days; she'd also booked the camels for a movie shoot near Greenville. When the Drakes learned that Murray had left town, they went looking for her. Eddie confronted her in a field at Bob Jones University, where a scene was being filmed. He told her the New Jersey court had awarded them everything.

"Who are you kidding?" she said with disgust. "He had every right to repossess."

"That don't matter," said Eddie, waving the court order. "We got the papers right here."

"You'll have to speak to the attorney."

"Give me the goddamn camel, lady, I'm warning you."

"Don't try that shit on me," Bunny said, and walked away.

Murray had trucked the girls back to his daughter Robin's in North Carolina, where he was waiting for Bunny. It was an awkward time. The kids were delighted to see their dad, and they made him welcome, but other people were living in the house, and Robin was trying to cope with both a new baby and her rocky relationship with the baby's father. She felt a special warmth for her mother just then—Denise had come down to help after Ian's birth, despite her own shaky condition. Robin and Nada had spent years getting out from under their father's thumb and, much as they enjoyed his visits, they were ambivalent about his taking up residence with Tory and Dutchess and his new love. Good for him, finding somebody, but why was he dumping their mother when she was practically helpless? And why had he never shown her the attentiveness and consideration he was showing Bunny?

Unmindful of his daughters' mixed feelings, Murray wanted to get things straight with Bunny before returning to Meadow Gate Farm. How were they going to play this? He'd never cheated before—not that it was cheating when you were practically divorced—and he wasn't entirely comfortable with the idea of living under the same roof as Leonard. Bunny told him that, though her marriage had long since ended, she preferred to keep their affair quiet.

"So Leonard ain't your husband."

"He was, at one time."

"You carry on like you're still married."

"Business reasons," said Bunny. "Now, what are we going to do about those people? Do you want them taken care of?"

"The Drakes?" said Murray. "It's just a lawsuit."

"They're going to take your elephants and your trailer."

Murray smiled, shaking his head in indulgent wonder. "Come on, Bunny, they ain't going to take a goddamn thing."

While Bunny trucked the camels back to Meadow Gate Farm and Murray stayed on at Robin's, Dick Drake was putting up posters in South Carolina, checking farmers' fields, and making inquiries at truck stops. A fellow at one gas station said two elephants had come through a couple of days earlier; that was as close as Dick got. He and Eddie caught up with Pat Guthrie in Kentucky, but Murray had phoned to say he and the girls weren't going to tour with the Guthrie show after all.

On the long drive back to New Jersey, Dick and Eddie hashed things over. It burned Eddie that Murray had his chimp and the borrowed camel, but the rig wasn't worth much and he figured they might as well leave the matter in Bunce Atkinson's hands.

Dick was more sanguine. In his view Murray had no right to anything but the elephants; he wanted to find the little thief and straighten this out. Where could Murray have gone? He'd avoid the obvious spots, like his place in Missouri and Meadow Gate Farm in New Jersey. What did that leave? Dick felt he'd probably work the elephants to feed them—which narrowed his options—and stay within shouting distance of New Jersey to deal with the legal situation.

After a pit stop near Philadelphia, Eddie took the wheel for the final jump to Dot's place. Dick, who'd hardly slept in three days, dozed off trying to imagine where you'd go if you wanted to keep two elephants out of sight.

"Give me my life to live over," said Al Campellone, a chunky, thoughtful fellow of middle age, "and I'd be Amish, out in the fields, working with animals. A labor of love—getting out of each day what you put in." He wore heavy work clothes, steel-toed boots, and a cap tilted back on his head. He was showing a visitor around a rural property near Philadelphia.

"My livelihood is utility construction," he said, "but my real love is horses. I've been into horses all my life. When I was growing up in Philadelphia, draft horses were still used by the dairies and the bakeries. The dairies had a competition on the care and beauty of their horses. One of the dairies was right next to our home. They had a large stable just down the street, and I spent many hours there.

"Later I worked for the dairy, and when Barnum and Bailey came to Philadelphia, it was our account. That gave me an opportunity to spend a lot of time with the circus animals, which I enjoyed. The tents were set up in our local neighborhood, so I could hang around quite a bit. I was fascinated by the animals— lions, monkeys, elephants.

"After I got out of the service in 1946 I bought myself a riding horse and became associated with local riding groups. I was subsequently appointed director of the Bicentennial Activities Committee; we worked closely with the Pennsylvania SPCA, and I became active with the historic societies in the communities where we took riding trips.

"It was through these involvements that I met Leonard Brook, up in Colts Neck, New Jersey, where he and his wife kept exotic animals for show purposes. One day he called and said he had a friend with two elephants who had business in this area. Could he lay over for a couple of weeks? I said sure. At that time, we were leasing and had twenty-seven acres fenced in. As you can see, the property adjoins a farm on one side and the Schuylkill Valley Nature Center on the other, so there are no immediate neighbors.

"I was working when Murray came in, but someone here showed him where to park the trailer. The people who owned the property didn't want a lot of activity, so the elephants mostly stayed up there behind the barn. We didn't make it known that they were here.

"The elephants were Tory and Dutchess. Tory, the smaller one, seemed the more pleasant. Dutchess appeared to be disgruntled—she had her head down and was weaving back and forth. Murray said, 'Is it all right if I let them go down and graze? They'll pull some of that tall grass.' He unchained them, and off they went. I said, 'What's the matter with her?' Murray said, 'She doesn't have all the freedom she'd like just now. Okay if I let her play?' I said sure, and he hollered down, 'Okay, Dutchess, you go play.'

"Well, Dutchess perked right up—let out one of those elephant calls you hear in the movies and trotted up the hill. She went into that clump of trees right there and started throwing her body around, shaking the trees, knocking leaves down, having a ball. After awhile Murray called, 'That's enough,' and she went back down the hill, letting it be known she was not too happy the fun was over. 'All right,' he said, 'go play some more.' She let out another yell and trotted back up.

"I spent quite a bit of time with Murray and his elephants. Their relationship was not what I'd seen anywhere else. In circuses, the guy has a hook, or he tugs the ear. Murray didn't use any devices to control his elephants; he had total voice control. They were like family to him, and I appreciated that relationship. It's common that people fall in love with their horses, but it was unique to see it with elephants. It was really something to see them understand their keeper and respond that way.

"I had Murray over to meet my mother, who was quite elderly. She enjoyed his visit. She likes to feed people, and I guess Murray's one of those skinny little guys who always looks like he needs to be fed. He took her to see the elephants—she got a kick out of that. Our conversation was always fairly general, but I got the impression, through things he said, that there were problems with his wife and they were in the process of splitting up, something along those lines. I didn't pry. He was good with his animals, which tells you a lot about a person.

"Murray was here a couple of weeks, then he said his business was over and he was leaving. He offered me compensation for the facilities. I told him it wasn't necessary. Having the elephants here was one of those unique experiences—how many times will you get the chance to have that sort of exposure to such magnificent animals? I felt fortunate just having them on the farm.

"He said if I was ever down Missouri way, I was welcome to stop in and see him. I said likewise, if you're ever back in the area and need to lay over, just let me know. I was unaware of his situation at that time, and I can't honestly say I had any idea I'd be seeing him and those beautiful elephants again."

After losing track of Murray in South Carolina, Eddie Drake had returned to California and found work as a crane operator. The state power authority was erecting wind machines on the mountains near Tehachapi; in the high desert, wind machines were an efficient way of generating power for the cities of the Antelope Valley—Tehachapi, Lancaster, Palmdale, and Rosamund. Like his father, Eddie was a skilled heavy-equipment operator. Though angered by the loss of his chimp and the borrowed camel, he assumed he'd eventually get them back. In the meantime, he had to get on with his life.

Dick, too, was starting to resign himself to a prolonged stalemate when, in mid-summer, Richie Novack called: "Hey, Dickie, I swung by Colts Neck this morning. Guess who's back at Meadow Gate Farm." Dick alerted Bunce Atkinson, who obtained a court order from the Superior Court of New Jersey. After reviewing the facts of the case, Judge Laurence Stamelman ordered that Murray turn over the camel and the chimp to the Drakes. Murray was entitled to possession of Tory and Dutchess, Judge Stamelman ruled, and could do with them as he wished. The rig, pending final disposition of the suit, was not to be moved off Meadow Gate Farm.

Murray was now being represented by a law firm Bunny had recommended. One of her help had been injured while working on a line-painting truck, and a firm in Elizabeth had handled his suit against the driver who had clipped him. Bunny put Murray in touch with Rinaldo and Rinaldo. Because he was broke, she also put up the $2,500 retainer.

Rinaldo and Rinaldo was a small, general-practice firm that specialized in personal injury and criminal law. One of the senior partners generally did the initial work with a client and established the fee schedule. Then the question of which of the firm's half-dozen attorneys did what became a matter of scheduling. Most evenings they'd look at the next day's roster of court appearances and divvy them up. You handle Ocean County, I'll handle Middlesex, and Gerry has to be in Monmouth County, doesn't he? Great. He can answer the interrogatory in the elephant-man case.

For a young lawyer like Gerry Martin, Rinaldo and Rinaldo was an ideal place to start out. It was small enough that you got involved in all kinds of things and, if you had a question, one of the senior guys could probably answer it. Matty and John each had thirty-plus years under their belts, and Tony must have had twenty-five. Being able to bounce ideas off them and kick around trial strategy gave young attorneys an accelerated education and bolstered their confidence in court.

Martin had graduated from Seton Hall, then run a small exporting business before going back to school. At twenty-four he'd entered Fordham Law School in Manhattan; he wound up at Rinaldo and Rinaldo through fraternity connections. He'd been at the firm for three years when he inherited Murray.

Much of what Martin did was drudgery, plain and simple, but he was happy to take this case on. Murray was a character, for one thing, unlike anyone he'd represented. Besides, as the suit played itself out, he couldn't help but learn.

Leonard Brook got on well with Murray Hill, but as weeks turned into months he came to view him as a stubborn little fellow with a chip on his shoulder and a reluctance to say thanks. Here they'd gone out of their way to help him and his elephants, and he acted like it was his due. He had a strong attachment to the girls—that would be what had won Bunny's heart—but couldn't she see the guy was a schmo? They fed him, kept him in tobacco, booked his elephants—the girls did a number of commercials and promotions, and Tory appeared in a Robert Mitchum movie, *That Championship Season*. They even gave him a bedroom. He did little more in return than drive the stock truck, tend the waterfowl, and throw hay to their elephants when he fed his own. That and fiddle with his kiln, trying to perfect a way of preserving elephant turds.

Murray had this harebrained notion of packaging turds in plastic boxes of the sort corsages come in, advertising them as a novelty—"Paky Poo" was one name he mentioned—and selling them by mail order and in stores. This was going to solve his problems! It would have been funny except that Murray had long since got on Leonard's nerves. What had started as a brief layover had turned into an extended stay. Talk about the man who came to dinner. Not much Leonard could do now except avoid the little loudmouth and hope the trial came soon.

As for Bunny, she was a marvel of haywire energy. She got up at five o'clock to feed the animals. Both she and Leonard worked eighteen or twenty hours a day. At six in the morning they'd be loading dogs for a shoot in Cleveland. At ten her daughter would pull in with monkeys, back from a job in Manhattan. Meanwhile the new goat was sick, the driver from Agway wanted to know where to drop the grain, the Bureau of Non-Game Animals needed information, the parrots were squawking, the dogs were barking, the guy from Atlantic Carting was hauling off waste, and the New York office, run by Bunny's sister, wanted to know if Leonard, at seven the next morning, could have two black dogs and a braying donkey at the studio in Queens where Woody Allen was shooting his new film. It seemed to Murray total bedlam.

Bunny was unbelievable. You'd be telling her something and she'd blurt out something unrelated, steamrolling right over you. She didn't even realize she was interrupting. She had her own agenda and the world had better respect it. She couldn't talk now—she was in a rush, had to nurse a lion cub—but she'd call you at ten o'clock. You'd sit by the phone until noon before calling her, and think she'd say sorry for failing to phone? Hell no, she'd get short with you! For interrupting! Her concern for animals and family was boundless; her treatment of other people was appalling. She was unreliable. She tailored the truth to suit her purposes. She promised things and forgot them. Murray took perverse pride in his own difficult nature, but he couldn't hold a candle to her.

He was smitten.

And so, it seemed, was she. When they did bookings together —in Englishtown, New Jersey, or Furlong, Pennsylvania, or Great Barrington, Massachusetts—it was bliss, the kind of sweetness he hadn't known in thirty years. They worked side by side, laughing and waiting to get back to the room. With her usual vagueness, she had mentioned a place in West Virginia they could use and perhaps one day live on. When he raised the topic, of course, she looked at him like he was crazy. Where did you get that idea? She was one of the most unreliable and abrasive people he'd ever met.

He was in love.

Because the house at Colts Neck was given over to animals, the domestic arrangements were unusual. A baby goat and baby llama lived in the living room; so, basically, did Bunny and Leonard. He slept in the big chair, she on the sofa—the only spots, besides Murray's bed, where sleep was possible. Murray worried that Leonard must have known she was tiptoeing upstairs in the middle of the night; she assured him he wouldn't mind. They'd been divorced for years and lived together for convenience.

"Why does it have to be a secret?"

"My daughters wouldn't understand."

"They're grown women, for chrissake. How come I'm having such a hard time believing you?"

"Want me to bring the divorce papers? You don't trust me?"

"Hey, it ain't that. I'm from Missouri. Show me."

Murray didn't doubt her love, but he couldn't help wondering about her financial generosity. At first he'd persuaded himself she was simply an animal nut concerned about Tory and Dutchess. As the relationship deepened, however, and they discussed the future, he saw that she assumed she'd end up with the girls. And indeed, as the months passed and the Drakes continued to pursue the suit, signing the girls over didn't seem such a bad idea. Counting room and board, feed, his use of her rig, and cash she'd given him—including $30,000 to prevent foreclosure on his farm in Missouri—she'd already sunk enough to have bought them outright. If she owned them legally, they'd be protected against the unforeseen. It was a long shot that things could backfire in court—Judge Stamelman had already ruled that Murray owned the elephants—but why take a chance? He'd sell the girls to Bunny. She'd file a lawsuit of her own, claiming Murray owed her for the time he'd spent at Meadow Gate Farm. He'd claim, in turn, that he'd been stuck at the farm because the Drakes had tied up his rig. Her suit might back the Drakes off; at the least it would provide a kind of insurance against an adverse judgment.

In the meantime, Murray's thoughts now encompassed the idea of a second marriage. His twin sons, he knew, didn't care for Bunny. They'd spent the summer at Meadow Gate Farm, lending a hand with Tory and Dutchess and sleeping in the barn. Murray had wanted them to stay for the school year, but they'd chosen to go home to their mother, even though it meant saying good-bye to the girls. Ah, well—adolescence was tough and at least the twins had each other. As for his daughters, they weren't crazy about Bunny either, but they kept in touch, phoning and sometimes visiting.

"How's your mother doing?" he asked Robin. "I haven't talked to her this week."

"She's good. I spoke to her on the weekend. She seems happy and goes to her group three or four times a week. How's everything there?"

"What's that?" said Murray, blocking one ear to muffle the din of cockatoos in the living room.

"How's everything there?"

"Same as ever," he said, kicking the little donkey that was peeing on his boots.

"How's your lawyer working out? Rinaldo."

"Now it's a young guy named Gerry Martin. I started out with one of the big shots and ended up with Gerry. Nice kid, but green. You know how these bastards work."

It was a time of infuriating complication in his life, and exhilarating change; he embraced the idea of spending his last decades with a new partner. The fight with the Drakes was turning into a prolonged mess, but he buoyed himself with thoughts of the future. Once the legal case had been resolved and his divorce from Denise finalized, he and Bunny and the girls would begin a new life together.

Neither Murray nor Dick Drake had had much experience of the legal system. Like most animal men of their generation, they had relied, in past disputes, on what lawyers refer to as self-help remedies. Neither understood the process that had been set in motion, neither anticipated its convolutions, and neither could have foreseen its end. How were they to know that a legal dispute is like a badminton match? To all appearances, the attorneys try to win every point by using all the shots in their repertoires. Mesmerized by the serves and returns, the lobs and smashes, a naïve client may take a while to appreciate that the attorneys do fine no matter what the final score. Their incomes depend not on who wins but on how long they keep the shuttlecock in the air.

Once Bunce Atkinson had filed the original complaint, Dick and Murray both imagined they'd go before a judge in weeks or perhaps months. Had they known, at the start, that before they met in court a notice of motion would be filed for an order dismissing the complaint and setting aside the order to turn over the disputed property, and the court would order that a responsive pleading be filed to the verified complaint, and that this would trigger, in turn, the counterclaim of the defendants; the proof of mailing and certification of Bunny Brook and Arlan Seidon a.k.a. Murray Hill; the answer to the counterclaim of the plaintiffs; a court order to show cause with temporary restraints; an amendment to the order to show cause to provide for substituted service; the certification of the defendant; the court order that the defendant turn over the camel and chimpanzee, keep possession of the elephants, and not move the tractor-trailer off Meadow Gate Farm; the certification of Arlan

Seidon aka Murray Hill; the notice of motion for an order compelling the depositions of the plaintiffs; a certification in opposition to the notice of motion for discovery; a failed settlement conference; a court order that the plaintiffs make themselves available for depositions within ninety days; a notice of motion to amend the counterclaim; the statement of depositions of Richard E. Drake; a court order that the defendant be allowed to file an amended counterclaim; the answer and amended counterclaim of the defendant; the answer to the amended counterclaim of the plaintiffs; an adjournment from April 8, 1983, to June 22, 1983; a further adjournment to October 17, 1983; a notice of motion to intervene with an affidavit; an amended affidavit of counsel in support of the motion to intervene; the certification of Gerry Martin; an affidavit in opposition to the notice of the motion to intervene; a court order that Bunny Brook be permitted to intervene in the suit; an answer to the complaint in intervention of the defendant; the complaint in intervention; another answer to the complaint in intervention of the defendant—had they known that the case would again be listed for trial, on October 17, 1983; then adjourned to November 28, 1983; then adjourned to March 19, 1984; then adjourned to April 16, 1984—had they known that, after the cumbersome apparatus of the law had been exploited, the list of pleadings would fill two columns in the Superior Court docket, the attorneys would run up billings that far exceeded the value of the tractor-trailer in dispute, and more than two years would elapse—two years of severely strained relations among Bunny, Leonard, and Murray at Meadow Gate Farm, and of the Drakes' repeatedly having to scrape up cash for yet another trip back to New Jersey for a deposition or court appearance—and that this excruciating pace represented typical progress through the system—had they known all this when the feud began, perhaps they would have found a way to settle their differences early on. Perhaps Murray would have signed over the rig and gone back on the road with Tory and Dutchess. Perhaps he and Bunny would have made a life together. Perhaps the Drakes would have put the whole thing behind them and got on with their lives.

During two years of legal badminton, however, both men invested so heavily in their cases, developed such scathing antagonism, and so deeply persuaded themselves of the rightness of their positions that—when the matter finally did come before a judge, in the spring of 1984—what seemed on paper to be a minor dispute about a tractor-trailer had become a blood feud.

5

THE VERDICT

You can't help feeling for them same as you feel for your own children. You never want anything bad to happen to them.

—Murray Hill, 1984

▼·▼·▼·▼·▼·▼·▼·▼·▼·▼·▼·▼·▼

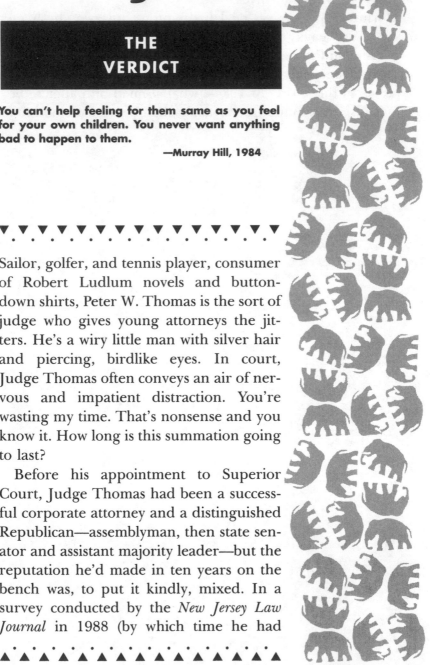

Sailor, golfer, and tennis player, consumer of Robert Ludlum novels and button-down shirts, Peter W. Thomas is the sort of judge who gives young attorneys the jitters. He's a wiry little man with silver hair and piercing, birdlike eyes. In court, Judge Thomas often conveys an air of nervous and impatient distraction. *You're wasting my time. That's nonsense and you know it. How long is this summation going to last?*

Before his appointment to Superior Court, Judge Thomas had been a successful corporate attorney and a distinguished Republican—assemblyman, then state senator and assistant majority leader—but the reputation he'd made in ten years on the bench was, to put it kindly, mixed. In a survey conducted by the *New Jersey Law Journal* in 1988 (by which time he had

▲·▲·▲·▲·▲·▲·▲·▲·▲·▲·▲·▲·▲

been assigned to Atlantic County), attorneys were invited to rate anonymously the sixteen judges in the vicinage in seven categories: knowledge of law; promptness of decisions; ability to handle complex matters; demeanor; ability to foster compromise; overall competence; and adherence to rules of practice. Judge Thomas ranked at or near the bottom in every category save one: adherence to rules of practice. Simply put, he was seen as one of the strictest judges, and one of the least competent.

Judge Thomas had sat in Essex County and Morris County before his assignment to the more affluent Monmouth County, an area of horse farms and country homes owned by the likes of the rock stars Bruce Springsteen and Jon Bon Jovi. Freehold, the county seat, lies midway between Asbury Park on the Jersey shore and Trenton, the state capital, on the Pennsylvania border. It's a pretty town of twenty-four thousand souls, historic old homes, mature shade trees, and graceful churches. Drugs aren't quite the problem here that they are in some other parts of America; still, Monmouth County carries a backlog of drug-related cases. These impede the proper functioning of the courts and lead them to seek ways of avoiding the time and expense of jury trials.

Judge Thomas was hopeful that case number L-42577-81 E —*Edward Elliott Drake and Richard Edward Drake, Plaintiffs*, vs. *Arlan Seidon a.k.a. Murray Hill and Murray Hill Enterprises, Defendants*—could be settled in chambers. He had the attorneys outline their positions, then asked if there weren't room for compromise. Could he not mediate a settlement? Surely, in a civil suit growing out of disputed ownership of a tractor-trailer, court proceedings could be avoided through pretrial negotiation.

The Drakes' lawyer, Bunce Atkinson, said his clients would accept $50,000 and the tractor-trailer in full settlement. Murray's lawyer, Gerry Martin, took the offer to his client. Murray declined, obscenely.

Bunce Atkinson returned with a better deal: they'd take the tractor-trailer plus $25,000. Murray told Gerry Martin no way he was giving them money.

Just before trial was set to begin, Atkinson told Martin in Judge Thomas's chambers that his clients would drop their suit in return for nothing more than clear title to the tractor-trailer.

Atkinson, Martin, and Judge Thomas all figured this was it; Murray would be nuts not to accept the deal. Judge Thomas, who had earlier expressed impatience at the lack of movement on the defendant's side, said pointedly, "It seems to me a very fair offer, Mr. Martin." Martin agreed, but said his client felt he had been fully justified in repossessing and had no legal exposure. "You might remind your client," said Judge Thomas, "that there's no such thing as having no exposure in civil litigation."

Martin himself thought the offer fair. In the parking lot outside the courthouse, he explained why. Murray listened with what little politeness he could summon. Having cut many deals with shopping malls and circuses over the years, he considered himself a decent negotiator and an astute judge of character.

"Why do you think they keep backing off? They've got no right to the rig, and we can prove it."

"Murray, I know you feel strongly. But go before a jury and you never know what might happen. It's a roll of the dice. Different juries can do different things with the same facts."

"If I'm supposed to back off, after two years of getting jerked around, then I don't understand what the law's for."

"No matter what the circumstances, the repossessor isn't usually perceived as the guy in the white hat. I mean, whatever the merits of your case, you do have possible exposure. Judge Thomas said so himself."

"The agreement's right there in writing. Why the hell should I give them the rig?"

"Partly because Judge Thomas made a point of saying that he thinks this is a fair settlement."

"He wouldn't, if he knew the whole story."

Martin was determined to stay out of the courtroom, and for good reason. Judge Thomas, on hearing that Murray had taken Eddie Drake's clothes and tools as well as the animals, had said to Martin, with real feeling, "A young man of limited education

—do you have any idea what his own hand tools mean to him?" It seemed odd that he would express himself so forcefully on a tangential point. Martin felt that the judge was sympathetic to the plaintiffs, and he knew that Murray's abrasiveness could only reinforce that bias, especially after the pretrial negotiations had foundered on Murray's intransigence.

"Murray, look. When a judge helps negotiate these things and one side won't budge an inch, he gets frustrated. He can never quite put out of his mind which side is making him hear the case."

"Them bastards abused the girls. They lied to me. They stopped sending money. I don't owe them a thing."

Martin hadn't realized what a flinty character this was. Murray had come to hate the Drakes, he knew, and that colored his judgment. But wasn't he shrewd enough to understand that, if he wanted revenge, another opportunity would present itself? He and the Drakes worked in the same field, after all.

"Suppose it goes smoothly. Let's say the jury sides with us completely—which, incidentally, almost never happens. Your costs are still going to exceed the value of the tractor-trailer. You said yourself it's not worth more than four or five thousand. Save yourself some money. It's time for us to make a concession. We're fortunate it's a minor one."

Murray shrugged. "I pay taxes, I raised four children, I fly the flag. I believe in the justice system. It's what makes our country what it is. I want my day in court."

"As your attorney, I urge you to accept the offer. The Drakes aren't going to settle for voluntary dismissal and go home— they wouldn't have taken it this far if they had any thought of doing that. But they're offering the next best thing. They need something to salvage their pride. Let them have the rig. Wait a minute, Murray, don't blurt out an answer. Stop and think about it."

Murray paused long enough to light another Camel. "I've thought about it. I'm not paying any tribute to those mother-fuckers."

After the court clerk had opened proceedings in a windowless room on the third floor of the Monmouth County Courthouse, and a six-member jury (four men, two women) had been empaneled and sworn in, Bunce Atkinson got to his feet, buttoned his suit jacket, recounted the Drakes' version of events, and summed up their position:

"This is basically our case. We say that Murray Hill had no interest in that tractor-trailer and wasn't entitled to take it. He had our chimpanzee and our camel for four months before they were returned. He had no right to take the chimpanzee and the camel."

Atkinson argued that the elephants, having been sold for $80,000, served as full collateral for an $80,000 note. "That collateral, when he took it, satisfied his obligation." But the Drakes had paid off several thousand dollars and so wanted "the difference between the $80,000 and the amount we had reduced the loan indebtedness to." As well, said Atkinson, the Drakes were seeking damages from the American Express commercial and the Greenville elephant ride. They sought $20,000 for the tractor-trailer, plus compensation for unrecovered personal items that had been in the truck the night Murray took off.

As for Bunny Brook's suit, in which she sought expenses in excess of $100,000 for maintaining Murray and the elephants, Atkinson pointed out that wherever Murray had maintained his elephants, whether at his own place in Missouri or at Bunny Brook's farm in New Jersey, it was an expense he himself had to bear. "We contend," said Atkinson, "that they are Mr. Seidon's—Murray Hill's—elephants, not our elephants."

It was Gerry Martin's turn to address the jury, and he got off to a fumbling start. Noting that his client was referred to in court documents as "Arlan Seidon a.k.a. Murray Hill," Martin told the jury, "A lot of times people see that 'a.k.a.' and all of a sudden they think of a crime figure." During a long career in show business and animal training, said Martin, his client had always been known professionally as Murray Hill. He had "never used any other name to defraud people."

Murray had brought a countersuit; its basis, said Martin, was that "the entire lawsuit that the Drakes have brought here today was brought with one intention, and that was to injure my client maliciously, intentionally, and without foundation."

"You cannot bring a cause for malicious prosecution," Judge Thomas told Martin, impatience in his voice, "until the original action upon which it is based has been decided."

After Martin had summarized Murray's version of what had happened, and Bunny's attorney, Tom Smith, had outlined the basis of her claim for expenses, Judge Thomas, consulting his watch, said irritably, "You gentlemen told me this case is going to take one day to try. It took you an hour and a quarter just to open to the jury, and I tell you again—if this case is not finished by four o'clock on Wednesday, there will be a mistrial and you will start all over again at some later date before another judge."

In retrospect, Murray would be unable to say when he'd had the first hint of disaster. It might have been on the first day of testimony; it certainly grew out of Judge Thomas's unsympathetic treatment of Gerry Martin. Judge Thomas was short with all the attorneys, calling them "windy," but he found particular fault with Martin's demeanor and technique. At the start of proceedings, when Martin objected to something Bunce Atkinson had asked, Judge Thomas replied, "I can't hear you, Mr. Martin." Martin repeated his objection. Judge Thomas said firmly: "I still can't hear you." Only then did Martin realize he had better get to his feet.

During Martin's cross-examination of Eddie Drake about the disposition of money earned from Reid Brothers Circus, Eddie gave an answer so long-winded and circuitous as to be incomprehensible.

"Very nice speech, Mr. Drake," said Martin. "Now—"

"Don't make any remarks, counsel," Judge Thomas said sternly.

During Martin's direct examination of Murray, Judge Thomas again took him to task: "Mr. Martin, I heard all the words, but I didn't understand what the defendant said. If that was an explanation as to why there was no security agreement . . . Is that what it was? It was supposed to be an explanation of that?"

"Yes, Judge."

"Did you understand it?"

"Well, Your Honor, I appreciate—"

"Don't do that again," said Judge Thomas.

Martin felt like a schoolboy dressed down in front of the class. He had started badly, he knew, but it wasn't until Judge Thomas excused the jury to confer with the attorneys in private that he first had a sense of foreboding. Bunny's lawyer, Tom Smith, clarifying her role, said, "Judge, in July of 1983 Mr. Seidon turned the elephants over to her, gave her clear title to them."

"Then there is no lien claim here?"

"No," said Tom Smith. "we own the elephants—"

"You might not own the elephants when this all winds up," Judge Thomas interrupted. "You might have a bill. The way this case is shaping up, you might not have the elephants because your client might not own them."

For Bunce Atkinson, here was the first glimpse of a more promising outcome than he'd imagined; for Gerry Martin, the first premonition of disaster. Continuing his direct examination of Murray, Martin asked about the replacement act for the Pennsylvania date Eddie had failed to make. Again Judge Thomas intervened.

"What are you talking about this for? Any claim arising out of this?"

"Well, no," said Martin, "Your Honor inquired as to whether or not there was a contract—"

"He already went into it," said Judge Thomas. "There was no contract. Why are we discussing it?"

"I don't know. Your Honor inquired."

"I don't know either," said Judge Thomas sourly. "That's why I asked the question."

Shortly thereafter Judge Thomas chastised Martin for repeatedly saying, "Thank you, Your Honor," even when his objections were overruled. Martin explained that it was a habit meant to convey respect. "A bad habit," said Judge Thomas. "In many instances it could be deemed to be sarcasm, Mr. Martin."

During Bunny Brook's testimony, Judge Thomas once again became exasperated with Martin. Bunny's answers were sometimes Joycean in their stream-of-consciousness rambling, and Atkinson objected.

"You'd better ask specific questions that require specific answers," Judge Thomas told Martin, "instead of letting the witness go on."

"Yes, Your Honor."

Murray felt that the judge disliked him personally and was showing up Gerry Martin as a way of communicating this dislike to the jury. Murray, too, was getting an ominous feeling about where the trial was heading; that feeling crystallized when, on the third day of testimony, Martin said, "If Mr. Atkinson will represent to me that he's releasing any and all claims to the elephants themselves—"

"I'm not going to let him do that," said Judge Thomas.

Murray was stunned. Atkinson, Dick Drake, and Eddie Drake had already released their claim to the elephants. They had all agreed that the repossession was legitimate. Atkinson had stressed the point: "We contend they are Murray's Hill's elephants, not our elephants." Now, however, Murray's own lawyer had again raised the matter, and with one brief pronouncement—"I'm not going to let him do that"—Judge Thomas had turned the whole trial around.

"What were you going to do in return for getting extra collateral?" Judge Thomas asked Murray. "Were you going to hold off foreclosing on the elephants?"

"At this point I was not figuring on foreclosing on the elephants," said Murray. "I wanted to see them work. I was not looking to take back the elephants."

Judge Thomas began to entertain the view that the second collateral agreement had become enforceable—that Dick had actually sent it off just before the elephants were repossessed, and that Murray had verbally agreed not to repossess so long as Dick provided this additional collateral. If the second agreement had indeed become enforceable (even though Murray had never received it), and if he had indeed waived his right of repossession (in return for the unreceived agreement), then Murray was suddenly vulnerable in ways nobody had foreseen.

"Now's the time to call the vets," Murray said during the next recess. "We need them to testify about the abuse."

"Too late," said Martin. "He won't let them take the stand now."

Judge Thomas had other court matters the next day, Thursday; Friday was a holiday; and he'd be away on vacation the following week. There would be a break in proceedings. Gerry Martin figured it was time to exit this mess gracefully. In a coffee shop near the courthouse, he and Bunny—whose help he had enlisted—tried to persuade Murray to give up his claim to the tractor-trailer. The trial was not going well; the rig was a small price to pay to end it. Murray would never have gone to court if he'd known there was a chance of losing the elephants. Now that the prospect was real, he agreed to sign over the rig.

Martin approached Bunce Atkinson with this settlement offer —the same one Murray had earlier rejected. But Atkinson suddenly held a stronger hand. He'd been dealt a trump and intended to play it. The Drakes would no longer settle for just the rig. Tell your guy to throw in $25,000, Atkinson told Martin, and my guys might consider it.

Martin, though disappointed, hoped to use this counter as the basis for a new round of negotiations. Murray, however, despite Bunny's repeated urging during the anxious week of recess, resisted the idea of giving the Drakes anything more than the rig. He slept badly each night, spent hours with Tory and Dutchess each day, and walked the property, brooding.

Gerry Martin urged him to reconsider Atkinson's counteroffer. Murray refused. In his mind, Judge Thomas had sided with the Drakes, strengthening their case and weakening his. Now he was supposed to buy his way out of the hole dug for him by someone paid by the state to stand back and weigh the arguments of the two sides? That was justice?

The Drakes could take their offer, he told Martin, and put it where the sun don't shine.

When proceedings resumed, ten days later, Murray believed he had only to recount in detail the truth of what had happened. Any right-thinking person would see the legal and moral justification behind his actions. The judge and jury were bound to see—all he had to do was explain the whole deal from the start.

For reasons he couldn't quite grasp, however, he never got the chance. Once again Martin got off on the wrong foot. Bunce Atkinson had presented a request to charge the jury a second time, and Martin had submitted his objections to the request. Reviewing Martin's submission, Judge Thomas looked up over his glasses and asked, "Is there any reason why you couldn't get this typed?"

"Yes, Judge," said Martin. "It was prepared over the weekend. I apologize for the handwriting."

"What did you do all last week?"

"I tried another case, Judge."

In the end, the trial was a morass of conflicting testimony. It came down, as trials do, not to truth in the absolute but to the acuity of lawyers and the credibility of witnesses. Murray's fate had been hinted at by Judge Thomas's unexpected upholding of the second collateral agreement; it was sealed by Bunce Atkinson's astute cross-examination. Murray proved, ironically, to be Atkinson's best witness and Gerry Martin's worst.

Everything about him was wrong. His testimony—he had jury members glancing skeptically at one another half a dozen times. His attitude—snickering aloud in court and scoffing at the testimony of the Drakes. His attire—the same polyester leisure suit day after day. Why, Atkinson wondered, would Martin not have prepped his client properly? Lawyers took seminars on these things. If Murray Hill was supposed to be an elephant trainer, why didn't he dress like one? Why not wear jeans and a work shirt? In his lime-green leisure suit he looked like a carnival pitchman, selling a bill of goods to the gullible public. To trusting, naïve people like Eddie Drake.

Eddie was perfect in the role of the well-meaning young man duped by the shyster, every parent's image of the fundamentally decent son. Gerry Martin took him for a kid with street smarts and a mean streak who turned dumb at convenient moments; but he feared that Judge Thomas and the jury were buying the performance.

Dick, for his part, had been on enough movie sets to understand the force of image. On the witness stand he was variously self-effacing, uncomprehending, and aggrieved. He dressed suitably and was expert at modulating his deep voice—he could have been a radio announcer or a mortician, so easily did he shift from lightheartedness to grave sincerity. He even got away with admitting he'd put up someone else's camel as collateral. If he'd crossed anything out on the paper, he explained, he feared it would have voided the whole deal.

Murray testified that the market for Asian elephants had dried up and the girls were worth less than when he'd sold them. Africans were now in demand, he said, and the price of Asians had declined sharply. Asked to put a number on the current market value of Tory and Dutchess, he said $20,000 each, maximum. Dick, meanwhile, had testified that their value had gone up. Faced with conflicting testimony, jury members had to decide whom to believe. The mouthy little showman, or the concerned father doing the best for his son? If there was any doubt, Atkinson dispelled it by reading back Murray's earlier deposition, in which he had said the elephants were still worth the $80,000 the Drakes had paid for them.

Eddie testified that the ticket booth was worth $1,500, Murray that it was worth $350. Whom to believe? The little smartass in the green leisure suit, or the hardworking young fellow who'd sunk his life savings into the deal and spent his last $340 for diesel fuel just before the rig was taken?

Eddie testified he'd put a stereo system in the truck. Murray said the stereo system had indeed been there when he repossessed but wasn't there any longer. Asked by Atkinson, "Do you know what happened to it?" Murray replied, "Not really."

Eddie testified that on Reid Brothers Circus he had paid Murray's expenses; Murray said he had paid his own way. Under skilful cross-examination by Atkinson, however, Murray admitted that Eddie had indeed paid for most of the permits, fuel, and motels. (He never got a chance to explain that, in the animal business, it was routine for the buyer to pick up the tab.)

Atkinson elicited Murray's admission that he had moved the chimp and the camel out of state, hiding them in South Carolina; that he'd added interest to the Drakes' late charges, even though there was no provision for interest in their agreement (Murray never got a chance to explain that he'd given them thirty days' notice, and got no response); that it would have been simple enough at the Pocono Truck Plaza to have removed Eddie's personal possessions from the rig and left them in the motel room; and that Murray, in his counterclaim for damages, was seeking agent's commissions from jobs Eddie had been unable to do because Murray himself had the elephants.

Atkinson was patient and incisive. Stroke by stroke, he painted a picture of Murray as a shifty, calculating cheat. He established that it costs roughly $1,000 a month to board an elephant, and that Bunny Brook's exorbitant claim of $76,000 included a personal loan of $30,000 made to prevent foreclosure on Murray's farm in Missouri. Cross-examining Bunny, Atkinson established that Murray had signed over the elephants on the understanding that she, too, would sue the Drakes. He established that her claim for damages included charges for room and board of the camel and chimp—the animals Murray had refused to turn over to Eddie. He established that Murray could have rented or bought a tractor-trailer to work Tory and Dutchess, rather than leaving the elephants at Meadow Gate Farm and running up a bill with Bunny. He established that, although Bunny had supposedly bought the elephants the previous July, she had continued to bill Murray for storing them. He established that, by the terms of her purchase agreement, she could have sold Tory and Dutchess to recover her expenses rather than incurring new ones. Patiently, deftly, he communicated to the court his certainty that she and Murray were in cahoots.

Murray could scarcely believe that the past three years could be depicted in a light so favorable to the Drakes. "What about the thousand they promised and never sent?" he asked Gerry Martin during a break. "How come that hasn't been brought out?" Martin said they'd get to that. "How come the judge can't see Dick nodding and signaling answers to Eddie? Why aren't you objecting?" Martin explained that objections were based on points of law. "See the dirty look he gave me when Eddie was testifying?" "I told you, Murray, don't show that kind of emotion in the courtroom." "Yeah, well, he didn't give Eddie no dirty look when he snickered at my answers." "Just tell the truth as you know it. Don't worry about what the Drakes are doing."

But he never got a chance to tell the truth as he knew it—just bits and pieces. Martin had counseled him to keep his answers to Atkinson short; anything that needed elaboration, they'd cover during redirect examination. Murray testified that Eddie had done "a very nice job" of handling the elephants and that he was a "talented animal man." Afterwards, Martin chastised him for speaking highly of the plaintiff. "I told the truth," Murray shrugged, "like you said. Why should I lie? I wouldn't have let them have the girls if he didn't do a good job."

Murray's disenchantment grew by the day. Each question and answer was a brush stroke. By these measured, tedious applications of paint to canvas, a picture was being painted that had little to do with reality. So agitated did Murray become during cross-examination that he said in frustration, "You're not getting the whole story! You're not asking the right questions to the whole story!"

"Mr. Seidon," Atkinson said calmly, "I'll ask the questions. Your attorney will be given an opportunity to ask questions."

Murray testified that he had intended to throw in the howdahs, the ride stand, the ticket box, and the chains for free, but that in December, once the Drakes were in arrears, he had started billing them for this "free" equipment.

Murray testified he had paid off the bank that had a lien on the tractor, so he could sell the rig free and clear. Under cross-examination he admitted he had told the Drakes the lien had been removed but had not actually removed it. He testified that he had doctored some paperwork on the truck after the repossession. He testified that he had told Eddie sure, you can leave your chimp cages at my place, never discussed a storage fee, then started charging two dollars a day.

"But you have to—"

"That's all, Mr. Seidon."

Wasn't the court interested in finding out why he'd done these things? He'd had good reasons. These people had lied. They'd failed to meet their financial obligations. They'd mistreated the elephants he'd raised from infancy. Eddie had refused to do the Florida run that would have allowed him to keep up the payments; meanwhile, he was booking Murray's regular dates himself, cutting Murray out of an agent's fee. Why wasn't the other side of the story—the empty promises and lies and reassurances—allowed to come out? Each time Murray tried to elaborate, Atkinson cut him off. Each time he looked to Martin for guidance, Martin busied himself with notes. By the time Atkinson had finished his damningly incomplete portrait—and his flattering picture of the Drakes—Murray knew there could be only one answer to the silent question Atkinson was asking the jury members every time he glanced at them: the wisecracking pitchman who's been caught in all these evasions, or the handsome young man he left stranded at a truckstop without so much as a change of clothes?

. . .

"Sure I remember you," said Al Campellone, the contractor and horseman down Philadelphia way who'd let Murray lay over on his property two years earlier. He'd been interrupted at dinner by the telephone. "How are those beautiful friends of yours? Tory and Dutchess."

"Just fine," said Murray. "Reason I'm calling, you said if we were ever back in the area . . ."

"You coming in again?"

"I'm in New Jersey right now. I'll bring the girls in later tonight, if that's okay. They'll just be there for a couple of days." If asked why he'd moved the elephants off Meadow Gate Farm, Murray would say he was preparing for his next date. The girls were, in fact, booked to give rides at a mall in Pennsylvania the weekend after the trial. What the hell, the rig was restrained by court order, but nobody had said anything about not moving the elephants while the trial was in progress. When he'd asked Gerry Martin if it mattered where they were kept, Martin had said, "If they're now at the Brooks' farm, that's where the court expects them to be." To which Murray had replied, "I'm supposed to be a mind reader? How should I know what the court expects?"

That night, using a borrowed rig, Murray trucked the girls down to Al Campellone's farm, left them in the care of his son-in-law, and returned to Colts Neck, pulling into Meadow Gate Farm just before dawn. Later that morning, back in court, he felt better knowing the girls were safely out of state—until, that is, Bunce Atkinson raised the notion of inspecting the rig to determine its condition and arrive at an accurate idea of its value. That afternoon a party trooped out to Bunny's.

Murray figured his goose was cooked. At the very least, he'd have some explaining to do. Miraculously, however, the Drakes paid such close attention to the rig—checking to see how bald the tires were, noting that the howdahs were gone, and the ticket box was missing, and the generator had been removed— they failed to notice that the elephants were gone.

•   •   •

When the jury foreman announced the decision, Eddie Drake clenched his fist in a victory salute. Dick, grinning, shook hands with friends and family. Murray was numb at first, disbelieving; then the anger welled. He'd gone to court to contest his right to the tractor-trailer. His own lawyer had refused to raise the issue of abuse and call the vets to testify because the girls weren't part of the suit. Now, after six days in front of a judge who'd taken an instant dislike to him, who'd swallowed Eddie's poor-dumb-elephant-boy routine, and who'd turned the case around in a way that had stunned everyone—after six days of pure bullshit stretched over two weeks, of things taken out of context and twisted around, of partial answers and unasked questions, the jury says hand over the tractor-trailer, and while you're at it hand over Tory and Dutchess, the equipment, and $106,000 in damages? Two years of waiting, of borrowing from Bunny and his mother, of sinking deeper into debt, with the rig tied up in Colts Neck and the bills piling up, for this?

As for Bunny Brook's suit—filed as insurance against just such an eventuality—the court ruled that it had no substance. Since the elephants had been improperly repossessed, and thus had been owned all along by the Drakes, Murray had had no right to convey them to her. Despite all the money she'd given him, in other words, she had no legal interest in the elephants. Nor could she look to anyone other than Murray for financial relief.

In the parking lot, Murray and Bunny huddled with their attorneys. Murray and Bunny were highly emotional; Gerry Martin was vague and consoling. He told Murray a substantial bond would have to be posted for the court to allow him to keep the elephants while the decision was being appealed.

"Just tell me one thing, Gerry. If I take off with the girls, does that screw up the appeal?"

"I didn't catch that," said Martin. "Tom and I didn't hear what you just said. Do you understand?"

Mealy-mouthed lawyers, covering their own ass first. The whole racket was an outrage. He'd petition the governor, god-damn it. He'd do whatever it took. Anybody with half a brain would see right off what a sham the trial had been. Meantime, if that little black-robed prick thought he was going to take this lying down, he didn't know Murray Hill.

That night, at Dick's sister's place in Far Hills, the Drake clan gathered in triumphant celebration. "Good for you, honey!" Doy said on the phone. "All your hard work has finally paid off. We're all real proud of you." Dick could whoop it up with the best of them, but he found his victory glow dimmed by the uneasy feeling that maybe they should have gone right out and taken possession of the elephants, or at least left somebody at Meadow Gate Farm to keep an eye out. Who could say what Murray might try next? He'd been agitated as hell by the decision, anybody could see that, and the idea of leaving the elephants with him overnight while he brooded and sulked . . .

Then the Meyer twins dropped over and the party revved up and Dick told himself hey, quit worrying. Murray felt close to the elephants—he wasn't stupid or vindictive enough to hit them up with Euthanol or open a vein. He cared for them too much to drop them. And not even old Murray would be fool enough to run in the face of the court decision. Go on the lam with elephants? For a start, the rig was in sorry shape—how would he move them? Where would he take them? What would he do for money? Besides, it would be outright theft. They jailed people for less.

No, the funny nagging tic in Dick's brain was just spasmodic relief after the strain of the trial. A little more Canadian Club would take care of it.

"Just a minute," said Al Campellone, dazed. He switched on the bedside light, squinted at his watch—midnight—and took a moment to get his bearings. He'd been wakened by the telephone at his home near Philadelphia. "Murray? You say you're down at the barn?"

"Sorry to call so late."

"Is there a problem?"

"Don't worry, there's nothing the matter down here."

"What's up?"

"I lost the case."

Campellone, confused, assumed Murray was talking about his divorce and wondered why he'd call in the middle of the night. "Sorry to hear that, Murray. I know these things are tough."

Murray's voice had been level, but now it broke. "They're not going to take the girls from me, Al. I can't let it happen."

"Take the girls? How do you mean?"

"We're leaving. I'm taking them with me. Tonight."

"Listen, why don't I come over. Give me ten minutes."

"I've got my helper here, we're almost done. See, I raised these girls since they were babies. You can't help feeling for them same as you feel for your own children. You never want anything bad to happen to them. I just didn't want you to think I was running out on you, that's all. Whatever I owe you, I'll make up to you."

Al Campellone told him it wasn't necessary and wished him luck. He switched off the light but had trouble getting back to sleep. It's not every night you find yourself trying to console a grown man in tears.

Next day, when the Drakes went to Meadow Gate Farm, they took along Dick's old buddy, Richie, and his nephew, Alex Wilkie. Two uniformed state troopers accompanied them. Despite the hangovers, the mood was buoyant. Aiming for an outer ring, they'd nailed the bull's-eye. They drove onto the property and pulled up beside Murray's old rig. They'd brought along diesel fuel and batteries, in case the tractor needed a boost. They planned to load Tory and Dutchess, take them back to Dot's place, then check the rig out carefully to see whether it could make the long haul back to California.

One of the farmhands wandered down from the barn, lit a

smoke, and watched as they laid out chains, checked fuel, oil, and water levels in the tractor, and opened the trailer doors.

"You guys are wasting your time."

Everybody stopped what they were doing. Dick tipped his cap back on his head. "How's that?"

"They ain't here."

"No way," said Eddie.

"Run that by me again," said Dick.

"They're gone," said the farmhand. "He's gone, too."

The so-called lower primates, when angry or frightened or agitated into tantrum, defecate uncontrollably. Eddie proceeded to throw what, in a gorilla, is known as a shit fit. Dick, ready to lose it himself, told his son to calm down. How far could Murray have got? They'd found him before, hadn't they?

"He's got a day's head start! We'll never find the little mother!"

True enough, Murray already could have crossed over into Canada. Hell, in eighteen hours he could have got to just about anywhere. But as Dick assured his son, they now had the law on their side. Once criminal charges had been brought they'd get help from every public agency in the land. Imagine—hundreds, maybe thousands of law-enforcement types combing the country.

No, Murray didn't have a prayer. They just had to think this through, call Bunce Atkinson, notify the authorities. How long could he last? How hard could it be finding somebody trying to hide two elephants?

6

DESTINATION UNKNOWN

It is neither a slight responsibility nor a trifling matter to have to keep and maintain an elephant for a month or two.

Louis Rousselet

▼ ▼ ▼ ▼ ▼ ▼ ▼ ▼ ▼ ▼ ▼ ▼ ▼ ▼ ▼ ▼

273 FILE 7 SP COLTS NECK NJ

REQUEST STATEWIDE AND NATIONWIDE
BROADCAST
WANTED FOR THEFT
ARLAN SEIDON AKA/MURRAY HILL. TRADING AS
MURRAY HILL ENTERPRISES, INC. W/M AGE/55 505/
125 GRAY HAIR AND BEARD. USUALLY WEARS
GREEN LEISURE SUIT. BELIEVED OPERATING
TRACTOR/TRAILER 1971 FORD TRACTOR GRAY AND
SILVER NJREG/XYP73R W/LETTERING ON SIDE
DAWN ANIMAL FARM, MEADOW GATE FARMS.
TRAILER 1964 FRUEHAUF, GRAY AND SILVER
NJREG/685/TDZ LKA RT 1 BOX 248A, FORDLAND,
MISSOURI.

IT IS BELIEVED SUBJECT DEPARTED NEW JERSEY
OPERATING ABOVE TRACTOR TRAILER ON 5-3-84
DESTINATION UNKNOWN. TRAILER IS CARRYING
TWO FEMALE INDIAN ELEPHANTS FULL GROWN
AGES 20 AND 21 YEARS.

▲ ▲ ▲ ▲ ▲ ▲ ▲ ▲ ▲ ▲ ▲ ▲ ▲ ▲ ▲ ▲

In twenty years with the New Jersey State Police, Bob Britton had worked on some odd cases, but this was one for the grandchildren. Ever since the wanted for Murray Hill had gone out on the teletype, he couldn't mention it without somebody making a wisecrack. People tore *Far Side* cartoons out of the newspaper and left them on his desk. One of the troopers at the Colts Neck barracks asked him, almost keeping a straight face, if the elephants were still . . . at large. Another stuck his head in: "Hey, Bob, see Dumbo's on TV tonight?"

Like most law-enforcement types his age—he was forty-four—Britton had come to police work via military service. He'd served in the air force (too late for Korea, too soon for Vietnam), then worked in a paper-products factory before joining the state police. After seven years in uniform he'd moved into plainclothes, working for Troop C. Over the years he'd been assigned to Laurelton, Keyport, Princeton, and Fort Dix, before moving to the casino gaming unit. On his promotion to sergeant a year later, he was transferred back into the troop. His first assignment was Colts Neck. He'd been sergeant of detectives for four years when Dick Drake walked in and introduced himself.

Driving out to Meadow Gate Farm from the Troop C barracks, Britton tried to think who Dick had reminded him of. Dick had said he worked in the film business in California, and he looked the part—tanned and glib, with a high-voltage smile that added little warmth to his expression. You saw that smile on desk clerks and car salesmen of a certain age, men who never dreamed, when they took the job, they'd still be doing it twenty-five years later. Leslie Nielsen? No. George Peppard! That was it. Give Dick a fifty-dollar haircut, a few inches in height, and a safari suit, and presto—George Peppard on *The A-Team.*

Dick had come prepared with the paperwork from the trial. There was no disputing his claim. What had started out as a civil suit was now theft, cut and dried. Murray Hill had no legal right to the elephants. A bench warrant had been issued when he'd failed to abide by the judgment, and a fugitive warrant had been issued for his arrest. Dick figured Murray had fled to Canada and wondered what sort of cooperation might exist between the two countries. He suggested it might be useful to chat with Bunny Brook.

Like everyone in the area, Britton knew Meadow Gate Farm by reputation. In the years the Brooks had been there, the area had been gentrified. As farms disappeared and estate homes took their place, Meadow Gate Farm began to seem outlandish. It was more an open zoo than a farm: you saw strange animals in the fields and corrals. The people who owned it kept exotic and show animals, Britton knew, and were not particularly friendly. The police had not had complaints from neighbors, but the Brooks had the reputation of being eccentric.

Britton had never noticed that you couldn't just drive or walk onto the property. It was carefully fenced, and when he stepped out to ring the bell, a gang of barking dogs slammed against the gate, fangs bared. A farmhand came down from the barn and asked what he wanted, then went up to the house. A minute later Bunny came out, a dark-haired, mile-a-minute woman wearing filthy jeans and a work shirt. She talked across the gate rather than asking him in. Her appearance was harried, her manner unambiguous: she didn't like this, and she didn't have all day.

Britton had been a sportsman in his younger days, and Bunny reminded him of people he'd encountered while hunting deer at Great Swamp in Basking Ridge. One time, having taken a buck, he was confronted by a group of animal-rights activists. They had been intelligent, well-meaning people, willing to risk jail, and he could easily imagine Bunny among them —she had the same air of obsessive caring, of willingness to act on her beliefs. Animals were her life and she'd do whatever it took to protect them.

Bunny made clear that she hated the Drakes. Her first concern was the elephants and she believed Murray was the best person to have them. If she knew anything, Britton realized, she wouldn't let on. She wasn't much concerned about her missing tractor-trailer, though she claimed Murray had taken it without her consent. He had left a note promising to return it. Could Britton see the note? She said she had turned it over to her attorney, Tom Smith. Britton suspected that she had given Murray her blessing, or at least turned a blind eye. No point pressing the matter. They had enough particulars on the rig that it would show up in a routine stop.

"Heard from him since then?"

"No," said Bunny.

Murray had vowed not to contact her, since he'd jeopardize her—and, perhaps, himself—by doing so. Still, Britton believed that Murray would get in touch sooner or later, if only to let the Brooks know where to pick up the rig. The important thing at this stage was not to alienate Bunny. If he could come out every so often to chat, that would be worth more than what she might betray if he probed more deeply into her role.

"Will you let me know if he contacts you?"

"Yes, of course," said Bunny. She ran a dirty hand through her hair. "Now, is there anything else?"

"I was just thinking, must keep you busy, all that stock. How many animals have you got here?"

"Six hundred."

"Well, I won't hold you up. Thanks for your time." Britton clicked his pen and put it in his pocket. Watching her eyes, he said, "I wonder where Murray went with those elephants."

"You tell me," she said, and locked the gate between them.

"One day somebody was trying to get me into an A.A. meeting," Charles C. recalled, at the kitchen table of his home in the Hudson Valley north of New York, on land his family has farmed since the eighteenth century. He has no close neighbors, and views the world with great skepticism, an outlook he brought home, along with his addiction, from Vietnam. He sipped orange juice as he talked.

"The whole world knows a drunk's a drunk—everybody knows except the drunk. I told this guy, 'I'm not going to any A.A. meeting.' I thought they stuck crucifixes up each other's asses, what did I know? The monster in you, the alcoholic, is whispering, 'That's where you'll get help, and you don't want help.'

"Well, that same night my cousin blew his brains out with a shotgun. I realized he wouldn't have done it if he hadn't been drinking. I finally made the connection—alcohol is a problem. I went to the meeting and almost instantly I knew I was in the right place. Suddenly nobody's arguing with you, telling you you're a stupid son of a bitch. You're no longer the odd man out. It's like being from Mars and finally, after twenty-five years, meeting a colony of Martians.

"All my life I'd been interested in antique cars. After I quit drinking I found I had extra money, so I put together a Model T Ford. A guy mentioned that they were advertising for antique cars for a James Cagney movie. Cagney grew up in Hell's Kitchen, but when he got some money he bought himself a farm up the road here. We used to see a lot of him when we were kids. I thought great—how many people can say they were in a James Cagney movie? So I called. The guy said, 'What color's your Model T?' I said, 'Bright red.' 'Bring it down,' he said.

"I took the car down to Eleventh Street in Manhattan, between A and B Avenue. It was supposed to be 1905, and the art director wanted these bright colors to contrast against the poor Hasidic Jewish neighborhood. There's all these horses and wagons and chickens and shit. The guy tells me, 'When you drive through, toot your horn—you're one of the rich people impatient to get through the poor people.' I'm crawling along in the Model T, hitting the horn, when a horse rears up in front of me. This guy with a beard shakes his fist in my face and says, 'Blow that goddamn horn once more . . .' The movie was one of the last Cagney made before he died, *Ragtime*. The guy with the beard was Leonard Brook.

"It turned out Leonard was in charge of all the animals in the film. I wanted to get involved in the movie business, so I started helping him. He'd go eat, and I'd watch his chickens so the Puerto Ricans wouldn't steal them. I watered the animals. Must

▲ 121

have been a hundred and ten degrees, and every time we got a shot done I tried to get them into the shade.

"I saw how they did the vehicles. I turned my Model T into a truck, took the backseat off and tied on chicken cages, working with Leonard. I noticed he had some water tanks, and I told him I did, too, old horse-drawn wagons. Next movie he made he used one of my wagons. That's how I got to know Leonard and Bunny Brook, and through them many other people in the animal business.

"One day one of the people I'd done some work for phoned me and said, 'A trainer I know, he's got his elephants on the road. Do you know someplace they could park on grass for a few weeks?' I said sure, up here. An old man in Massachusetts does oxen for this guy, and I figured here's another old fart who works for him. Probably down and out, can't afford to go wherever elephants go to take a break. He'll get a freebie here, hay and water for the elephants, eat with us up at the house. The tradeoff for me was, be great for my kids having elephants around. How many people can say they've had elephants?

"So this little guy arrives with his elephants in a tractor-trailer. He came in down by the old farmhouse and parked behind the shed. You couldn't see him from the road or from the house here—he was perfectly protected. He said my family was welcome to go down, fool with Tory and Dutchess, he'd give us rides, he just didn't want the general public knowing they were here. He stayed with them most of the time, slept with them, maybe came up here for breakfast or dinner.

"My wife says I'm a magnet for weirdos. They find their way to me, or vice versa. Murray Hill was a funny little guy—you could tell right away you weren't going to jam this square peg into no round hole with all the others. He seemed like the biblical madman, the guy who goes out in the desert for forty days and nights and comes back screaming. He was broke, and he'd been trying to come up with some way to make money from elephant dung. I told him, Murray, people don't want to take home dung. Understand? Any dung. Gold-plated dung. Petrified dinosaur dung, I'll bet nobody would buy it. Might make an interesting museum display, but people won't pay money for it. Every day these elephants dump a ton, and Murray's determined to turn this pile of crap into dollar bills.

"He reminded me a bit of the drifters that used to work on the farm when we were growing up. What's a drifter? A person who never gets established anyplace. One morning you wake up and he isn't there. Some of these guys, they'd been in every state of the union, like Murray. There's a whole part of America that never gets fully understood. When there's a census, it's the part that doesn't show up. They want nothing to do with the system, and vice versa. They breathe in and out, they take up space, but nobody ever gets a handle on them.

"Murray told me some of his experiences—the days when he had chimps, his TV shows, taking animals on the road, working the elephants. I was surprised when I found out he had a wife and kids—he never spoke of them. His orientation was toward the elephants. They were his family. You could tell they'd been together a long time.

"The elephants, man, they were great. They're like bulldozers you can tell what to do. 'Take that tree out of the ground, Dutchess, bring it over here.' I was working on my place, and they rolled boulders around for me, did some heavy work. Murray could make them do whatever he wanted with his voice.

"You know the way pilot fish hang around the mouth of the shark, or the little bird sits on the lion's ass? They don't get harmed because they eat the ticks or whatever. They're mutual caretakers, that symbiotic relationship. Murray reminded me of that, him and his girls, depending on each other. He'd feed them, water them, clean up after them, exercise them. They'd go down to the swamp and muck around. I remember one day they took off and Murray ran after them, giving them shit. He was like a mother chasing kids who want to play, trying to sound mad but really having too much fun to pull it off.

"My sister's family used to come over every night to visit Murray and play with the elephants. My niece was always accused in school of making up wild stories, and one day in show-

and-tell she said, 'We have elephants at our farm.' The teacher made her write a hundred times, 'I will not tell false stories to my friends.' I felt sorry for the kid—that's no easy task for a seven-year-old. Next day, down goes her mother with a Polaroid of the kid standing between Tory and Dutchess. Of course the end result was that she got away with some bizarre tales. After that, the teacher never knew whether to believe her or not."

Charles C. went to the fridge to pour himself more orange juice. Half the fridge seemed taken up with orange juice. A poster on the wall showed a skeleton in a fur coat, posing like a fashion model. The caption read: "Fur, the 'look' that's dead."

"My daughter put that up," he said. "Kids get into this animal-rights thing at an early age now. The way we're being taught to look at animals is changing. The other day a guy accused me of stealing one of his leg-hold traps. He caught me in the right mood, so I pulled him out of his truck and beat the shit out of him. He was bigger than me, but he really pissed me off. Guy's trespassing on my property, accusing me of stealing his trap.

"Some poor animal had dragged the trap into a field, then chewed off its own foot—raccoon, a big one, judging from the foot. I took that goddamn trap and smashed it. Now, if I've got a rat in my house, I'll go after it. If a dog attacks my kid, I'll kill it. But I do not hunt animals. And if I did, I'd kill them instantly, not leave them for twenty-four hours before coming back for the goddamn skin. I told the guy, 'Don't you ever trap here again, you son of a bitch, or I'll set a Vietnamese head snare for you.' I tell you, everywhere you look things are going down the drain. It's not animals that are ruining the world. It's not droughts, or insects, or natural catastrophes. It's people. People ruin everything."

Charles C. wanted to get back to his latest project, the restoration of an antique cannon. He keeps busy, working on four or five jobs at once and drinking orange juice. He showed his visitor to the rental car. Two jays were doing a dive-bomb maneuver, over and over. Charles C. stopped to watch. The crickets had set up a low-grade din, the kind of background noise that, if you listen too long, changes from pleasing to insidious.

"Once when I was drinking," he said, "they had me locked up with some real screwballs over in Middletown. There was a one-armed Indian from Quebec, likable guy but crazy with alcohol. He'd jumped out a window, trying to kill himself. He landed in a garbage pail and succeeded only in ripping his arm off. In Middletown he tried swallowing foam cups. He almost made the grade, but not quite. They put him in a straitjacket. Next night, after lights out, they came in with mop handles and beat him. I mean, they beat the shit out of him. They had his mouth taped shut and he was screaming right through the tape.

"Next morning I said to one of the guys who'd done it, 'Look, you've got to tell me. Why?' The guy said, 'When someone tries that hard, he'll eventually succeed. His emotion is gone. That's the problem—no spark. We can't get him to love us, but we can get him to hate us. That hatred will keep him alive for a couple of weeks, get him over the hump.'

"In Murray's case, you could see how much he cared for the elephants, but hatred was the driving force. He hated the justice system, he hated the guys who'd abused the elephants. That hatred fueled him.

"What was going to be a few days with him and the elephants turned into a few weeks. That was fine, but Murray's the kind of guy who can get on your nerves after a while. When he left, I remember, the truck had been sitting idle. Murray got down here on the county road but couldn't get up the hill because the clutch had burned out. I had my pickup and hooked it up to the front of the tractor. Murray unloaded the elephants and got them pushing with their heads. It was windy and rainy, getting dark, and I've often wondered what people thought, on this little back road, at the sight of two elephants pushing an eighteen-wheeler up a hill."

Charles C. started for his house, then stopped. "You know what I think of Murray? You know Johnny Appleseed? The other day one of my kids was asking me about him. Who was

he, Daddy? Why did he go around planting apple trees? I
mulled that one over. Maybe he was nothing more than a Murray Hill, a little guy who took it upon himself to do something
most people wouldn't bother doing. When Murray was here, I
didn't know the real circumstances. Later, when I found out, I
just shook my head. I said to myself, 'You've got to hand it to
the little son of a bitch.' "

"Murray?"

"I'm at a pay phone—"

"Wait!" said Gerry Martin, at the offices of Rinaldo and Rinaldo. "Don't tell me. I don't want to know."

"What about the appeal?"

"I'm glad you called." Martin didn't sound glad. "I wanted to
talk to you about that."

"What the hell's to talk about? I thought we'd agreed to go
ahead with it."

"That's not my recollection of our conversation in the parking lot," said Martin. "What I recall saying is that we'd proceed
with a motion for a new trial to preserve the issue of the verdict
being, in my view, inappropriate in light of the weight of the
evidence. The motion would simply keep open the possibility of
an appeal."

Murray fed in quarters. "You did the best you could, Gerry,
but I got a raw deal. You know it and I know it."

"I agree that Judge Thomas made legal mistakes in the way
he allowed the case to be presented to the jury, and I think
there'd be a good possibility of getting the decision reversed.
But the court has made its ruling for the moment, and getting
the thing opened and looked at again could be a tricky process,
especially in light of your decision to resort to a self-help rem-
edy."

"You mean taking off? I wasn't going to hand the girls over to
those bastards."

Outside, a police cruiser had parked alongside the rig. Two
troopers got out and slammed the doors. One said something

to the other; both looked at the rig, which was rocking from side to side. The other replied and they both laughed. DAWN ANIMAL FARM was emblazoned on the trailer. It might as well have said AMERICA'S MOST WANTED. Murray turned his back.

"Ordinarily," Martin was saying, "to retain possession of the elephants after the court's decision, while an appeal was pending, you'd be required to post a bond. That's because, in the eyes of the court, the elephants now belong to the Drakes. The bond would be substantial. Money becomes a factor. And things like the bond question become more complicated given that you're no longer in the jurisdiction."

"Nail them on the abuse," said Murray, watching the troopers head his way. "It's right there in the contract. I got it in writing that they wouldn't mistreat them."

Martin had resisted Murray's efforts to raise the issue of abuse because the elephants, at the outset, hadn't been in dispute. But he was relieved not to have had to litigate the matter. Proving abuse, he knew, would have been tough. It's hard enough to get expert testimony even in cases of child abuse.

Martin hadn't looked deeply into the legalities of animal abuse, but knew it was a can of worms. To a judge or a jury member—to anyone who had never worked with exotic animals —the distinction between a good trainer and a bad one, between a firm hand and abuse, would seem subtle indeed. Before you can train any big animal you must get around it safely. This you can do only after it has been broken. You must fracture the link between instinctual impulse and physical expression. The instinct is not eradicated, merely suppressed, and each time it resurfaces—when a chimp flees, or a bull elephant challenges his trainer—it must be driven back down.

Animals soon establish among themselves a hierarchical structure. The trainer must place himself at the head of the hierarchy to make the animals do his bidding. Some trainers use brute force. Others achieve excellent results using a reward system, reinforcing the responses they seek. Most trainers combine positive and negative reinforcement, a pragmatic blend of what works best with a particular animal.

In the end, though, what gives you control over a much larger animal is not your ability to bribe it with lemon drops but your power to inflict pain. The aggressive chimp's incisors are pulled, his mouth kept sore so that he resists the urge to bite you. The elephant mustn't forget having its leg chains hitched to a pickup and being slowly pulled off its feet; then it will do a laydown on command. It must never quite lose the sensation of being conked with an ax handle, gigged with a can opener, jolted with an electric prod. If it tests your authority, you must beat it until it relents. The animal abandons the challenge—cowering, defecating—as unmistakably as a schoolboy, tortured by a bully, cries, "Uncle!"

Here the good trainer stops, mission accomplished. The bad one continues to whale away, bringing more to the task than mere reinforcement—he brings his own impacted rage, or warped notion of machismo, or sadistic pleasure at inflicting the sort of abuse he himself once endured.

Some parents whack an obnoxious child. Whether such treatment is ethical can be debated. What's indisputable is that, to be effective, corporal punishment must be a calculated proscription of misbehavior, not a violent loss of control. It must be instructive rather than vindictive. Many trainers liken their handling of animals to a parent's way with children. Just as some parents abuse their kids, they argue, some trainers abuse their animals. That doesn't mean all disciplinarian parents and all firm trainers are abusive. How, except in extreme cases, do you persuade the court that a parent—or a trainer—has crossed the line? Good luck to the attorney who tries.

"My understanding," said Gerry Martin, "is that Bunny Brook has instructed her attorney to go ahead with an appeal. That would raise many of the same issues we'd be seeking to have reexamined."

"I'm the one who should be appealing," said Murray. "I'm the one got screwed."

The troopers, at the cash register, said something to the hostess and took a window booth. Were they keeping an eye on the rig?

"—your fugitive status," Martin was saying, "an appeal would be an even more complicated, time-consuming process, involving many additional hours of work . . ."

"More money? Is that what you're saying? I don't have any money, but I'll pay you when I get some."

Martin didn't want to sound mercenary but the fact was that he belonged to a firm, and the firm would fire him if he took on an appeal when the client still owed for the trial and the firm had received nothing toward the cost of transcripts and appellate fees and so on. It would be a substantial undertaking. Until the trial portion of the representation had been looked after, Martin really couldn't—

"Murray? Murray?"

Eddie Drake's girlfriend had given birth to a baby girl, and before he was quite used to the idea of being a father she announced that she was pregnant again. More than ever, Eddie needed a way of generating regular income. When he got the chance to lease a female Asian from the Gatti Circus for a hundred dollars a day, he jumped at it.

Doy, meanwhile, waited tables at Brewers Café in town. She enjoyed the social contact, and it was useful to work at a place where your family could drop by for breakfast. The money came in handy, too. Dick was preoccupied, spending hours every day on the phone, writing letters, trying to get a line on Murray. He figured Murray was probably broke and working the animals to feed them; if so, there were people in the business who knew about it. Somebody had heard from somebody else that Murray had crossed into Mexico. Someone else figured he was up in Canada. Another elephant man had heard from an animal dealer that Murray had made inquiries about finding a third-party buyer. When Dick tried to nail down these rumors, however, they evaporated. Everyone had a theory but nobody had anything solid.

Dick waited for news from New Jersey, and when none came he called Bob Britton. He said he'd seen Murray's name in an ad in *Circus Report* for All-Risk Insurance. He also said he and Doy had received an anonymous letter suggesting they'd find the elephants back at Meadow Gate Farm. The writer claimed that Murray had vowed to kill them before giving them up. Britton said he'd look into it.

Britton phoned Jim Greenstreet, the insurance man at All-Risk, who had no recent knowledge of Murray. He called Dale Tuttle, who said that Murray had donated a bull to Dickerson Park Zoo but that he hadn't seen him in a long while.

Britton drove back to Meadow Gate Farm. Bunny wasn't thrilled to see him, but again came down to the gate and gave him a few minutes. No, she still hadn't heard from Murray. Yes, Murray still had the tractor-trailer. No, they had no wish to lay charges; they believed it would eventually be returned. Yes, Murray had indeed threatened to kill the elephants—and himself—rather than turn them over to the Drakes. The court proceedings had so distressed him that she made an appointment for him with a psychiatrist. Nothing had been accomplished; Murray wasn't one to tell his problems to a stranger. But that had happened during the trial, she said, months earlier. The information in the letter, she told Britton, must have dated back to that period.

Britton called Dick and reported this conversation.

"What do we do now?" said Dick.

"Sit tight," said Britton. "I know it must be frustrating, but a guy with elephants? He'll turn up."

Nothing in their backgrounds suggested that Howell Phillips IV and Skip Mantha, on meeting in Manhattan in the late 1960s, would become best friends. Howell was the grandson and son of prominent investment bankers in Boston. His parents had assumed he would follow them in the family business, but Howell had always been keener on animals and causes than bonds and debentures.

One of Howell's grandparents had owned a six-hundred-acre farm in Indiana, and Howell's most pleasing childhood memories were of his visits there. From morning to night he searched for frogs and snakes and butterflies. One of his uncles had thoroughbred horses, which were sometimes kept at his grandparents' farm. Howell was taught horsemanship and animal husbandry. His parents raised collies and joked that they'd had to evict him from the playpen so the puppies would have a place. They took him to pet shows and bought him beautifully illustrated books about moths and butterflies. By the time Howell was fifteen he was spotting errors in books on lepidopterology.

Summers were spent at a sprawling summer retreat in Nova Scotia. The place had been in the family since the early years of the century. Vast but primitive, it included twenty-three buildings spread over thirty-six square miles. There was no electricity; the cooks and maids relied on kerosene and their wits. Everything had to be rafted in across the largest of the six lakes, or pulled on sleighs in winter. The closest neighbor was eight miles away, the nearest town twenty miles. Deer and moose were so abundant you felt like an intruder in paradise. At night you could hear the haunting calls of owls and wolves. As a child, Howell imagined that the whole world was pristine and would stay that way forever.

The land itself had originally been leased in the name of a sportsmen's club, but Howell's great-uncle, in a coup that became part of family lore, managed to con the Canadian government out of a good chunk of it. By uncertain means the great-uncle obtained a deed from the king of England. When the Canadian government sought to revoke the club lease and sent a letter saying, in effect, get your buildings off our land, the great-uncle was able to produce this deed as proof of ownership.

Eventually the snowmobile did what the government had been unable to do. Without year-round caretakers it became impossible to maintain the place in winter. Theft and vandalism by snowmobilers led the family to sell off the land, which was turned into a summer camp for underprivileged kids. Howell went up to see it years later, with a maid who had worked for the family. Long, barrackslike, prefab buildings had been put up; the undergrowth had been burned off; the forest had been scarred by service roads. The maid's eyes filled with water when she saw it.

Howell, like his grandfather and father before him, enrolled at Harvard. He had thought of becoming a veterinarian, decided instead to attend medical school, but did so poorly in chemistry he was not accepted. He studied commerce and finance instead, obtaining his bachelor's and master's degrees. He wasn't sure what he wanted to do, but he wanted to do it out of range of his family. He moved to New York.

To appease his parents—to be able to say he'd tried it and hated it—he took a job at the family firm on Wall Street. Meanwhile he debated whether to buy a good place in the city or to keep an apartment there and sink his money into a country home. In an expensive area of northern New Jersey he found the property that made up his mind, a spacious house with a barn and outbuildings, on a stunning acreage that backed onto the Appalachian Trail and included a pond, a trout stream, plenty of pasture, and abundant hardwood forest. He planned to spend time out of the city, and he wanted to keep animals. He also felt the acreage might be a better investment.

In his mid-thirties, Howell was still unsure what to do with his life. His work on environmental and animal causes felt marginal, with nothing at the center. Moving from project to project, and from woman to woman, he felt unfulfilled; he was good at investment banking, but there was something disturbing about a prescribed career. Fighting his parents' expectations, unable to sustain a love relationship, fearful of wasting his life, he joined a Gestalt group.

That was where he met Skip. An Atlantan by birth, son of an auto mechanic, Skip was a lifelong hippie. He, too, was confronting himself, and Howell found they had much in common. Both were adult children of alcoholics, both had woman problems, and both felt spiritually vacant. In the course of group therapy the two men became friends with an intimacy new to Howell—the kind of friends who write long letters instead of phoning, drive each other to the airport, and discuss the unmentionable with easy candor.

All the group members were close, and Howell often invited them out to his farm. These weekends were glorious experiences, made possible, it seemed, by the special optimism of the sixties, ten people brought together in an honest exchange of pain and acceptance. Howell lived for two years with a woman from the group. There was talk of starting a communal house. But the sixties turned into the seventies; the group ran out of steam, and its members began going their separate ways. Howell's work as an investment banker—lunching with CEOs, identifying takeover targets, arranging corporate financing— demanded more of his energy. He began to find it impossible to keep a lunch open for Skip each week; they talked on the phone regularly, then occasionally, then lost touch altogether.

One day they bumped into each other on Lexington Avenue. Each was astonished by the changes in the other. God, it had been years! They exchanged bear hugs and jokes about receding hairlines. Over dinner, Howell found his old friend in tough shape, desolate and adrift. Skip had returned to Georgia and married an old girlfriend who ended up leaving him for the next-door neighbor. Despondent, he'd returned to New York a few months earlier to pull himself together.

It was now 1984, and Manhattan was turning out masters of the universe. Howell was earning a small fortune; Skip continued to lead an existence more suited to Ken Kesey than Tom Wolfe. His blue jeans and fisherman's sweater might have been the same outfit he'd worn to group weekends at Howell's farm. He was a lovely man in a time warp, happier experiencing life than seeing what he could wring out of it. When he pulled his golden hair into a ponytail, Howell noticed the gold stud in his earlobe. He ordered a vegetarian meal, heavy on the tofu, and drank herbal tea. Afterward, for old times' sake, they went back to Skip's place and smoked a joint. The dismal basement apartment stank of incense; there was a tattered collection of Afghani cushions on the floor, and nowhere else to sit. All that was missing, Howell thought, was Vanilla Fudge on the stereo and Peter Max posters on the wall.

Howell had long since ended his dalliance with the counter-culture. Closing in on fifty, he looked back on the sixties as a useful aberration and his career as a kind of inevitability. Helping corporate predators identify prey, and helping prey avoid corporate predators—this was what he'd been born to do. Many of his Wall Street friends would view Skip as a Frisbee, but Howell admired the choices he had made. It had always impressed Howell, for instance, that Skip had once earned a scholarship to MIT but decided not to spend years among people motivated by nothing more inspired than a high-paying job. A fine craftsman, gifted with his hands, Skip was content to scrape by doing odd jobs of carpentry or cabinetmaking. His decision to live in the East Village, selling soft drugs to pay the rent, allowed him to explore t'ai chi and Rolfing and crystals.

At the time of their dinner, Howell needed someone to take care of his country place. It had been burgled and he'd lost more than fifty thousand dollars' worth of the inherited wealth for which he'd once had disdain—antique firearms, his father's gold studs and cufflinks, and his great-grandmother's magnificent service for sixteen, from Shreve, Crump & Low, Boston's finest silversmith. Even with a sophisticated motion-detection system, Howell felt nervous about leaving the farm unattended all week. As his new woman, Veronica, bluntly put it, he needed a caretaker but was too cheap to hire one.

Howell arranged for Veronica and Skip to meet. After a lunch in Tribeca, Veronica, whose intuition was usually sound, dismissed Skip as "flaky." He was not flaky at all; he was steadfast and dependable. Howell knew how it felt to founder in the wake of love and figured Skip might appreciate time to himself. What better place to recover than the prettiest spot in New Jersey? Here was a way for Howell to combine generosity of spirit with his own practical needs. Too bad if Veronica didn't warm to the guy. Howell asked him if he'd like to move in.

Skip wondered what would be expected of him. His carpentry might be useful, Howell said, but otherwise it would simply be a matter of tending the garden, keeping an eye on the ever-growing number of animals, and giving the place occupancy. Skip moved in two weeks later; his possessions fit in the trunk of Howell's Acura. Crossing the Triboro Bridge, leaving New York behind, Skip wistfully recalled group weekends at the farm. Chatting with Howell in the car, he felt the rejuvenation of their friendship. Turning into Howell's drive, he was stirred anew by the beauty of the place.

It truly was a superb property, worth millions. At the rear, rolling meadow gave way to mature forest—a mixture of oak, maple, and hickory. Laurel and hemlock grew in the gorges, and berry bushes took hold on the ridges—huckleberries, pokeberries, and a type of purple berry Skip couldn't identify. Sycamores lined the creek banks, along with graceful willows and the odd silver maple. Jewelweed sprang up in direct sunshine; rhododendrons thrived in the dappled shade. The first week Skip was there, he saw white-tailed deer, pheasants, and a coyote. Sunsets were spectacular, evenings beautifully tranquil. Skip used his muscles for the first time in months, and his sleep was the sleep of the untroubled. Tea in hand, he began each day by checking the progress of the cutting garden and the vegetables, an inspection that sometimes took hours. In late morning, when the air was not yet fuzzed by humidity, and a breeze swayed the meadow in slow undulation, the property spread out before him like a vision of the Peaceable Kingdom.

Skip thanked his lucky stars that he'd reconnected with Howell. They'd been close in a way men seldom are, and he looked forward to resuming the friendship in depth. He didn't much like Veronica—he'd never admired Howell's taste in women—but she came up only on weekends, and Skip often used those times to visit friends in the city or his mother on Long Island. In a few weeks his spirits had lifted. By the time he'd spent six months at the farm his divorce no longer embittered him, and solitude had restored his appetite for company. He'd been there almost a year when, one afternoon, he got a call from Manhattan. Howell spoke in his office voice.

"How would you feel if someone stopped in for a couple of weeks with his elephants?"

"You pulling my leg?"

"Two Asian elephants. Adult females. He'll look after them. It won't mean any additional work for you."

"You're serious."

"I'm serious. Would you have any objections?"

"I can't think of any. What the heck, I enjoy animals."

"That's great. He'll be there later this week."

"Fine," said Skip, who knew Howell well enough to understand that, in the ensuing pause, a sentence was being carefully framed.

"Skip, this particular set of circumstances is not necessarily a set of circumstances we want the whole world to know about."

"Really."

"I'll explain on the weekend—it just happens to be one of those weird situations. Mum's the word. For now, at least, we don't want people to know the elephants are there. Understood?"

"Right on," said Skip, who had always enjoyed tossing darts at Howell's sober pomposity. "I'll hide them under my bed until you get here. Then you can help me knit wool sweaters for them, and we'll mix them in with the sheep."

7

HIDE AND SEEK

In the beginning of all things, wisdom and knowledge were with the animals; for Tirawa, the One Above, did not speak directly to man. He sent certain animals to tell men that he showed himself through the beasts, and that from them, and from the stars and the sun and the moon, man should learn.

—Pawnee Chief Letakots-Lesa

▼ ▼ ▼ ▼ ▼ ▼ ▼ ▼ ▼ ▼ ▼ ▼ ▼ ▼ ▼

I've had the opportunity to turn the girls loose in a wild wooded area. I usually spend about three hours, twice a day, letting them roam without any supervision whatsoever until I'm ready to bring them in.

The girls are tethered in one spot in the woods, and we have to walk about three-quarters of a mile to a watering hole (natural spring coming out of the ground). The land lay here is mountainous with large outcrops of rock, all the natural wildlife, deer, coon, snakes, etc. Very little ground graze but thick tree cover. There are some old manmade trails. There is also some excellent swamp area. There are probably untold underground water supplies.

When we first arrived I would lead the girls to the artesian well. The water is extremely cold but tastes excellent. It runs down the hill and turns into a narrow stream. I have only followed it downstream for about a mile, where it runs

▲ ▲ ▲ ▲ ▲ ▲ ▲ ▲ ▲ ▲ ▲ ▲ ▲ ▲ ▲

into the swamp. On its way downhill it picks up several runoff streams during rains or wet seasons.

At first, Dutchess drank directly from the well where it surfaces. Tory has finally found a spot where she seems to like the water. It is an area about thirty feet from the stream where the ground is always moist. During their treks through the woods they passed this spot many times and recently one of their footprints started filling with water. Tory goes to this footprint right away and starts to drink. After a few days other footprints filled with water. Dutchess will drink from any of them but Tory drinks only from the one. If Dutchess is drinking from that one, Tory waits until she finishes. After a few days there were no more individual footprints, just a single water hole about five feet long and two feet wide.

These drinking habits are contrary to everything I have observed in the past. Normally they would not drink water that had been standing even for a brief time. They'd only drink if I put a hose with running water right in the bucket, and then Tory would try to get the water directly from the end of the hose.

We were here for more than five weeks before either of them really drank well. They seemed to drink only a minimum amount. We had a period of five straight days of fairly heavy rain. Neither of them drank anything. I assume they were getting enough from browsing, the moisture on the leaves. There was also a period of five days that were extremely hot and humid. Much to my surprise they drank far less than normal. But they made mud holes and mudded down. Temperature does not seem to be the major trigger for mudding. Humidity is more important. The higher the humidity, the more they mud themselves.

At this point their intake of food is mostly striped maple leaves. On a few occasions Tory will also graze on a type of wild grass. Dutchess eats the same, plus she also eats a certain kind of fern, I believe they are called fiddleheads. Their hay consumption is down from six or seven to about three and a half bales of hay a day. I would say they are now eating sixty percent leaves and forty percent hay, but their stool looks the same as if they were eating exclusively hay.

Their social pattern is to stay within forty or fifty yards of each other. At certain times they come within touching range. Usually they spend two or three hours on their own each morning and another three hours *in the afternoon. When I call them (whistle signals), they usually appear within three or four minutes, sometimes together, sometimes from different directions. They do their normal salutations after being separated. Spending so much time with them in this type of setting is a first and it's interesting to see how they behave on their own. . . .*

Skip had been curious about Murray ever since the rig had turned off the county road, started down the driveway, and promptly got hung up. Skip had come over from the barn to introduce himself and help out. Murray had climbed down gruffly to shake hands. The girls' trunks were wagging out the side of the trailer, and Skip went to pet them. Murray told him to stay the hell away. He crawled under the rig, cussing, and discovered the trailer had been riding so low that the tire holder had caught a rock ledge. Skip volunteered to go for help, but Murray wanted to get out of sight with no fuss. Skip lent a hand, and after a good deal of work they chipped away enough rock to free the rig. Murray said thanks and disappeared.

Skip had never met anyone quite like him. A leery, jockey-sized, cocky fellow with a deep voice and firm opinions, he spent hours with his elephants each day and slept with them in the trailer—or in the woods—each night. During the week he and Skip were the only ones at the farm, and they began spending time in one another's company. Some days they fished and had dinner together, cooking up their catch—the pond was stocked with pickerel and bass—in Howell's kitchen. Murray helped Skip with the garden and the farm animals; Skip sometimes tagged along while Murray took the girls into the woods, or worked on their feet. Murray described his legal situation and how it had come about, but otherwise said little about himself. He was not planning to stay long and saw no sense in giving too much away. Every so often he phoned his brother, Wally, in Arizona for news of his family and of Bunny's appeal, which seemed to have bogged down. He longed to call Bunny, but wasn't sure how she'd feel about the tractor-trailer, and wondered if she'd ever cared as deeply as he did. Besides, he'd vowed not to communicate.

Skip, curious how anyone could end up with elephants as companions, related bits of his own background in hopes of learning more of Murray's. At first, each offhand inquiry ("How'd you get your start in the animal business?") prompted a one-liner ("First time I got drunk I got married. Second time I bought a chimp, so I quit drinking"); but one afternoon, after they had weeded the vegetable patch, Murray recounted how he and Denise had got their first chimp. A year after their marriage, he said, they were playing nightclubs in Quebec—the Cat Girl dancing, Murray doing stand-up and playing accordion. The star of the show had been a young chimp named Jinx, whom they both adored. Jinx did five minutes a night, and his owners, Ed and Darlene Sellick, Murray learned, made $650 a week. Murray and Denise did the rest of the show—nearly two hours—for $250.

"Makes no sense," he told her backstage one night as she, in her Cat Girl costume, centered his bow tie and smoothed the shoulders of his tuxedo. "That's not Bob Hope out there, for chrissake. It's a monkey."

"Not a monkey," said Denise, "a chimp."

It hadn't escaped her notice that Darlene wore a different outfit every day, Ed had a Nikon camera, and they drove around in a new Coupe de Ville. Here she and Murray were killing themselves to get by, while Ed and Darlene were practically retired. On their day off Murray and Denise took Ed out for a drink to ask how he'd started with chimps. Murray, who didn't normally drink, ordered a second round, one thing led to another, and before long he was inquiring where a fellow might buy a chimp. From a teacher in Maine, Ed said, a woman who had done her doctorate on chimps and treated them like pets. Murray reached her by phone. I just have one at the moment, she said, and quoted a price, $650. A week's pay for Jinx. We'll take it, said Murray. Next morning, while he nursed a headache, Denise told him what he'd done.

They drove to Maine and met Alita Wescott, who taught

school in Portland. The chimp was an infant male, seven pounds, instantly lovable. Murray asked how you trained a chimp. Treat it like a child, said Alita, never forgetting it will always be a wild animal. Murray and Denise, childless, nodded wisely. When Alita cautioned that it was tricky and demanding, they nodded again. How hard could it be? Darlene was a housewife and Ed was a tool-and-die maker.

They loaded the chimp in the Buick and drove back to Murray's parents' house in Connecticut. Poor Shirley, when she saw what her son had done. Bad enough that he worked in clubs while Wally was going through as an engineer. A chimpanzee? For this they'd given him a proper education and encouraged his musical talent? When Murray assured her he'd make good money, she bit her tongue. She should tell him he was crazy as a loon? Any mother should tell her son he's a heartache?

Murray, who'd always been handy, built a wooden cage and removed the backseat of the car. In the yard he spent hours trying to teach Chatter simple things. They hadn't been in Meriden a week when Ed Sellick called.

"Pick up that chimp?"

"Sure did," said Murray. "Cute little guy, too."

"Want to go to work?"

"You kidding?" said Murray. "All it does is eat, sleep, shit, and piss. No way I can train it that quick."

"You know the TV show Jinx does? Well, the same people are opening a Super Circus tent in Chicago."

Two of the partners, pro wrestlers, planned to wrestle alligators and box kangaroos in the tent. They needed somebody out front working the Bally stand, pulling customers and pitching the show.

"But Ed, Chatter can't do a thing."

"It doesn't have to do anything. Let it fool around while you talk. They'll eat it up."

Before driving to Chicago with Denise in the front and Chatter in his cage in the back, Murray looked up "chimpanzee" in his parents' encyclopedia. He learned, among other things, that chimps have a life expectancy of thirty-five years, attain full growth by age eleven, and feed mainly on fruit, plant shoots, insects, and bird's eggs. "In contrast to the other great apes," said the encyclopedia, "they are temperamentally extrovert and endowed with considerable intelligence, involving even a degree of insight. They are consequently educable, though attention is inclined to wander if a particular problem eludes them, whereupon they are liable to tantrums."

He and Denise would have found it more helpful to have been told, "They're fierce little bastards, mischievous as hell, unbelievably strong. They can destroy a room in thirty seconds. If you take them on, it's a fight to the finish. When an elephant goes after you, you generally wind up dead. When a chimp does, you only wish you were dead."

"A chimp did this," Murray told Skip, pulling up his pant leg to expose a scarred knee, "after I'd started importing them myself. We were living in Downers Grove, Illinois, only house we ever owned. I don't like houses. They tie you down and cost too much in taxes and utilities."

"A chimp?" said Skip. "Looks like you fought a grizzly."

"I was importing different exotics by then. I knew all the dealers in Asia and I had a good thing going with Pan Am. You could make a buck in those days."

"Before they had laws governing the trade in animals?"

"Before the little old ladies in tennis shoes started squawking."

Kneeling, muscling the chimp into a shipping crate, Murray had been knocked off balance. The chimp had scooted behind him and bit him. It felt like being shot in the butt. Murray hollered and unloaded a left hook, but the chimp ducked, came underneath, grabbed Murray's leg, and sunk his teeth. By the time Murray had subdued him there was blood all over the basement and Murray's kneecap wasn't where it was meant to be.

"Twenty-five-pound chimp. Somebody'd already bought him and I was loading him to ship. He figured there were other places he'd rather be."

"Right on," said Skip. "I don't think I'd want to be forced into a cage in somebody's basement in Illinois, either."

"We didn't know what the hell we were doing," said Murray. "Made it up as we went along. I got hurt, I caught hepatitis, you name it. But we were crazy about Chatter, and by the time our first daughter came along he was part of the family. He did backflips, knuckle walk, impersonations of Elvis and Ed Sullivan, great act. We toured Quebec again the next year with him and Robin in the back seat. Robin was a baby and Chatter looked after her. When she started crying, he patted her head."

One afternoon, while they were playing a nightclub in Hull, they crossed the river to see the Parliament Buildings in Ottawa. It was an ugly November day and Parliament Hill was bleak and deserted. While they were taking pictures at the War Memorial, two gentlemen in expensive wool topcoats and fedoras happened by. The elder man, like many people, was intensely curious about the chimp.

"I'm Louis St. Laurent," he said, removing a leather glove and offering his hand.

"Nice to meet you, Lou. Murray Hill. My wife, Denise, our daughter, Robin, and this here is Chatter."

They answered his questions, talked about chimps and babies, discussed the weather, then shook hands all round—Chatter included—and it wasn't until they were back at the club and Murray happened to mention the incident that he found out the fellow they'd met was the prime minister of Canada. Murray shrugged; politician or not, Lou had seemed like a nice enough guy.

A chimp was the ticket, all right, and soon they were making $500 a week. "Chatter and Murray," said the newspaper ads, "Chimp and Chump, the only Father and Son Act of Its Type." Before each show Denise slipped into the audience to ask people at a distant table if they were afraid of chimps. Could Chatter come over as part of the act? Denise left an open bottle of Coca-Cola on the table and Chatter noted where it was. During the show, at Murray's cue, Chatter leaped off the stage, scurried up the aisle, hopped on the table, and guzzled the Coke. The audience roared.

Chatter loved soft drinks, loved being the center of attention, and started taking off while Murray was still doing jokes stolen from Henny Youngman. To stop him, Murray bought some 250-pound test and a heavy-duty rod and reel. He fed the line through Chatter's tuxedo jacket. When Chatter broke lead, Murray grabbed the rod and reeled him in—"Come back, old buddy, c'mon back here!"—jerking the chimp off his feet and dragging him backward up the aisle. People howled, figuring it was part of the act.

Truth was, though, Chatter was growing unmanageable. Chimps tend to, as they get bigger and older, which is partly why Murray bought more babies. It would be good to have two Chatters in case one took ill, or they got two bookings for the same date. And Murray realized he could turn a buck selling chimps to zoos, circuses, and private owners.

Just as Robin had a strong bond with Chatter, the next child, Nada, had a special connection to Cobby. Robin had been a sweet girl, content to amuse herself, early to talk and walk; Nada was hyper and rebellious, scooting across the floor instead of crawling, jabbering incessantly. Each chimp, like each child, was distinct in personality and required unique handling. Cobby, for instance, had a huge appetite and an annoying bathroom habit. He kept leaving a puddle of urine on the linoleum. One day Murray snuck down the hall after him, waited a moment, then peeked in. Cobby was straddling the bowl, as he'd been taught, but holding his penis so that urine shot up in the air.

"You dirty little—"

Before Murray could finish, Cobby had looped his penis around his finger, a one-eighty, and hit the bowl. His expression was priceless: How's that, boss? This about right? Murray and Denise were laughing too hard to discipline him.

"What times we had," said Murray, lighting another Camel. "You can have a lot of fun with chimps."

"What about the chimps?" said Skip. "Think they had fun, too?"

"What do you mean?"

"Seems like a pretty unnatural life for a wild animal."

"Hell, they were part of the family. We treated them same as we treated our kids. We all sat down to meals together."

Young chimps ate as much as you gave them, Murray said; they pushed back from the table as their bellies expanded. The kitchen had a bay window. Robin and Nada sat at either end of the table and the chimps faced out. Some mornings, when Cobby had finished his own breakfast, he'd spot something in the yard. He'd jump up on the table, agitated—"Uoo, uoo, uoo!" Chatter, twice his size, hopped up on the table, grunting, elbowing Cobby aside, and Robin and Nada had to see, too, and the boxer started barking, and during the commotion Cobby swiped the bread from Chatter's plate. By the time the others had decided there was no cause for alarm, Cobby was politely eating bread and jam. Chatter looked at his empty plate dumbfounded, but he never twigged, perhaps because Cobby was smart enough not to try it too often. He always pulled it on mornings when they had strawberry jam.

Skip had never seen Murray laugh before, really let loose, and each anecdote was more uproarious than the last. Like the time in the elevator at the television station in Chicago, where they filmed *Chatter's World,* a show Murray did for years. Murray got the chimp into one corner, but the elevator was crowded and a blonde got too close. When Cobby goosed her, she wheeled and slapped Murray's face.

"I tell her, 'It wasn't me, lady, honest.' She gives me this look, like, 'How low can you get, blaming it on that sweet chimp.' Meanwhile Cobby's innocent as an angel, like he don't know what the fuss is all about."

Murray's and Skip's laughter carried across the meadow and subsided. It was dusk. The geese had come into the pond and the sheep were gathering near the barn. At their tethering spot in the woods, ready to be loaded in the trailer for the night, Tory and Dutchess chirped and trumpeted back and forth.

Murray got up to leave, wiping water from his eyes. "The stunts we pulled? The characters we met? I tell you, Skip"—he wasn't laughing anymore—"we're divorced now, me and Denise, but we had some times back then, seemed like the fun would last forever. . . ."

Skip sat in the fading light, watching Murray limp across the yard—like Tory, he favored one leg after he'd been inactive— and Skip's own tears, born in mirth, changed into something else, though he couldn't have said whether he was lamenting his own impending divorce and uncertain future, or the predicament of this strange little man who'd happened into his life.

The girls have gotten to know these woods pretty good. Different areas have different foods. Their normal feeding is to go where there is water in the morning and then start browsing on striped maple. The pond that started out as a single footprint filling with water is now about twelve feet long and six feet across.

In the afternoon they go to areas where there is no water but has oak and chestnut. (As I'm not much on flora I cannot pinpoint the exact subspecies.) Socially they are getting to be more of themselves. Tory is gentle but she is basically a loner and doesn't really care if she has company. Dutchess is tougher and a better worker but she does have a sense of humor and it's starting to come out again. She enjoys playing and likes interaction.

Something that always intrigued me about elephants but I never really noticed before is the bone above the eye, how it protects the eye and how the elephant uses it. Just above that bone is a hollow, and the hollow also serves a purpose. That formation of the skull is not often observed in use. Occasionally when an elephant pushes an object, the object will slip to the side of the head. Normally the elephant uses the center of the upper part of the trunk, or the front plate of the head, to continue pushing.

In the woods here we often go through heavy underbrush. For bush that's low to the ground, the girls use their feet to kick through it. From about three to five feet off the ground, they arch the trunk forward, tilt the head back and push. If it's higher than that, they tilt their heads down and push with the top of the frontal plate on the skull. In thick brush, the vines, limbs and brush slide by the eye on that top bone, and the girls don't even close their eyes in these situations. I've also seen them push dead trees or bent-over trees by resting the tree on the top of the eye bone and letting the tree trunk slide up that hollow as the elephant moves forward.

Yesterday the girls headed south to the swamp. They drank a little and mudded down good. On the way back we saw a deer grazing up ahead about twenty yards alongside the path. We kept on walking like we didn't see it. When we got within about five yards the deer moved a few feet uphill and continued grazing. It looked directly at us but didn't seem disturbed in the least. We passed within eight or ten feet of it.

This morning I was afraid I'd lost Dutchess. Usually when I call them in, they come, but this morning only Tory came. Dutchess had been gone for over an hour and I hadn't heard any of the forest noises that usually give her away. I whistled for her and got no reply. If she wanted to stay hidden I'd have a hard time finding her. It amazes me how quietly they can move through heavy woods and how hard it is to spot them when they don't want to be seen. Even when I'm moving carefully I make at least three times as much noise as they do. I began to worry—I sure can't afford a lost elephant. I said to Tory, "Let's find Dutchess. Where is she?" Her ears came forward and she immediately started off toward the east.

She moved at a steady pace, grabbing wild grass here and there but not stopping to browse. I followed her for ten minutes until she stopped. Then I whistled again. Dutchess started her chirping (it came from far off, way down in the swamp). Tory turned in that direction and slapped her jaw with her trunk. They both trumpeted at the same time and Tory headed toward the swamp at a brisk walk. They both kept trumpeting. I followed Tory down the hill over rock outcrops, then I spotted Dutchess coming up the far side of the hill. It took seven or eight minutes before they met, greeting each other with the usual touching, smelling, and talking. I'm sure Tory understood exactly what I'd said to her. I'm starting to see a much closer relationship between the three of us. . . .

•   •   •

Even as he worked grueling hours on Wall Street, helping acquisitive companies devise new ways to incur debt, Howell Phillips IV kept up his many outside interests. He was careful not to call himself an animal activist or animal rightist, since those he'd met were naïve. Unlike most activists, he had a working knowledge of the law, and his upbringing had exposed him to the subtleties of political influence. He brought to his animal-rights work a highly developed—and highly unusual—talent for blending idealism and pragmatism.

It was at a meeting of a group formed to lobby for humane slaughterhouse practices that he had met Veronica. Somebody had misquoted the statute that applied to a particular case of cruelty. Howell was familiar with the case, which involved a puppy factory, and couldn't resist piping up, "I'm no lawyer, but I happen to know you're mistaken." He was invited to take the microphone and explain why, under law, it was proving so difficult to shut the place down.

Veronica introduced herself after his impromptu dissertation. She was a mercurial woman in her late thirties, more handsome than pretty, with shining eyes, mannish shoulders, and good skin. An inheritance had left her free to pursue her own interests; Howell became one of them. He was competent, well bred, and committed to his work in a way she had always found attractive.

Howell became increasingly involved with the group, and with Veronica. Though he was also seeing a woman at his office, he claimed, week after week, to be on the verge of breaking up with her. Unless he did so soon, Veronica threatened, month after month, to end their relationship. The months passed. A fragile equilibrium was struck. Veronica, who had a complicated emotional life of her own, saw Howell not at all during the week but spent weekends with him at the farm.

Veronica had first heard of Murray Hill through friends who told her he'd gone underground with his elephants to protect them from abuse pending the reversal of an unfair court ruling. She loved elephants—she had traveled to Africa and Southeast Asia to watch them and learn about them—and she had embraced his cause before even meeting him. She was charmed that, on the phone, he referred to the elephants as "the girls." They needed a place to lay over for a couple of weeks, he'd said, and she'd thought immediately of Howell's farm. It had taken some lobbying, but Howell had finally capitulated. When Murray next called, Veronica had told him she couldn't wait to meet them.

Tory and Dutchess turned out to be adorable, though in very different ways. Tory, the more approachable, had a rounded back and shortened hindquarters that gave her a rather roly-poly look. Her puckered cheeks, bright eyes, and damaged trunk—split open at the tip and imperfectly healed—made her instantly endearing. To the touch, her trunk felt as mighty as a boa constrictor, yet strangely delicate and unthreatening. She returned Veronica's curiosity and they became instant friends.

Dutchess was longer-legged, with a flatter back and a leaner, more graceful appearance. She reminded Veronica of one of her New York aunts, an embittered spinster, haughty and skeptical, never seeking your approval or offering hers. Her deep connection to Tory was evident at once; it struck Veronica as the sort of bond that exists between sisters who are especially close. In certain lights her skin seemed a deeper gray than Tory's, and the rounded dome of her skull was more bulbous.

As for Murray, he was not what Veronica had expected at all. A tiny man with a roguish, masculine charm, he was clearly devoted to the girls and willing to do anything for them. But when she first heard him command them she was taken aback. She'd assumed one spoke sweetly, as brides did in Thailand when they sought to ensure fertility by touching the sacred creatures. Murray was brusque and tyrannical. "Move up, Dutchess. I said move up, goddamn it!"

He was a disappointment in other ways, too. The first time she caught him with a fishing line in the pond, she was aghast. What gave him the right to hook living creatures, wrest them from their element, and slit them open? She couldn't understand how anyone who would go to such lengths to protect his elephants could possibly be so callous.

But Howell was a lifelong fisherman. Patiently, he tried to persuade Veronica that, so long as you ate your catch and used the remains for fertilizer, there was nothing wrong with fishing; in fact, it did the pond good. Veronica wasn't buying. She was also, it turned out, dead set against selling lambs in the spring, killing chickens, or otherwise intruding on the natural order.

The farm was costly to maintain, Howell argued; he needed the income and the tax benefits. Besides, he took pains to do things as humanely as possible. He wasn't rigorously vegetarian, as she was, and his briefcase was hand-tooled Florentine leather, but he was not insensitive. He supported many positions she and other activists espoused; he'd done volunteer work; he'd taken in abused and neglected animals. He'd even invited a group of animal rightists up one spring to shear the sheep.

Purportedly this he had done to show how open-minded he was. In fact, he'd done it to confirm these people's idiocy. They amazed him. They had complained about the brutality of traditional shearing methods, and Howell had said they were welcome to shear his sheep as they saw fit. A whole delegation showed up; many had never set foot on a farm. Howell's sheep were robust—some weighed almost two hundred pounds—and they grew jittery and wild-eyed as the volunteers advanced on the stalls, shears in hand, calling softly, "Heeere sheep, here sheepie-sheep." When the sheep bolted, the volunteers went down like bowling pins. Dumb luck, he realized later, that no one had been seriously hurt.

Many of them were like that. One organization Howell belonged to found itself at odds with another during a march in Manhattan. Both were protesting against conditions at the zoo in Central Park, the oldest in North America. When they reached the zoo, one group wanted to march through it, the other to march around it. The discussion became an argument; the argument grew heated; the two groups marched off on their separate ways. The two leaders never spoke again.

If only these people—Veronica included—would focus their energy, see that it's more productive to fight your enemies than your friends. Slowly, the world was changing; each year brought broader coverage of protests at research laboratories. Cosmetics firms announced an end to testing on rabbits; fur-wrapped women were assailed on Fifth Avenue; a Massachusetts man was jailed for beating his dog. Questions of animal rights were publicly debated every day. As with drunk driving, protection for nonsmokers, and child abuse, the moral issue had only to be raised for popular opinion to bring about legislative change. Animal-rights people had a glorious opportunity, Howell believed, but infighting was crippling them.

One woman—the great majority of activists were women—shot down ninety percent of the legislation proposed by her organization because it was imperfect. She could not be made to see that all progress is a halting sequence of compromise and accommodation. Another woman, the head of a national animal-rights group, stood firm against proposed legislation to govern animal auctions because it would imply recognition that such auctions existed. But they do exist, Howell pointed out; we've documented ninety of them in the state of New York alone. Perhaps, she said, but how in good conscience can we acknowledge them? It would be a kind of legitimization.

To Howell, that was the movement in a nutshell: well-intentioned, impractical, naïve. Much as he admired Veronica's fierce dedication and enjoyed her affection—she was as ardent in love as in her defense of animals—he found himself siding with Murray against her more extreme positions, and relying on Murray's support when she complained about the practices of husbandry at the farm. And so, as Howell and Veronica tee-ter-tottered back and forth, Murray found himself at the fulcrum of their relationship—the point at which the slightest shift upsets the whole precarious balance.

The next time Dick Drake came east, he stopped in at Colts Neck to see Bob Britton and find out how the New Jersey State Police investigation was going. Britton's reassurances did nothing to end Dick's growing disenchantment with the law-enforcement system. The months were passing and what had been done? Sure, Britton had spoken to Bunny's attorney, who'd been no help, and he'd phoned people in Missouri, who had no useful information. He typed out his reports and called Dick every now and then and that was it. Why, Dick wondered, wasn't anybody out there looking for Murray?

Britton explained that a wanted had gone to the State Crime Information Center computer in Trenton. They had good identifiers—Murray's description, date of birth, and Social Security Number, as well as the plate, serial, and vehicle identification numbers of the rig. New Jersey was plugged into the National Crime Information Center, which meant the Trenton computer automatically loaded the federal computer in Washington. Almost every state was hooked up to the NCIC computer. No matter where in the country Murray got stopped, the police would radio in for a Signal 15, a computer check of driving credentials, and a Signal 16, which checks the wanteds. Even at a weigh scale they might well run a check on the plate number.

"It's just a question of time," said Britton. "He'll show up."

Dick had come back to New Jersey to pick up Murray's old rig, which was still at Dot's place. He planned to load his Ranchero in the rig and take both vehicles back to California. Dick had received a tip that the elephants were in Texas and planned a route back that would let him check it out. He was also going to snoop around Fordland, see if he could turn up anything in Missouri. He'd done up some wanted posters, and Doy had made a stuffed Murray doll, complete with porkpie hat and pins piercing the heart, a voodoo-style calling card he'd leave in Murray's mailbox.

Word of Murray's flight had spread quickly through the grapevine. Dick pumped everyone he talked to, but he was at a disadvantage. Murray had more friends in the business than he did, especially in the East, and elephant men tended to stick together. The circus underground was a tightly knit web: the slightest vibration on one strand registered throughout, an early-warning system Dick would have to overcome. Most cops and customs officials couldn't tell an African from an Asian, much less distinguish two female Asians, which meant Murray could easily work Tory and Dutchess using a sympathetic owner's papers. Elephants had disappeared before, reappearing months later under different names. Without tattoos or formal identification of any kind, how do you know that Frances isn't really Rosebud?

The only way for Dick to be sure was actually to look at every elephant he could find. To that end he was compiling a list of places in Canada and the United States—circuses, game parks, zoos—where elephants might be kept. When he traveled, he checked out any likely spots in the area. And he made a point, everywhere he went, of mentioning the elephants. They'd be an odd enough sight that anyone who spotted them—waitresses, truckers, gas jockeys—would remember.

Before heading back to California, Dick made a run up the Hudson Valley. He stopped at a bar and got talking to the girl serving drinks, who'd noticed the California plates on his pickup. Dick said he was a circus nut who traveled the country whenever he had the chance, attending circuses and state fairs. He especially loved elephants. Did she know of any in the region—carnivals, game parks, even privately owned elephants?

She mentioned a local circus and the Catskill Game Farm up the valley, but then the bar got busy, and it was only later, after he'd left, that she recalled overhearing something about a couple of elephants. It had been months earlier and probably didn't amount to much, but somebody at the bar had been talking about elephants pushing a tractor-trailer up a hill, something like that? Over Columbia County way?

Then again, you heard all kind of crazy stories serving drinks and the guy who'd told that one, if she recalled right, had been three sheets to the wind. Actually, no, come to think of it—he'd been drinking orange juice, record quantities of it. That's right, she remembered now. Who could forget him? He'd been a Vietnam vet, telling stories to strangers, with a desperate laugh and a faraway look in his eye.

•　·　•

Back in the chimp days, before the twins had come along, when Robin and Nada were still babies and Chatter did the TV show and Denise hardly touched a drop before supper, Murray had had a photo made up each year as a Christmas card. A couple of his favorite shots, worn and cracked, he carried in his wallet. One afternoon at Howell's, while Murray and Skip were fishing, Dutchess broke her chain, reached into the fifth wheel, and ate everything she could find, including Murray's shirt, jeans, socks, and underwear. Murray didn't realize what had happened until he went to bed.

An elephant's digestion is inefficient, and he knew the more durable items would pass through her. For the next few days he pulled clothes out her rear end. His jeans reappeared, chewed to pieces, and a wristwatch—still ticking—turned up in the manure, but the rest of his things were gone, including his wallet. Losing two hundred and seventy bucks was tough enough, but losing the old photographs was a crying shame. One shot he especially loved showed Cobby holding an open book; Robin and Nada, aged four and two, in pajamas, seemed to be listening attentively to the chimp's bedtime story. The book, from a Time-Life series, was entitled *Evolution*.

Along with photos and cash, Dutchess had eaten his identification. Murray hated his growing dependency on Howell and Veronica—and on his mother in Arizona, who had begun sending money to a box number each month—and the loss of his driver's license galled him. What if he had to take off on short notice? At a novelty store he had a little ID card made up with his picture, name, and a false address. In a pinch he could say he'd lost his wallet but happened to have this in his pocket. But to get proper identification—driver's license and Social Security number—he needed a birth certificate. He couldn't risk applying for one in his own name. What to do?

One night he and Skip happened to watch a television movie that gave him an idea. Next morning after Murray had fed and watered the girls, Skip drove him to town. He hopped the bus to Manhattan and made his way toward Forty-second Street and Fifth Avenue. Under the watchful eyes of the marble lions and the hustlers, he made his way up the wide stone steps. Inside, he felt daunted by the vast extent and solemn air of the New York Public Library. The ceilings were high and ornate, the floors and columns marble; reading rooms had built-in lecterns and lamps on the desks; people spoke in hushed tones.

Back issues of daily newspapers, he was told, could be found in the Public Catalogue Room, third floor. He climbed the winding stairs beneath a ceiling painted with an interpretation of the Promethean legend. At the microfilm desk the clerk gave him such a disdainful look that he realized he should have bathed and changed his clothes. He said he needed to see old issues of *The New York Times*.

Once he'd figured out how to feed the spool of microfilm into the projector, he cranked through issues of the *Times* from 1929 and 1930. The layout looked old-fashioned, but readers of the day evidently hungered for the same things that appealed to their modern counterparts: "H. E. White, lawyer, admits theft, pleads guilty to taking $25,000." "Lady Mary Heath, the flier, files for Reno divorce." "Macy's cuts prices of cigarettes, carton of 200 sells at 99 cents." Among the death notices, he searched for reports of male infants who would have died without a Social Security number. The library also had bound volumes of births and deaths by borough. From the Brooklyn records he got names of children born the month he'd been born, who had died in infancy.

To get a birth certificate, he had to go to a municipal building near City Hall. He hopped the subway and emerged near the Brooklyn Bridge. In the Bureau of Vital Records, a worn gray fellow in a worn gray uniform gave him a form to fill out. The last time Murray had needed his birth certificate he had simply written away, saying he'd been born in Brooklyn on April 30, 1929, and would they please mail a copy. Within a week he'd received it, with a bill for fifty cents. The fee was now five dollars and they wanted your mother's maiden name, hospital, attending physician . . . Hell, they wanted everything but your hat size. The form also said something about sworn affidavits, which meant an attorney.

Somehow, during Murray's life, attorneys had moved from the edges of daily enterprise—drawing up wills and searching titles—to the center. They had insinuated themselves into every undertaking, agreement, and transaction, no matter how minor or straightforward. Unwanted, unbidden, unnoticed, they had taken over. Look at the dispute with the Drakes: in the end, no matter what the decision had been, who could have won but the lawyers? Gerry Martin had refused to raise the issue of abuse and had blown the case completely—for which Murray owed him thousands of dollars. He grew agitated at the thought. It wasn't Gerry so much—he'd tried his best—it was the rotten fraternity he belonged to. Attorneys were scoundrels. They fed you a line, cut deals among themselves, turned the simplest matter into a legal maze. Nowadays you could hardly tie your shoes without one—what if you broke a nail and had to sue the shoelace company? Murray didn't like attorneys. He didn't like forms or sworn affidavits. He liked looking you in the eye, cutting a deal, and shaking on it. His best circus and elephant-ride contracts had always been handshakes—he'd taken the girls out to Utah for the Donny and Marie Osmond show on a handshake, and up to Canada to tour with Garden Brothers Circus on a phone call—but things didn't work that way anymore.

Hell with it. The world could change, but who said Murray Hill had to? Hire an attorney just to get a birth certificate? He crumpled the application form, threw it in the garbage, and headed back to New Jersey.

It's been so hot and muggy (bugs biting like hell) you'd never know it's already September. When I called Robin she told me Bunny's appeal isn't going ahead. Where that leaves me legally I can't say, but maybe Howell and Veronica can help me find out.

Unfortunately, Howell isn't dependable, which Skip warned me about. Howell said he'd get copies of the transcript for me, but that was weeks ago and still nothing. They know a lawyer in California and they talked to him about working something out with Drake before they even told me what they were doing. In my situation, I have to depend on them, but I sure as hell wish they'd let me know what they're doing supposedly on my behalf.

It's good of them to let me stay here, but I'm starting to get a funny feeling about them. When they offered to help get my legal situation straightened out, I told them all I was interested in was an appeal or a new trial. We never discussed anything about a settlement. I never was and am not now in favor of that, but they just went ahead without consulting me. Sometimes I get the same worry about them that I had about Bunny, that the real reason they're helping me is so they'll end up with the girls.

Yesterday the girls went up the hill, then Tory crossed the trail and started browsing. Dutchess headed south until she was out of sight. I'd hear her flap her ears, and Tory would answer. After ten minutes or so, Dutchess chirped. Tory became very alert and headed in that direction. She traveled about 200 yards and then stopped. Dutchess was still out of sight, but every so often I could hear her tear off a branch. Then I couldn't hear her at all. After she'd been gone an hour I whistled and called her. I tried to get Tory to call her, but Tory wouldn't do anything. I headed Tory down toward the swamp, as neither had had any water yet. Still I heard nothing from Dutchess, and I started wondering again if we had lost her.

When we got to the big pond, there she was, throwing debris on her back and squeaking. She was wet and muddy up to the elbows and knees. It's the first time she's gone into the big pond by herself. They greeted each other with their usual sounds and gestures. We all went to the big pond. For the first time they both went all the way in, completely submerged, with their trunks sticking out like periscopes. They played in the water for almost an hour. I've seen Dutchess play, but this is the first time I've seen Tory start playing that way in years. She's starting to come into her own. I really enjoy watching them play.

Returning from town one Sunday afternoon, Veronica was alarmed to see Murray and the elephants in the open area between the house and the barn. After watering them, he was taking them back to the trailer. From the road, she told Howell, the elephants had been perfectly visible. There was fresh snow on the ground—the first that winter—and it made them stand out like a billboard. Was he aware of Murray's recklessness? If the elephants weren't kept hidden at all times, they were bound to be detected. Howell and his immediate neighbor, a retired diplomat, hated each other with a passion. The neighbor, Veronica knew, wouldn't hesitate to blow the whistle.

Howell had long since concluded the best way of hiding the elephants was to let the locals know they were there. In small communities, you knew everybody's business anyway. No matter what efforts were made at concealment, somebody was bound, sooner or later, to see them or hear them. Murray had already been there so long that questions were probably being asked about all the hay purchased by the farm; they'd have to buy even more in the cold weather. Being straightforward would deflect suspicion. Howell had kept many exotic animals over the years, and the neighbors thought nothing of it when they saw a llama or a camel among the cattle or sheep.

"How would you explain two elephants?"

"Say they'd been abused and were here for rehabilitation. Just like other abused animals we've had."

"Are you even allowed to have them here?"

"I don't have any reason to think otherwise."

There was no local ordinance prohibiting exotic animals, and while the keeping of elephants might have contravened some obscure state law, the state wasn't forceful in policing such matters. Howell had once been made to get permits for his swans. A year later when he got a renewal form, he simply said all the swans had died, and that was that. People didn't ask questions unless they had reason to. Once everybody knew the elephants were there, said Howell, they wouldn't think twice.

Veronica disagreed vehemently.

"It's more logical to give people an explanation than to pretend they don't exist," said Howell, a rational fellow—or, as someone in the Gestalt group once put it, an incurable head case. "The open approach is likely to be more productive than a policy of concealment."

"Nonsense!" said Veronica, an emotional woman—or, as Skip

had described her to Murray, a lit firecracker. "Wrong! Wrong! Wrong!"

"I'm not suggesting we advertise their presence in the local newspaper," Howell continued, gazing down at the kitchen table and rubbing the bald dome of his skull, "but it's practically impossible to conceal them twenty-four hours a day in any case."

"What do you think will happen to your reputation and your career if it gets out that you harbored a fugitive? He's a fugitive from justice! It's a serious crime."

"I'm aware of that."

"He's not only charged with theft, he's in possession of the stolen property."

"I know that."

"An endangered species."

"Veronica, I know."

"For which he couldn't possibly have the necessary USDA and USDI permits."

"By the way," said Howell, "I spoke to John in Sacramento and he's willing to approach the Drakes. Maybe we can get this sorted out in the next few weeks. If they're the kind of people I think they are, they'll be open to the possibility of a buyout."

"You know more law than I do, but if we get caught they could prosecute us for being accessories. Am I right?"

"It's possible."

"If they decided to make a big thing out of it he'd end up in jail. We could end up there, too. Isn't that true?"

"Not likely, but possible."

"Well, then," Veronica screamed, *"why are we even discussing it? If we're found out we might go to jail, and you're saying let's not bother making sure we don't get found out!"*

"That's not what I'm saying at all."

"How did I ever get involved with anyone so thickheaded? Tell me how!"

"We're in danger of losing our focus here," said Howell, getting to his feet. He tried to embrace Veronica, who'd have none of it. He sat back down at the kitchen table—a beautiful antique piece of Nova Scotia pine—and resumed massaging his scalp. This was not the moment to remind Veronica that the whole thing had been her idea and that, when she'd first suggested it, dragging him out of a meeting and practically begging him to call Skip and pave the way, he'd expressed the very concerns now troubling her.

"Three points," said Howell. "One: we're doing this to help Tory and Dutchess—let's not lose sight of that. Two: this has gone on longer than anticipated, and it's time to seek a resolution. And three: however this plays out, we're not going to let it get in the way of our relationship. Agreed?"

I've moved the truck from its location in the woods to a spot right in back of the barn. I need the electric hookup in the cold temperatures. As the weather got progressively colder the girls started watering from a stock tank alongside the barn, then out of a tub in the truck.

With the exception of two or three days, I've gotten them out of the truck for at least half an hour. I have them situated where there is no wind, and what sun there is, they can get at it. I don't know how long they would survive in real cold temperatures, but they stand up to the cold surprisingly well. Their diet now consists of six or seven bales of hay and twenty-five pounds of grain a day.

I've been lucky enough to find a decent timothy hay. Skip helped me pick up a big load the other day from a farm about twenty miles from here. When they joked that we must be marking it up for resale, I said we were at a place where they were bringing in sixty or seventy horses to make a movie. Howell doesn't seem too concerned about people knowing the girls are here, but I like going as far away as possible to buy hay. I figure the more people who know, the more chance of something going wrong. Veronica is real concerned about getting caught but Howell treats it as a lark. I don't think he understands what could happen if I got arrested on his property. They asked me again if I wanted to settle with Drake. They know a lawyer who could make the approach. I told them I don't want to settle. I want a new trial and complete vindication.

The truck is facing west, with wind protection in front of it and wind protection on the north. The south and east are completely open and unprotected. On the outside I've piled manure all the way from the ground up to the bottom of the trailer so no wind can get under it. But it still gets so cold at night it wakes me up. I can't get warm sometimes and I can hardly move my fingers. My back bothers me off and on, and I have pain in both arms and my left shoulder. First thing in the morning is the worst, before I get any coffee and aspirin in me. Nothing like winter to let you know you're getting old.

The back of the trailer is used for hay and grain storage. I have a pipe-framed partition filled with two-by-ten lumber to keep Dutchess out of the feed. I also had to hot-wire that section so she wouldn't break it down. The girls are head to head in the center of the trailer (gives them enough room to lay down at night). The fifth wheel is set up for my living area, tools, etc. Between me and Tory is a little gate that also had to be hot-wired, as did the loading door on the side of the trailer. The ceiling (still leaking) has been insulated and hot-lined. The walls are not insulated and there is always a sweat problem. I have a portable kerosene-fired salamander heater, operating on a thermostat set at forty-five degrees. It faces into the middle, where the girls are. The heater and their body heat keeps that area a good twelve or fifteen degrees warmer than where I sleep. I have a thermometer on the south wall so I always know the temperature. So far the girls are doing well and holding their weight, but I sure hope we get off light this winter. I don't know how long we could stand up to a real cold spell.

Early this morning Tory accidentally (while sleeping) touched the hot-line on the door. It woke her with a start. It's really not good to have an inside wall or door hot-lined, but they have to stay in for the warmth of the heater and without the proper equipment and materials I don't know how else to keep them from knocking the door open. The ground is frozen solid and covered with ice. I can unload them only long enough to clean out the truck. Today they watered outside (about forty-five min-utes) and shuddered at first but then didn't show any signs of chilling.

Several days ago I noticed Dutchess's trunk was peeling. The outer layer of skin was coming off as if it was scabby. It's about seven or eight inches above the finger (on the front) and started on the left side. There is now a bad patch on the right side also. I'll just watch it for several days as it doesn't seem to bother her. The only thing I can figure is several weeks ago, before the hot-line was installed, Tory took some things off the fifth wheel, including a can with some kerosene left in it that they crushed. Dutchess must have got some on her trunk. Many years back I remember the same thing happened when they got into some diesel fuel.

Some mornings there's frost on all the metal toward the back of the truck (hay storage) and condensation dripping throughout the trailer. Condensation is a real problem and if it got real cold the inside of the trailer would be solid ice. When I unload to clean out the manure, the girls break the ice on the outside tank to drink. On warmer days I've taken them down to the pond and chopped a hole through the ice for them. I'll bet they're the only elephants in the world who've watered through fourteen inches of ice.

Tory has started pushing on the double door that's bolted shut. I'll have to hot-line that door also. Spending the winter in a trailer with the girls isn't what I was planning on. There's a lot of work and the accommodations aren't the best. My back keeps bothering me and I get these pains in my arms. To top it off, my lower bridge is slipping and I've been having a problem chewing and eating. Today I also have a miserable headache, which might be connected to the bridge or bad teeth.

So far we're holding up all right, but if I get to the point where I can't look after them properly, keep them warm enough and fed, I may have to throw in the towel. I'll do just about anything to keep them away from those bastards, but I sure as hell don't want to end up punishing the girls.

During afternoon rush hour, on the George Washington Bridge between Manhattan and New Jersey, the Ranchero sputtered and quit. Dick Drake cursed himself and pulled off as far as he could. There wasn't much room; traffic roared by eighteen inches from his door. He squeezed out the passenger side to await help. Passing cars and trucks flung frozen grit in his face; the thumping whine of tires was painful on the ears. Two hundred feet below, the wind-scoured Hudson River shone like burnished steel. Fine place to run out of gas.

Eight million stories in the naked city and who stops? Two young guys from New Jersey, who, as it happened, had gone to school with Dick's nephew Alex, the martial-arts master. Dick told them he was staying with his sister in Far Hills; he'd had a beer with Alex just the night before. Small world, one of them said, and Dick wondered why, if it was so small, he and the police—who could always find a few ounces of marijuana—were having such a hard time finding tons of elephants.

Dick was on his way to Connecticut, having heard that Murray's brother, Wally, lived in Middlefield. The young guys were on their way to Cape Cod. They took Dick across the bridge to a gas station, then back to the abandoned pickup. By then, of course, there was a citation on the windshield. Dick, thankful for out-of-state tags, tore the ticket into pieces and flung them off the bridge.

It was late evening by the time he found Wally's house. He parked down the street, cleaned his glasses, and smoothed his hair in the mirror. He was an old friend of Murray's, just passing through, and remembered Murray saying something about a brother in Middlefield. Dick wondered what his old pal was up to. Heard from him lately? Got a phone number for him?

A surprisingly young woman answered the chime. Dick started his spiel, but it turned out she and her husband had only just bought the house. Wally Seidon had recently moved out of state—where, exactly, they weren't sure.

It was getting late, so Dick bought a Quarter Pounder, found a parking lot, and slept fitfully in his sleeping bag in the front seat. In the morning he thawed out with coffee, then went to the post office and got Wally Seidon's forwarding address in Tucson, Arizona. He drove to his sister's place in New Jersey, collapsed into bed at four in the afternoon, and slept for sixteen hours. Next day, before heading home to California, he dropped by Colts Neck to see if Bob Britton had any news.

Dick himself had learned that anyone taking animals into Canada by road had to use one of the 150 border crossings monitored by the Canadian Department of Agriculture. More than a million animals passed from the United States to Canada each year—pets, research animals, livestock, birds, and poultry, as well as exotics for show purposes—and the Department of

Agriculture assigned each animal a number. In Canada, the Department of Environment had responsibility for endangered species, but Agriculture manned the points of entry, did the check, and kept computerized records.

On the phone from California, Dick had got through to Ottawa and persuaded Réal Bonin, who worked in the animal-health branch of the Department of Agriculture, to run a computer check. Had any elephants come into Canada earlier in the year—say, April, May, or June? Yes, said Bonin. Two of them, traveling together, had crossed from New York to Ontario in late April. Were they both Asians? Yes. Both females? Yes again.

Something else, said Bonin. According to the database, the same elephants had left the country a few days later, come back into Canada the following week, gone out ten days later, and returned a third time in early June. Dick figured Murray had been working them when he could in upstate New York, then taking them back across the border to work in Canada or to hide out.

The animals, said Bonin, had traveled under the papers of somebody named Morris. Dick had found a Ron Morris of Big Top Productions in Sarasota, Florida, and he'd heard a rumor that, a couple of years earlier, Murray had laid over at a place called Jungle Larry's in Naples, not far from Sarasota. Bingo! Dick was sure this was no coincidence. He was willing to bet that Tory and Dutchess were the Asians that had gone into Canada.

"With that to go on," he told Britton, "your guys ought to be able to track him down."

Britton was dubious. "The timing doesn't sound right. That would mean he took them out of the country before the trial even started."

"We don't know for sure when he moved them off Meadow Gate Farm," said Dick. "Bunny and Leonard could have done it for him. They've got elephants; they could have used fake papers. They've both worked up in Canada before. They've got connections all over. That's also right around the time Murray transferred his farm over to his brother."

Murray Hill met his wife Denise, when they worked the same Illinois nightclub.

He bought his first chimpanzee in 1956 and made it part of his comedy routine.

After the wedding in Meriden, Connecticut, Murray and Denise spent their honeymoon on a vaudeville stage in Baltimore, then worked together all over the U.S. and Canada.

When they bought Denny, their first Asian, they knew little about elephants.

When they had Robin, their first child, they already raised one baby—Chatter.

Chimps were part of the family, an paid their way. Both Chatter and Cobl had their own shows in the early days television.

The stage fights were faked, but pro lems crept into the marriage and Deni took refuge in alcohol.

Both Robin (above) *and Nada worked as aerialists and handled animals. Murray and Denise also have twin sons, Adam and Allan, both of whom followed in their father's footsteps. Allan is now an elephant keeper at the zoo in Springfield, Missouri.*

Besides booking his elephants, Murray for a time produced his own circus.

The Mitie Mites—Tory, Dutchess, and Onyx—were Murray's meal ticket for many years: When he first took them out, they were the smallest performing elephants in circus history.

Season's Greetings

Orlov, Elaine, Robin
Noda

Robin spent much of her childhood terrified of the animals around her.

While Murray was hiding, Dutchess at
all his things—clothes, wallet, watch, and
the old photos he used in the family car
(left) each December.

As the Mitie Mites got older, the cost of feeding, insuring, and transporting them grew exorbitant
Then Onyx (front), in musth, turned on Murray and nearly killed him.

After selling the girls to the Drakes, Murray tried his hand at insurance.

To replace the elephant girl in his act, Murray trained a chimp (above right).

After attacking Murray, Onyx (right) was donated to a zoo in Missouri.

Tusks (on females they're called tushes) are regularly cut as a precaution.

Asians carry less ivory than Africans; still, Onyx's tusks have always been formidable.

For the movie Hawmps!, *Dick broke came*
and even got an acting credit.

An expert rider at an early age, Dick Drake
grew up wanting to be a stuntman.

One of his feats was to help train an elephant
to waterski on a movie shoot in Florida.

A jack-of-all-trades, Dick did stunts, wrangling, and animal handling on TV shows such
Quincy *and* Big Valley, *and movies such as* Evilspeak *and* B.J. and the Bear.

*ddie Drake, Dick's eldest, thrived on circus,
he camaraderie and sleepless nights, the good
imes that rolled through one day and contin-
ed into the next.*

*Vhile in Florida working on a box-office dis-
ster called* Honky Tonk Freeway, *Eddie
ked to play with Daisy, the female Asian in
he film. The use of an elephant hook on Tory
nd Dutchess angered Murray, who used
and and voice signals.*

*ddie, too, made a living around animals, and worked on many sets with his father. They bought
ory and Dutchess so Eddie would get more bookings for his circus act.*

Bucky Steele's home ne[ar] Jefferson, Texas, whe[re] Murray hid the girls f[or] a year. His plan was [to] take them to Mexico, b[ut] the regulations gover[n]ing endangered spec[ies] get tighter all the tim[e], and he was unable [to] devise a way of movi[ng] them safely out of t[he] United States.

FBI agent George Kien[ast] (with Dick) organize[d] the operation to sei[ze] Tory and Dutchess. Du[r]ing Murray's five year[s] as a fugitive, Dick mad[e] twenty-two trips out o[f] California looking fo[r] the elephants, which he'[d] been awarded by a cou[rt] in New Jersey.

Injuries to elephants' feet lead to many deaths in the wild. While hiding with the girls, Murr[ay] had problems with infection in Tory's foot and a crack in one of Dutchess's nails.

Dick had done some checking in Missouri, he explained, and found that a deed transfer on Murray's property had been started on April 27, 1984—the day the trial began—and completed just before the trial ended. Ownership of the farm at Fordland had been transferred to Wally Seidon. Murray had covered his ass in Missouri; he could easily have done likewise with the elephants.

"Here's the brother's old address in Connecticut. I went and knocked on the door, but he's moved down to Arizona. Here's the new address in Tucson. And here's the phone number of the guy I've been talking to up in Ottawa. French-Canadian guy."

Showing Dick out of the barracks, Britton thanked him for stopping by and complimented him on his detective work.

"One more thing," said Dick. "There's a lawyer in California who says he has a third party interested in buying the elephants. He doesn't say who the third party is. I wonder if Murray's behind it."

"I wonder," said Britton. "Take care of yourself. And let us know if you come up with anything else."

Dick, about to drive sixty hours nonstop back to Tehachapi for a job with his bull elephant, was struck by that remark. Shouldn't it have worked the other way around? Dick was the victim; Britton was the cop. Weren't the cops supposed to do the legwork? It had been six months since the trial. The police strategy, so far as Dick could tell, was to nod politely every time he gave them something to work with. They hadn't done much but make phone calls, and there was no reason to think they'd do more. As time went on, in fact, they'd do less. They'd have reasons—overworked, understaffed, rapes and murders and drugs to worry about. But the real reason was that they, like everybody else, thought it was a lark that somebody could hide two elephants.

Once, as a young man, hunting deer with Richie Novack, Dick had been tormented by a wisdom tooth. His jaw had swollen out to here and Richie had said for chrissake buddy the tooth's impacted, go see a dentist. Doy had tried to get him to go, too, but that wasn't Dick's style. If he could drain it, he knew, the infection would clear up. With his hunting knife he sharpened a little twig, then worked it between his gum and the bad tooth. He counted to three and bit down as hard as he could, driving the point in. Richie heard the scream a quarter-mile away; he hurried over and found Dick on hands and knees, moaning, spitting blood and pus. Looking up, Dick managed a pasty-faced grin—sure beats going to the dentist, huh, Richie?

If you have a problem, you don't rely on others. You take care of it. Too bad he and Eddie had gone to the police in the first place. What good had come of it? Eddie was broke and dispirited. He had a growing family and did any work that came his way, but in winter that wasn't much. Mostly he sat with a beer in his hand.

"Forget it, Dad," he'd said before Dick's latest trip. "The little son of a bitch beat us for them elephants. Two years just getting it into court? We're still twelve thousand in the hole to Bunce— he's been phoning and sending letters. Ain't worth the trouble of going through the whole thing again."

Dick felt otherwise. He didn't like seeing his son crunching beer cans, and he blamed Murray. The jury had made its ruling —the elephants belonged to the Drakes, fair and square. Murray had stolen them. Dick had got the sharp end of the stick more times than he cared to remember, and it wasn't going to happen again. Maybe Eddie could put it behind him, but Dick wasn't about to. If the police weren't going to find Murray, he'd find the little bastard himself.

Well, here it is, Xmas morning. Last spring, when I came here, I sure never thought I'd be here this long. This really has been one hell of a year. I've basically lost everything I've worked my whole life for. I don't have too many options right now or many prospects of things getting better. They say justice is blind but I've learned it is also deaf and crippled.

It's 6 A.M. and I've been up since 3 A.M. coughing and hacking and feeling like shit. My teeth are killing me and my plates are falling out. The lower bridge is slipping all over. My left arm hurts like hell most of the time and my right elbow bothers me sometimes. A few days ago I pulled my back again. I must have done a pretty good job because it really slowed me up. Skip gave me a pill and it helped a bit, but when I shoveled the shit out of the truck it seemed to take forever.

Veronica is starting to drive me nuts. I have to keep my cool with her. She said they spoke to that lawyer friend of theirs in California again, and he has contacted the Drakes about selling the girls to a third party. She said this lawyer said the Drakes wanted to think it over. Did she really contact this lawyer? Did he really talk to the Drakes? Or is it all B.S.? She stretches the truth and Howell usually backs her up.

When I said I wanted to talk to this John, Veronica said that wasn't such a good idea. They both say they want to help me but I'm just a novelty to them, and now the novelty is wearing off. Howell's in a bad mood more and more. They want to get me out of here without me having any say. They won't give me any information about what they're doing. I told them I don't want to settle with Drake. I want a new trial and the truth of what really happened to come out.

Howell told me they are going to have some people over for New Year's dinner and asked if I wanted to come. I thought it over and decided not to attend. I can't see sitting down to dinner with other people, stinking like I do. Living in the truck and having my clothes in there, there's no way I can't stink like an elephant. Besides, the last time I ate dinner with them Veronica kept telling me I was wrong about everything, including elephants, and I told myself then and there it was the last time I'd ever sit down at a table with that broad.

I still miss Bunny, but I have to ask myself if she ever had the same feeling for me that I had for her. She lied about so many things and I wonder if she lied about that. It was a bad situation living in the same house and I'm better off out of it. If she and Leonard really are divorced, how come he still introduced her as his wife? She never did show me the divorce papers, even though I asked several times to see them. Maybe I was just her private stud.

When I called Missouri the other day Denise was out but Robin and Allan were there. Denise is doing a good job staying off the bottle and I'm real proud of her, it couldn't be easy. She spends a lot of time with her group, getting help and helping other people who are sick with booze. I still love her, but in a different way than I used to.

I realized after I hung up that the kids never even asked me how I was doing. Sometimes I feel like I'm nothing but a big embarrassment to them and they don't give a shit about me. I sure miss my family and would love to see them, especially my grandson. Skip is away right now and except for the girls I feel totally alone here. Howell and Veronica gave me a couple of Xmas gifts—shirt and sweater—but I wish they hadn't. I already feel helpless and things like that just make me feel worse.

I've learned that the Drakes are going after the property in Missouri. I don't see how they can get it since Wally owns it, but when lawyers get together there's no telling what can happen—I'm an expert on that. I always thought the farm would eventually go to the kids. I am very depressed right now as I feel like everything is going down the drain and there's nothing I can do. My health is bad, I have no money, and I'm depending on people I can't trust. Me and the girls are trapped here.

8

I have to get the girls out of here but can't figure out how. I'm tired of this situation but I feel absolutely powerless as there is nothing I can do that wouldn't jeopardize the people who have helped me.

—Murray Hill, in his journal, 1986

▼ ▼ ▼ ▼ ▼ ▼ ▼ ▼ ▼ ▼ ▼ ▼ ▼ ▼ ▼
· · · · · · · · · · · · · ·

Murray woke at dawn. The parts of him that didn't hurt were numb. In the dim frigid stink, his breath made a cloud. The girls, on their feet, squealed when he stirred. Condensation had frozen on the hairs around their mouths. No wonder it was so bloody cold—the heater was off in the trailer and the power was out. "I'll get us warm in no time," he said, brushing straw out of his beard. Slowly, deliberately, he began to rub his hands, easing the painful stiffness in the joints.

Fiddling with the heater, coming to his senses, Murray remembered. God damn! Out of kerosene. How could he have been so forgetful? Skip was away for another week. There was nobody else at the farm; he had no choice but to walk to the Union 76 station—three miles into town, a laborious three back out. He hurried across to

▲ · ▲ · ▲ · ▲ · ▲ · ▲ · ▲ · ▲ · ▲ · ▲ · ▲ · ▲ · ▲ · ▲ ▲

the barn, boots crunching the snow, and got a bale of hay for the girls.

An hour later, at the gas station, he filled the jerry can, trying his damnedest to look like somebody needing a ride. But only one car stopped in, heading the wrong way. He started back to the farm as the first spokes of sun fell across the road. Another day of brilliant blue sky and subzero temperatures. It was almost spring. How long would the frigid weather endure? Trudging along, Murray thought again of turning himself in. Clean sheets, a dentist, hot meals . . .

. . . the judge's steady drone, Dick Drake's beaming victory grin, the girls' head-shy manner when he'd unloaded them at Bunny's place . . .

Screw that. He tried to walk more quickly, but the weight of the can seemed to have doubled. First he'd get the heater fired up. He'd warm the girls in the trailer before chopping a new hole in the pond. Then he'd make coffee, get the chill out of his blood and the ache out of his bones.

Who'd believe the sight of elephants drinking through ice? In the cold, oddly, they seemed to need more water than in warm weather. He was learning things about them he had never known, and at the time he'd sold them to the Drakes he would have said he knew it all. It was amazing to see the nuances of their personalities, the complex connections between them, the choices they made at liberty. An unfettered life was what they'd had coming before somebody put them in a crate and shipped them halfway around the planet. Strange that he'd never given a second thought to what they were beyond his ownership of them. He'd got them for their economic potential and turned them into a cash equation: sums of money spent on the transportation and maintenance and feed that enabled them to earn heftier sums.

Murray shifted the kerosene can to the other hand, tramping along the roadside, exhaling white breaths. What the girls were —really were—had nothing to do with money. They were playful, inquisitive creatures who frolicked in mud, knocked trees down to get at the tender shoots, and chased ducks as if planning to stomp them. Fifty-seven years old was kind of far along to start changing your thinking, but what the hell. . . .

Murray heard a vehicle behind him. He was close enough to Howell's that he didn't bother sticking out his thumb. The car slowed anyway. It was the state police. Rodney, the young trooper, leaned across and opened the passenger door.

Murray knew he smelled, but it must have been worse than he figured. When he stepped in, Rodney grimaced. Murray opened the window halfway.

"You're up early."

"Need some heat," said Murray. "Power's out up here and I ran out of fuel."

"All by yourself this week?"

"Skip's down South right now. The others'll be up again Friday night."

Rodney was a nice enough kid—he'd given Murray a lift before—but he was always full of questions. Murray steered the conversation toward the weather and kept it there. When Rodney turned in the driveway, Murray thanked him and climbed out. Rodney, despite the cold, opened his door and kept chatting over the roof of the cruiser.

The trailer was in back of the barn. Dutchess, hearing Murray's voice, let out a long, trumpeting call of the sort familiar to viewers of Tarzan movies. Though muffled, the sound was distinct in the frigid air.

"What was that?" said Rodney.

Murray felt a stab of panic. Most of the locals knew about the elephants. Didn't Rodney know? Was he joking? Or was this his way of saying he was officially unaware of the elephants and planned to keep it that way?

"What was what?"

"That noise," said Rodney. "Didn't you hear it? Almost sounded like an elephant."

Murray laughed, hoisting his jerry can and starting up the drive. "Rodney," he said over his shoulder, "have you taken any holidays lately? Sounds like you could use a break."

Skip enjoyed working in the garden at Howell's estate, and under his expert hand it had thrived. He had expanded and beautified the main bed by splitting clumps of lilies, phlox, and iris, planting borders of alyssum and arabis, and grouping the annuals—which he and Murray planted in April—to brilliant effect. Howell and Veronica looked forward to seeing the changes each week and complimented Skip on his green thumb.

After Murray had begun adding elephant manure to Skip's mixture of sheep and cow manure, the vegetable garden had also prospered, turning out tomatoes, squash, zucchini, lettuce, beans, cucumbers, bell peppers, cabbage, beets, and brussels sprouts in comical abundance. Skip and Murray had given vegetables to neighbors and visitors, and frozen more than enough to see them through the winter.

A nondrinker, Skip smoked pot. His first year in residence, prompted by the difficulty of scoring locally—and by the exorbitant prices when he did—he had sprouted cannabis seeds in wet Kleenex, then stuck the budding plants in among the delphiniums and cosmos. Deer had eaten most of them, and the few that survived had been stunted and undernourished. He asked Murray about elephant manure and its properties as a fertilizer.

An elephant, said Murray, is a single-stomached animal with a poor digestive system—more than half of what it eats, blue jeans included, passes through it—but the end product is marvelous. Because it's hot, you should let some of the acid wash out of it. It's best when it's been outside for a year or more. The manure pile in Missouri, he said, had always been a magic mountain, sprouting huge specimens of whatever fruits and vegetables the girls had eaten—cantaloupe, zucchini, watermelon.

"One time in Florida, they promised me a dumpster as part of the contract, but the dumpster never showed up. I'm giving rides at this mall, and the shit pile's growing, and the weather's hot, and I'm starting to get desperate. So I phone up the local paper and get a reporter out. She does a story about what great fertilizer it is, and next day people are dropping by, asking can they have some. Before you know it they're backing their cars up to the shit pile, hauling it away in bushel baskets. Shriners, I used to tell them to use it right away, put a good six inches on the lawn."

"What's the best way to use it?" said Skip.

"Best of all is to get an old turd, soak it in water, pop a seed in it and then, once the seed has sprouted, plant it in the ground, turd and all."

Skip had collected some of the older, intact balls of dung and been amazed at the growth rate, size, and potency of the resulting cannabis plants. A dozen plants had yielded far more pot than he could use. Having done the odd carpentry job in the area, he had made contacts; to some of the locals he supplied more than his manual skills.

One such customer, Roger, who taught at a nearby college, had become a friend. One thing led to another, and, over mugs of Red Zinger, they hatched a scheme. This year they'd grow the stuff not only at a remote spot on Howell's property but on Roger's and Peggy's land as well, camouflaging the patches in case of aerial surveillance, screening them with mesh to keep the deer out. They'd be fifty-fifty partners. If one patch got infested or ripped off, they'd split the proceeds from the other.

Skip, broke as ever, was beginning to think about his future. He'd always wanted to visit India and Thailand. Roger and Peggy planned on using Roger's sabbatical year to travel the world, a trip they'd had to rebudget frequently as the American dollar lost ground. Some bucks would be useful to them all, sure, but it wasn't just the money. The enterprise had its nostalgic side. These were people who had marched in Chicago, chanted, "Hey, hey, L. B. J., how many kids did you kill today?" and trekked out to Haight Ashbury in a Volkswagen van. Roger claimed to have got it on, way back when, with Grace Slick. He and Peggy still listened to the Grateful Dead and Sir Douglas Quintet, albeit on compact disc. No, quite apart from the money there was something deeply appealing about the sixties-like alchemy of transmuting the shit from purloined ele-phants into what might have been the finest dope any of them had ever smoked.

Because Tory and Dutchess were supplying the magic ingre-dient and, in a sense, the inspiration for the venture, and be-cause Murray was in such straitened circumstances, Skip felt duty bound to offer him a piece of the action, which raised a delicate problem. He and Murray, though good friends, were not much alike. Murray's values were a generation removed from Skip's, and Skip didn't want to give offense. On the other hand, Murray was destitute and mired in debt. He seemed to Skip a Homeric figure, embarked on an impossible odyssey, and Skip's heart went out to him. Murray had told Skip of his hope of turning elephant turds into a commercial phenome-non, like pet rocks. Maybe he'd be interested after all.

Skip had been discreet about his habit and wasn't sure if Murray had recognized the cannabis plants. A good introduc-tion to the subject might be simple disclosure. Late one after-noon, when he saw Murray approaching the house, he casually lit up. Murray greeted him, crinkling his nose in distaste.

"Would you like some?" said Skip, offering the reefer.

"Do I look like a hophead?"

Skip sucked deeply, then held his breath like a diver. "I really don't know," he said finally, smoke wafting out. "I'm not sure I know what hopheads look like."

Murray waved his hand to dispel the smoke. "Some of them are grown men with ponytails."

Skip chuckled, studying the live tip of the joint. He suctioned off another hit. "Do they get headaches if they go without cof-fee?"

"They don't drink coffee," said Murray. "Just herbal tea."

"Do they have nicotine-stained fingers?"

"They have little gold earrings in one ear."

"Do they climb the walls if they run out of Camels?"

"Smoking cigarettes is better than smoking that shit."

"The government certainly agrees with you," said Skip. His

eyes had reddened and his face had taken on the dumb, blissful expression of a ruminant. "So do the executives and shareholders of some of our mightiest corporations. No doubt about it, man, cigarettes are the best thing since sliced bread."

"Look, pal, you're not going to get any argument from me that the government's a bunch of assholes. You don't have to look no further than the New Jersey justice system. If you ever—"

"Anyway," said Skip, heading him off, having been down this road before, "that's not the issue right now. The issue is this"— he proffered the joint. "Would you like to admire the sunset and discuss something that might be to our mutual benefit?"

"I'd like to get dinner," said Murray. He started for the house, then hesitated. "Listen," he said, "I got no business in your private affairs. Just don't go dragging me into whatever the hell you're up to, understand? I got enough problems of my own. Now, you going to put the lasagna in, or me?"

At certain spots the trail drops off considerably, and the spring rain makes it very slippery. There are flat rocks on angles, soft spots that become mud holes, hard spots that become extremely slick. The girls change their walking habits according to the conditions. They know exactly where and how to plant their feet to get the best footing.

I have also noticed how differently they use their feet climbing up the mountain versus coming down. Going up, if the ground is soft or covered with leaves, they bend the foot down and forward so the nails dig into the softness. On rock or on hard ground they put the whole pad of the foot on the surface (flat-footed). They bring the hind foot right up to the back of the front foot (same side), then use the hind leg to push forward.

Going down on a soft surface they use the heel of the front foot, digging in. On a hard surface they use the whole pad, but push backward with the front feet, working against gravity. On a slick surface, as the front foot comes up and forward, the hind foot (same side) does the same, a split second later, touching the ground exactly where the front foot just vacated.

This afternoon I was making notes, not watching them, as they went north up a very steep incline of soft ground covered with leaves and heavy outcrops of rock. Both got themselves into a position where they could not go any farther uphill and didn't know how to turn around. They were not more than ten feet apart. Both started slipping backwards and it could have been a disaster. Tory was stopped by a tree, Dutchess by a big rock.

It took me a few minutes to make the climb up to where they were. This was dangerous and it was going to be difficult. I had to get them turned around, moved downhill a few yards, then moved along parallel to the top of the mountain. I also had to find a spot to take them uphill again, to the top, as I felt retracing their steps back down was too risky. There was too much chance of them slipping and tumbling.

I told Dutchess to hold steady while I moved Tory back and forth, changing her position a little bit each time (like getting a car out of a tight parking spot). I finally got her turned and onto a patch of moss that sunk under her weight but at least gave her some footing.

By this time Dutchess had also turned herself around, imitating Tory, but she couldn't figure out how to get over the ground between us, which was too soft to support her weight. Each time she tried, putting weight on her forward foot, she slipped. I finally figured the only way to move her out of there was getting her to put as much of her surface area as possible on the ground and hope she'd be able to keep her balance. It really wasn't safe (due to lack of footing and angle of incline) but I felt it was the safest way.

I told her to stretch out, then had her crawl on elbows and knees, with her belly dragging across the soft ground. On her right side, where the ground fell away downhill, she exerted more pressure, lifting that side slightly, which allowed her to keep her balance. Thank God she only had to cross about fifteen feet of ground this way. She made it across, then I told her to right herself in back of Tory and tail up, so she would follow in Tory's footsteps. We weaved in and out of big rocks, moving up and down the hill as required, till we finally reached the top. It was tough going but not as bad as what we had just been through.

When we finally got to the top, all three of us were exhausted. Tory patted her lower jaw with her trunk, and Dutchess started chirping.

From there we followed the sun back to the chain-up area. I sure wish I had a camera for these unusual experiences.

Several days ago I noticed a slight discoloration on Tory's nail (rear right foot) just below the cuticle (second from the outside). It seems to be an abscess right where the nail grows out of the cuticle. She shows no sign of favoring that foot, and the only sign of discomfort is when I press in the center of that area. The nail has become soft, softer the closer you get to the center. Yesterday afternoon it looked like it was starting to surface. This morning it started draining slightly.

When Dick Drake learned the New Jersey State Police had been tipped off that Tory and Dutchess were expected to cross from Canada into the United States the following day, he borrowed money for a flight to New Jersey. Finally!

Dick and Doy were busy preparing for the powwow they staged each summer at a campground in the mountains outside Tehachapi. Doy had some Cherokee blood and had come up with the idea of putting on a weekend celebration of native crafts and dances and costumes. The first Indian Hill Powwow, in 1985, drew only a couple of hundred people, but it got bigger and better each year and took more and more of their time.

Still, Dick figured he had to make the trip. This wasn't circus rumor; the tip had apparently come from the law-enforcement division of the Fish and Wildlife section of the United States Department of Agriculture. They'd be crossing from Fort Erie, Ontario, to Buffalo, New York. Dick wanted to be there to identify the elephants and enjoy Murray's humiliation.

Dick's sister picked him up at the airport in Newark and drove him back to Far Hills. It was dumb luck that she happened to live so close to Colts Neck. Without her place as a base of operations, he'd never have been able to continue his search. The meals and motels and rental cars would long since have bankrupted him—not that he wasn't already ten of thousands of dollars in the hole.

Dick borrowed Dot's car and drove down to Colts Neck. Apparently Bob Britton had been transferred out of the barracks.

His active cases had been turned over to a Sergeant Zupko, who was out. The barracks itself was in turmoil—offices were being emptied, filing cabinets wheeled out on dollies. Dick was told it was being shut down and a new Troop C barracks opened at Allenwood, twenty miles away. He asked the duty officer to tell Sergeant Zupko that he'd dropped in, left Dot's number, and explained that he was waiting for news of the border crossing. When he didn't hear back, he called the Monmouth County Prosecutor's Office. It turned out the tip had been a false alarm. The prosecutor's office had Dick's address on file as Far Hills, New Jersey—Dot's place—and didn't realize he'd come all the way from California. Sorry for the inconvenience.

The little bastard, causing all this grief and disruption! The mere thought of Murray was enough to make Dick hot under the collar. No way the little kike was going to get the better of him. Dick was going to find him and see him punished if it took the rest of his life. Dick had a couple of days before his return flight. He'd learned Murray's daughter's address in Pennsylvania, a rural property, and he checked the place out. Nobody was home, which gave him a chance to go through the garbage, where he turned up a letter from Murray's sister-in-law in San Diego. Mention was made of cosmetic surgery, and Dick wondered if he'd stumbled onto something. Was Murray undergoing an operation to change his appearance? Dick noted the sister-in-law's address; he'd check it out as soon as he got back to California.

Dick also called Murray's number in Missouri and got one of the twins. Passing himself off as a third party looking to buy the elephants, he talked Adam into giving him two phone numbers; Adam said these were the last ones they had for their dad. Dick knew one of them—Meadow Gate Farm in New Jersey—but the other was unfamiliar. It had a 212 area code and proved, when he called, to be the office of the animal-rental outfit run by Bunny and Leonard Brook and Bunny's sister.

Dick drove into Manhattan to check it out. The address, on Forty-sixth Street, turned out to be an old, nondescript six-story building. Dick spent the afternoon in a coffee shop across the street. When a beat-up old van parked in front and a man with glasses and a beard went inside, Dick hurried over and peered through the tinted glass. Two dogs lunged at the window, barking. There was also a donkey in the back. DAWN ANIMAL FARM was lettered on the side door.

A few minutes later the bearded man came out, got in the van, and drove off. By now it was the end of the workday; people were filing out of the building. Dick waited until just before six, then tried the front door. It was locked, so he went around back. A janitor was entering the service door, but Dick was too slow to keep it from locking shut. There was a wheeled rubbish cart by the door; Dick maneuvered it into place and waited until the door banged open again. When the maintenance man wheeled out another cart, Dick said, "Let me get that for you," and slipped inside. He got on the old, wooden-doored freight elevator and pushed the button for the sixth floor. Dawn Animal Agency had Suite 606.

One Saturday morning, Howell Phillips IV happened to over-hear a brief exchange between Veronica and Murray that made him furious. Howell was in the kitchen, washing dishes, but the windows were open. The summer air was warm and undisturbed, and their voices carried clearly.

Having watered the elephants, Murray was sanding a cane he'd fashioned from a downed branch. Besides experimenting with different ways of packaging elephant turds, he made handicrafts of various kinds—goose-egg belt buckles, hand-painted earrings, elephant-head coat hooks—and sometimes earned a few bucks at the flea market in town. Veronica, passing him on the way to the barn, said lightly, "Is it really that bad, Murray? You look so bored." Murray's reply—"There's not much to do"—made Howell's blood boil.

Not much to do? This was a two-hundred-acre farm with a big house, outbuildings, and dozens of animals; there seemed to Howell no end of things to be done. Since Murray's appearance there had been even more to do, yet it seemed to Howell that Murray did precious little of it. Howell rolled up his sleeves the moment he arrived, mowing the lawn and then working through the weekend on banking business, environmental causes, and chores. Oh, for the luxury of having the free time Murray had, time to write the articles he'd always wanted to write and, above all, to read the books he planned to read.

Howell's grandfather and his great-uncle had loved books and put together collections of international stature. Howell had inherited portions of their libraries. There wasn't a room in the house in which you couldn't have immersed yourself for years. Every room had overflowing bookshelves; two of the largest rooms held almost nothing but books. They were piled in corners, on the floor, on chairs and tables, on the back of the toilet—books galore, more than fifteen thousand volumes in all.

Not much to do? Murray busied himself with the girls or with dinky little projects when he could have been studying Roman history, German grammar, or the Delaware water dispute. He could have researched his own legal plight. He could have learned about the mythology of elephants or the geology of northern New Jersey. For a time Howell had wondered if he was illiterate; but his grocery lists, though misspelled, were quick and confident, he was keeping a journal, and every week he gave Veronica letters to be taken to New York, passed along, then mailed out from random locations.

One winter morning, watching the girls frolic in the snow, Howell had said something about Hannibal's extraordinary crossing of the Alps. Murray said the whole deal sounded like bullshit to him. Elephants would have died in the high passes, and so far as he knew they'd never found elephant bones up there. The story was most likely made up. Definitely not, said Howell. Hannibal crossed the Alps in the winter of 218 B.C. He recommended a book in his library. Murray shrugged, part indulgence, part dismissal: "A book's just one man's opinion."

In a room walled with books, Murray never took his eyes off the television set. He and Skip watched rented movies, quiz shows, and police dramas, Murray infinitely patient, Skip in a mellow daze. Murray spent endless hours with his elephants and then, especially in cold weather, endless hours with the television. The closest he got to cracking a book was tipping his chair back to rest his head. By the time Murray was in his second year of residence, his hair had left a greasy stain on the spines of several volumes of Balzac.

One Friday Howell drove out to the farm with Veronica and found the television screen so coated with electrostatic dirt he could barely see through it. He fingered CLEAN ME! on the glass. Sunday afternoon Murray came in and turned on the set. All Howell could see were the letters glowing through the dust. Did Murray not notice? Was he goading Howell? Did he not realize the message was intended for him? Could anyone be that oblivious?

Maybe so. Murray had a way of not even acknowledging that he was a guest in someone's home. He looked after his elephants lovingly and expected you to be as devoted to them as he was. You got the feeling he'd sell his boots to buy their hay—or, if it came to that, your boots. So long as the girls were fed and warm, nothing else mattered. Certainly the social niceties didn't. He smelled rank, for one thing. Howell joked to Skip that Murray must have been the source of the line about the guy who bathed once a month whether he needed to or not.

Skip smiled—not at Murray but at Howell, who was so cheap he'd urged both Skip and Murray not to shower more than twice a week, telling them they'd dry out their skin. Howell, meanwhile, left the electric heat on in his bedroom all week so it would be warm when he got there. Such contradictions drove Murray to distraction and fed his growing antipathy toward Howell. At times the two men seemed as petty as schoolchildren at recess.

Skip felt more rueful than amused. People. He realized he was becoming the conduit for the tension between Howell and Murray. Much as he liked Murray, he could see Howell's point. During the week, Skip could always tell how recently Murray had been in the house. Howell feared that the furniture—including antique pieces passed down through his family—was being ruined. Skip suggested putting an old chair in the living room and asking Murray if he'd mind using it, rather than the good chairs, when he watched television. Howell did so, and Murray obliged. He didn't take offense but he didn't take the hint, either.

Autumn gave way to another winter, winter turned to spring, and Howell's admiration of Murray's principled lunacy turned into abject frustration. From an upstairs window, watching Murray lead the elephants to the pond in a violent hailstorm, he was struck by a stunning realization. Murray and the girls had been at the farm for almost two years! This was no longer a layover, a stop, a visit. Murray had nowhere else to go. He and the elephants lived here.

For the past few weeks, before I take the girls out each morning, I've soaked Tory's foot. I'm soaking it in warm water and Epsom salts three times a day. I don't see any draining until she has walked on it for a while. It has started to drain, but very slowly. I've discovered that the center toenail is also infected. She has a history of low-grade infections and I hope this doesn't spread further. I laid her down yesterday, chained her hind right foot to two trees, and really worked on her nail. Had to stop after a few minutes due to pain in my back and arms.

Now that the weather's improved and I'm able to turn the girls loose again, I'm interested to see the differences in their personalities, which come out more all the time. Tory is a real loner who obeys only because she has to. Dutchess, on the other hand, is herd-bound. I'm surprised that she drifts as far from Tory as she does. Bringing them in, I've tried several things. One was to lead Tory and, as we started off, say to Dutchess, "We're going in now, see you later." The first few times I said this Dutchess came immediately and tailed up to Tory. Then she began waiting until Tory and I had actually started off before joining up. Then she didn't bother coming when we left, but kept us in range, making sure she could see, hear, or smell us. Just before we reached the chain-up area she appeared out of nowhere and tailed up to Tory.

Last night I got almost no sleep as both arms are killing me. Today I have trouble holding things—they just seem to fall out of my hands. The pain starts in the elbow. In my left arm it goes up and includes the shoulder. *In my right arm it goes all the way down into my fingers. I hope my arms don't get any worse, as they impair me from caring for the girls.*

My teeth have started bothering me again, so I started taking Anbesol and that seems to help. I wish I could do something about the lower plate which doesn't fit right and I have to take it out to eat most things. Of my three remaining teeth, two are all right, but the other one really bothers me if anything hot or cold comes in contact with it.

I've been starting the rig and letting it warm up every second day. It hasn't been on the road in two years and it's in bad shape. I don't know how far I'll get, but I got nothing to lose. I'm planning on leaving here. It's not the greatest timing, with Tory's nail and my health, but these people are driving me nuts. Howell gets in these lousy moods and doesn't say a word. I've only got about a hundred bucks and a quarter tank of fuel. I don't know where I'll go or what I'll do, but I see no improvement in the situation. The second winter here wasn't as bad as the first, but I sure as hell don't want to spend another one up here.

I've told Howell and Veronica many times that I'm against any settlement. I want a new trial and complete vindication, but they keep telling me they're dealing with this lawyer in California and what a great job he's doing. They won't let me talk to him or tell me what's being discussed. They want to decide my fate without me having any say. They treat me like a four-year-old. I'm just expected to fall into line and do as I'm told. I guess there are people who like having others plan their life, but I'm not one of them.

These people bug the hell out of me, but I still owe them. Skip says that Howell brags to his friends that he's got elephants here, even though Veronica and I have told him he's nuts. What if he tells the wrong person or somebody tells somebody else? The local trooper knows the girls are here, but either he don't give a shit (turning a blind eye because him and his wife buy lambs here in the spring) or else he's never checked me out and doesn't realize who I am.

In his own mind Howell's a goddamn hero. He doesn't think this whole thing is a big deal, but they could really nail him. If I got picked up here, there would be a lot of questions and I don't feel he would come up with the right answers.

Drake has given up trying to get the property in Missouri, for now anyway. Probably ran out of money to pay the lawyer. I've got reports that he's looking for me all over the country. I hear there was a break-in at Dawn Animal Agency in Manhattan and I wonder if that was Drake trying to get leads by going through back records of when I was doing dates with Bunny and Leonard. If it was him, he's barking up the wrong tree. There's nothing there that could connect me with Howell and Veronica. Even if there was any information, that office is such a goddamn mess he'd be lucky finding the telephone.

During the course of Murray's stay, Skip had become deeply attached to the girls and often found himself in their company. Sometimes he gave Murray a hand, feeding or watering. He had no wish to learn to get around them on his own—Murray, he feared, might then feel free to take off—but he enjoyed their presence, finding it restorative.

Now that he had read a number of the books about elephants in Howell's vast library, Skip had begun to appreciate the intricate role elephants had played in human affairs. Man's keen fascination was evident in prehistoric drawings, he knew, but he hadn't realized how fully elephants had suffused the art and literature of India, Greece, China, and Rome in the last few centuries before Christ. Even now the symbols and allusions were everywhere, from the Oakland A's logo to the white-elephant sale staged each month by the church auxiliary in town. (The American showman P. T. Barnum once procured a rare albino elephant that proved a disappointing attraction, costly to maintain, and difficult to dispose of.) While living briefly in London in the 1960s, Skip had frequented a Bayswater pub called the Elephant and Castle; it hadn't occurred to him that elephants, carrying soldiers in wooden "castles" on their backs, had once been widely deployed on the battlefield.

A merchant sea captain brought the first elephant to the United States in 1796, from India; it was displayed widely, to great hullabaloo, and in the early nineteenth century the first professional animal dealers—Murray's precursors—were supplying the burgeoning menageries and circuses. By the time

Barnum, in 1882, caused a public uproar in England by purchasing Jumbo, a male African, from the London Zoo, his circus featured no fewer than twenty elephants, including two born in captivity. Tory and Dutchess belonged to a tradition that was surprisingly long and rich, though not, it seemed to Skip, especially honorable. Much as he admired Murray's efforts to protect the girls, he was troubled by the moral premise on which the importation and ownership of exotic animals was founded.

"I wonder what they'd be doing if they were still in Asia," he said to Veronica one day, as they watched the girls set off with Murray into the woods.

"They'd probably be dead," said Veronica. "I used to fantasize about sending exotics back to their natural habitats. One trip cured me of that."

"You couldn't turn them loose in the jungle?"

"There's no jungle left that somebody hasn't planted crops in the middle of. Owners in Thailand used to turn their domesticated elephants loose to feed. Now they have to buy food."

"Which means the money the elephants earn goes into their own bellies instead of the owners' pockets."

"Elephants can't even earn their keep. With no jungle left, there's not much of a logging industry. The owners have a double problem. Now that they have to buy food, they've lost the ability to make money. Domesticated elephants are dying of starvation in Thailand, Malaysia, India, everywhere I went. I saw an elephant in Bangkok that had been killed in the street by a truck. It was used as a beast of burden. It was nothing but skin and bones."

"I knew about Africa," said Skip. "They're facing extinction in Asia as well?"

"The owners there can't afford medication, either, so you see a lot of disability and blindness. It's crazy, but we're at the point where elephants in America are better off than elephants in Asia. As a matter of fact, elephants here are better off than many of the people in Asia."

Skip took a redoubled interest in the girls and made a point of spending time with them each day. Just watching them

breathe was hypnotic, perhaps because the elephant's respiratory mechanism is unique. The lungs of most mammals occupy
a vacuum in the chest cavity. Spent air is expelled by the action
of respiratory muscles; fresh air is then drawn into the lungs by
the negative pressure in the chest. In an elephant, however,
there is no pleural space between the pleura and the lung. The
parietal movement works instead like a bellows, requiring free
movement of the chest wall. Which partly explained, Skip realized, why the girls usually slept on their feet. If they spent too
long on their sides, they'd have trouble breathing.

The better he got to know the girls, the more he was amazed
by their expressiveness. They showed excitement by bringing
their ears forward, pleasure by curling their trunks, apprehen-
sion by subtly intensifying their gaze. When you saw them every
day the littlest things took on meaning. The gentle flapping of
their highly vascularized ears—their air-conditioning system—
told you exactly how warm they were. A restive shine in the eye
suggested playfulness. An almost imperceptible change in
Dutchess's racking motion served as a warning. Funny, no matter how Skip approached her, Dutchess always seemed hostile
and cranky; one morning, hoping to befriend her, he brought
over a box of sugar cubes and asked if he could feed them to
her.

"Sure," said Murray, who had Tory down on her side and
was working on her foot, filing the nail with a rasp. "Long as
I'm around, she won't get out of line."

Skip offered Dutchess a cube. Her trunk approached his out-
stretched hand with its own form of curious intelligence, like an
alien being. She didn't pluck the sugar cube directly; she approached it with a swirling motion, taking the opportunity to
test the scent of his shirt and wristwatch and forearm, tighten-
ing the rough circle described by the tip of her trunk until the
cube was removed as if by magic—in fact, a combination of
suction and grasping with the "finger" at the tip. Almost at once
she was back for another one. Skip sensed that she registered
the source of this munificence and that it stood him in good
stead.

Or was that wishful thinking? On the basis of physiology, he had read, elephants could not be expected to demonstrate great intelligence. The brain of an adult elephant, though bigger than the human brain, constitutes a tiny proportion of the animal's total body weight. This ratio is a dependable guide to the mental capabilities of mammals; the elephant's reasoning powers could not scientifically be expected to exceed those of, say, a horse. Yet Skip found that to spend time in the presence of the girls was to be won over by their curiosity and—if not their intelligence, exactly—their air of primal wisdom.

"How smart do you think they are, Murray?"

"Smarter than some people around here. Without naming names, you might know who I mean."

"Seriously."

"I'm not joking. They figure things out. They know how far they can push you. Okay, Tory, that's it for the pedicure."

Like all trainers, Murray had a limitless supply of tales suggesting that elephants are indeed sage and resourceful. At one time, he told Skip, he had been the elephant man on the Polack Circus, having mixed his three elephants with Polack's three to create a six-act. One time in Washington state, he and his helper staked the elephants out for the night. It was late and foggy, and both men were beat; instead of putting the equipment away, they laid it out on a nearby table. Murray was still asleep in the morning when Dave poked him.

"Hey, Murray. There's something wrong in the line, but I can't say what."

"When you find out, wake me again. Meantime, get the hell out of here."

It turned out Onyx's back leg chain was broken. That had given the bull enough freedom to move forward and reach the table. He'd chewed up the electrical line and eaten the heavy-duty water hoses. And where were the headpieces? It wasn't until Murray walked down the line that he spotted them. Each was in the hay in front of the elephant it belonged to. Onyx had pulled them off the table, put the appropriate one at the feet of each elephant, then moved back in line, pretending his chain was secure.

"Think it don't take brains to pull a stunt like that?"

Quite apart from Murray's stories, Skip had the evidence of his senses. Watching the girls day after day, he saw firsthand examples of their ingenuity. Murray took them into the woods to work them, and Skip sometimes tagged along. One day Murray had the girls take down a stand of young aspen. He showed Dutchess which tree to take out first. She lowered her head and pushed until the tree began to yield; then she applied pressure with the underside of her trunk, popping roots in a spray of noise and dirt, forcing the tree down far enough that she could step on it, using her foot to finish the job.

Skip was astonished. Murray didn't even have to command the girls. Using only hand signals, he had them work unhurriedly but steadily; they cleared the area in less than an hour. Some trees were obstinately rooted, but the girls figured out how to deal with them. If a tree didn't stay flat to the ground, they stepped on it again. If it still had spring in it, they probed the dirt of the root ball, identifying the tenacious roots and tearing them out with their trunks. What was this act of problem-solving if not intelligence?

"How did you get started with them?" said Skip, as the girls made their leisurely way toward the chain-up area, browsing and stripping trees. "How'd you get from chimps to elephants?"

"Natural evolution," said Murray. "Our first elephant was a bottle baby I got real cheap. The night I picked her up at the airport in Chicago, I knew exactly two things about elephants. They eat hay, and they're not supposed to lay down or they die."

He'd built a pen for Denny in the garage, and she went from her shipping crate into the pen with no fuss. Denise—after whom Murray had named the elephant—had cut the finger out of a rubber glove for the formula. They had to lift Denny's floppy little trunk out of the way to feed her. She drained the glove and clearly wanted more.

"Funny I didn't think of it before," said Murray, "but babies got to be fed constantly, and this was a three-hundred-pound baby."

Murray took over the feeding, and Denise went back to bed. Denny took an extraordinary amount of formula, made a contented burping noise, then sank down in her pen and rolled onto her side. Her eyes closed and she lay perfectly still.

"No!" said Murray. "Up, goddamn it! Stand up!" He yelled and poked her but couldn't get a response. She wouldn't even open her eyes. He raced inside and shook Denise.

"Honey, wake up! She went down in her pen. She's dying! We got to get her up."

Half asleep, Denise trudged out to the garage and found Denny snoring contentedly. "She's tired, Murray. She needs rest. She just got off the plane from Asia."

Murray did everything he could to make Denny get up, but she wouldn't budge. He moved a cot into the garage and stayed with her, leaving the light on, checking every few minutes to make sure her chest was rising and falling. It was nearly dawn before he finally slept.

Denny had gone into her pen without resistance. Now, after a night's rest, the strange surroundings alarmed her. Murray, wakened by the commotion, read her expression—"What's all this?"—in the instant before she went berserk, knocking the pen to pieces and heading off.

"I'll bet it took half an hour to get a rope around her neck and tie her to a post," Murray told Skip. "How the hell were we going to control her? We got a collar specially made, with a lead. I remember the look on the trainer's face first time he saw it. He said, 'My God, you people don't know a goddamn thing, do you.' "

They'd hired a trainer only after realizing how difficult it was to sell her. Murray had placed ads in *Amusement Business*, the Billboard publication for circus and carnival: "Baby elephant for sale." When people called about other stock, he asked if they might be interested in an elephant. He called carnivals and circuses. When they found out it was a bottle baby, everybody had the same reaction: You nuts?

"We ain't going to sell her," he told Denise. "She's got to start making money or she'll break us."

"We don't even know how to train her."

"We'll find somebody who does."

By now they'd moved up to the farm in Wisconsin. The trainer they hired was a fellow who phoned in response to an ad. Sure he'd train the elephant, he said, but he was too broke to make the trip. Murray wired money. When Joe called back with his flight number, Murray said someone would meet him. On arrival day, Murray was late reaching O'Hare. He had Joe paged, and a big, gruff-looking fellow lumbered over to the counter.

"Joe Orth, by any chance?"

"You must be from Murray Hill's outfit."

"Truck's out this way," said Murray.

"So tell me," said Joe, once they were rolling along the shore of Lake Michigan, "what's this Murray Hill like to work for?"

"He's a tough son of a bitch but he's fair."

"Does he know what he's doing?"

"Hell, no. Don't know a damn thing about elephants. That's why he's hiring you."

"Does he bug you much?"

"He'll leave you alone. Screw up, he'll come down hard."

"What's the farm like?"

"Pretty basic. We're just starting to get it in shape."

"Much stock?"

"Monkeys. Birds. Quite a few chimps. Couple of cats. An eland, some ponies, few dogs, a camel. And the little elephant. Changes all the time."

"Does the old lady ride your ass? Got two bosses out there?"

"The old lady's fine."

"Is this the farm?"

The disappointment in Joe's voice made Murray see that, to a stranger, it must have been a shabby-looking operation—

twenty acres with a tumbledown barn, a mobile home ready for the scrap heap, and a corn-drying shed made of cinderblock.

"Man," said Joe, looking about. "What a dump."

Across the way, Denise, hearing the truck, stuck her head out the door of the mobile home: "Murray! Phone for you."

"Be with you in a second," said Murray, and went inside. When he came back out, he had to laugh—the look on the poor bastard's face. Joe stood six three and weighed a good two-forty, but right then you wouldn't have known it.

"Hey, I sure didn't mean—"

"Don't worry about it," said Murray. "You gave it to me straight and I did the same. Just remember one thing. If you ever cross me, you'll regret it. I got a long memory. Now come on, I'll show you around."

"So he trained Denny," said Skip, "and you and Denise took her on the road."

"Right," said Murray. "Denny worked out so great we got greedy. I figured let's get more Dennys—that way we could have her in two or three places at the same time. Then I got the idea of putting together a multiple act instead of a single. You made a lot more dough with three elephants, and the expenses weren't that different. When they got too big, we figured to sell them off and get more little ones. That's how we got Tory and Dutchess."

At the sound of their names, the girls paused in their browsing. When nothing developed, they voided themselves, caressed one another with their trunks, and resumed stripping bark in a stand of striped maple.

"How many elephants did you end up with?"

"It kept changing," said Murray. "We'd sell one, get two in, sell two more, then one would die. Most I ever had on the line at one time was thirteen. You needed two guys mixing formula day and night. You feed every few hours when they're on the bottle—finish one feeding and it's time to mix the formula for the next."

"It must have been terrible when one of them died," said Skip. "Must have shook you up."

"Sure, I felt bad. Real bad. Besides, when one of them died, it wiped out the profit on two or three others."

"Come on," said Skip. They'd reached the chain-up area; the girls picked up their chains for Murray and lifted the appropriate foot without being told. "I'm supposed to believe you're that coldhearted? Somebody who'd do what you're doing to protect Tory and Dutchess?"

"Look," said Murray, "ever since this happened, the reporters on the story, strangers writing in, all these people been trying to turn me into a hero. That ain't what I am. I just want justice—for myself and the girls."

"I sure admire what you're doing. I can't imagine sacrificing two years of my life."

"I'll sacrifice two more if I have to," said Murray. "These girls mean the world to me. They're all I've got left."

I'm worried about Tory's foot. It's getting worse by the day. She shows no sign of pain when walking on it, no limp, the only reaction is when I touch it. I laid her down and chained the foot so I wouldn't get kicked. I cleaned the surface with soap and water. I probed into the nail at the cuticle, then cut a hole at the swelling in the nail and probed that. There's pus in both, but the two infections don't seem to be connected. I cleaned both holes with peroxide, then put Betadine in both holes, then penicillin in both holes. Will continue this treatment daily.

All the years I've been around elephants I've heard how bad their sight is, that they rely on their sense of smell (which is excellent) and their hearing (also excellent). I've always felt that their sight, although not as good as some animals, is better than ours. For example, many years back on the Polack show, when I had six elephants in the herd, I had them all chained to the truck, as usual. The terrain was flat and vision was not a problem. Just at daylight all six of them became upset and I couldn't pinpoint the problem. I started walking in the direction they were all looking. In the distance I noticed there was a golf course, and people had started walking across it—that's what was bothering the elephants. The golfers were so far away they were just little specks on the horizon. When I mention this to people who supposedly know, they say it must have been either smell or hearing that tipped off the elephants. But the breeze was blowing the wrong way. I'm pretty sure the elephants saw them.

Here, when we walk down the trail the girls have made to the pond, we are often watched by deer, who stand on the outcrop of rocks. The girls always notice them before I do, even when the wind is blowing in the opposite direction. Also, one day as we were heading down the path, Dutchess suddenly stopped. It took me a long time to see what she had seen. A good distance ahead of her a little red newt was making its way across the path. Could it be that their sight is considered to be poor when it's actually very good, but the registry to the brain is slow?

I have to get the girls out of here but can't figure out how. I'm tired of this situation but I feel absolutely powerless as there is nothing I can do that wouldn't jeopardize the people who have helped me. I thought about the media and yesterday I walked to town and called one of the reporters who covered the trial for a paper in New Jersey. I asked him if his paper was interested in the story and would they keep it anonymous. He asked me to hold for a minute and put his hand over the mouthpiece. I got a bad feeling right then. I don't know if he had someone on the other line or if they could trace the call, but I hung up.

During the third year of Murray's stay, the color television broke down. Howell went to Sears and bought a new set, one of the last black-and-white models. It angered him that he should get stuck with replacing the set, but somehow, in the time Murray and the elephants had been at the farm, it had become easier to accommodate his foibles than to question them.

Howell kept a running list of petty grievances, but he never forced a confrontation until the day he swept out the garage and returned an hour later to find it dirty again. Murray was in the habit of stamping the mud off his boots, then shaking the straw out of them before entering the kitchen.

"Murray!" Howell said with a vehemence that shocked them both. "How do you manage to get so much fucking dirt in here? Keep the garage floor clean! Sweep up after yourself! Why can't you do a simple thing like that?"

Murray, stunned and apologetic, got the broom, vowing to do better. He swept out the garage and then, like a kid, told Howell he'd done so. For the remainder of the weekend they avoided each other.

The next Friday, when Howell and Veronica arrived, Murray greeted them in his usual genial fashion. Howell disliked conflict and was cheered to find relations back to normal. Unloading the car, he chastised himself. Perhaps Murray was difficult, but he was doing something heroic on behalf of his elephants—ruining his career, even jeopardizing his freedom—and it took certain character traits even to contemplate such a sacrifice. If some of those traits happened to be irritating, why should that prevent them from admiring his commitment and feeling good about the small contribution they were able to make?

His warm feeling lasted as far as the garage, which was covered with straw. Howell was already depressed, and the unswept floor plunged him into gloom. He'd been in a funk all week. A massive crash on October 19, 1987—the worst since 1929—had brought an abrupt end to the bull market of the eighties, reducing his own net worth by a good twenty percent and making half the suits on Wall Street expendable. The farm had always been his refuge, the one place he could suspend the worries and pressures of work. Now it, too, seemed beyond his control.

As usual, Veronica bore the brunt of his dark mood. When she'd finally had enough of his irritated glances and brooding silences, she blew up and gave him hell for ruining her weekend. He couldn't even muster the energy to vent his anger.

"You selfish jerk!"

"Mostly he baffles me." Howell's voice was uninflected, barely audible. "If you were living at someone else's place, wouldn't you feel a certain debt of gratitude, which you'd try to repay? I mean, am I missing something?"

"He does a lot," said Veronica. "You used to buy firewood before the girls started hauling out the dead trees. He fixed the gate and built that garbage dolly. He did that concrete work.

He and Skip tiled the floor. And he's good with the girls—that's the main thing."

"He seems completely unaware of social convention. I don't think I've ever met anyone so obtuse."

"He's used to going his own way. I'm sure it's not easy for him, being dependent on others."

"It's the little things. Is it such a big deal to pick up a broom? After Tory and Dutchess tore the shingles off the roof, I had to ask him three or four times to do the repairs. You'd think I was asking for a favor."

"To hear you tell it, he deliberately bugs you."

Having persuaded Howell to let Murray stay at the farm in the first place, and having fallen in love with the girls, especially Tory, Veronica felt obliged to take Murray's side even after she, too, had lost patience with him. Like Howell, she had been charmed by Murray at the start, viewing his eccentricities with detached amusement. Gradually, however, fascination at his independence of mind had turned into angry frustration at his opacity. Long before Black Monday came along—exposing the overpriced takeovers and untenable debt loads that firms such as Howell's had helped to arrange—weekends at the farm had taken on the aura of undeclared war.

At least, Veronica realized, she'd been able in the past to steer clear of both Howell and Murray. Some weekends she barely saw either of them. Now, though, in the aftermath of the crash, Howell's mood became inescapable—a black hole, sucking everyone's energy into the void of his despair.

"You know," said Dick Drake, "I heard the weirdest thing—I heard there's somebody out this way that has elephants."

Dick was sitting on a porch in backwoods Arkansas with two elderly women. When he'd stopped to ask directions, they'd noticed the California tags on his truck and invited him to have iced tea.

"There is," said the elder woman, a toothless, frail, watery-eyed soul with hair as fine as spider's silk. "He comes into the store once a week. He's always short. He pays with nickels and pennies. He wears big rubber boots."

"With the trouser legs tucked inside," said the younger woman, who was old enough to be Dick's mother.

"My sister loves elephants," said Dick. "Think there's any way I could get a picture of that elephant?"

"Nobody goes in back where they keep it," said the elder woman.

"Maybe I could speak to the owner of the property."

The woman slowly lifted a bony hand misshapen by arthritis and extended the crooked forefinger. "That stone house down the way there? He's the owner. But he don't like nobody snooping around."

"His stills are back in them woods," explained the younger one.

Dick chuckled. "Makes moonshine, does he?"

"Believe me, mister," the elder woman said deliberately, "you don't want to go wandering around in there."

Dick thanked the ladies for the iced tea and drove down to the stone house. When he got out of his pickup, he heard festive sounds from the rear of the property. He went around back and found himself in the middle of a lawn party or family reunion. Before long he was munching peanuts and drinking beer.

"I just stopped in to get directions," Dick explained to the owner of the house, a fat man whose air of jollity ended abruptly in his tiny, appraising eyes. "My truck's not running good and I need to find the closest town."

"Well, hell, have another beer while you're here."

Dick let it be known that he was crazy about elephants and had heard about this gentleman's. The fat man started waving his glass of bourbon around, giving Dick directions. "It's a tough haul, nine miles, but you're welcome to go in if you want."

An hour later, driving up a shallow river, crawling along, Dick figured he'd have done better with a mule and wondered if he'd make it back out. If he died in here they wouldn't find him for years. Finally he spotted the red clay track that crossed the river. It, too, was rough going, and he scraped the oil pan so noisily that hounds started barking way back in the woods. Rounding a corner, he came on a decrepit shack that was home to eight people, all of them sitting on the porch. A shotgun was propped against the step. Dick waved and kept going.

After another mile the track opened into a clearing. At its far end, a few hundred yards distant, was a Quonset hut and scattered mounds of elephant manure. His heart raced in anticipation—the more trouble it was tracking down some elephant, the more likely it seemed he'd find Tory and Dutchess. He drove into the clearing, looking for signs of life; when he finally spotted the elephant, tethered to a tree at the edge of the woods, he slumped in his seat, exhausted. It was a tough old bull in musth.

Each time Dick found another elephant, the letdown was more acute. Going to such lengths and coming up empty gave him the same feeling of melancholy he'd had when he'd put down Silver, the Lone Ranger's horse, a task that had fallen to him back in his days at Africa USA. They'd rigged a sling to keep the old stallion on his feet, doctored him for weeks, but he was thirty-two years old and they needed the stall. Dick had to get him out, find a vein, and jab the needle in. Silver didn't react at first; then he tottered and sank to the ground. It was strange, waiting for the life to ebb out of him, hooking him up to the tractor and dragging him out to the grave. It was a beautiful Sunday morning in Southern California. There was nobody around. Dick couldn't help thinking of all the other people for whom the Lone Ranger had been a part of childhood, thundering across the screen to the *William Tell* overture —"A cloud of dust, a flash of light"—outfoxing the bad guys each week, the proud stallion rearing as the Lone Ranger waved, then galloping off to close the episode. Here Dick was dumping that old sack of bones into a grave he had dug. Somebody had to do it, of course, but it felt weird all the same. No more "Hi-o Silll-ver, away!"

Dick sat in the Ranchero, despondent, watching the bull elephant rack in his chains. It seemed that the tens of thousands of miles he'd driven might as well have been done on a treadmill. It seemed that all the money he'd earned and borrowed to pay for these trips might as well have been thrown into a bonfire. It seemed that the two and a half years he'd spent looking for Murray had aged him ten years—Doy had told him as much. It seemed that the only sensible thing to do now was head back to Tehachapi, put his efforts into making a buck, and forget all about Murray Hill and the elephants.

Before starting the torturous drive back, Dick opened his notebook and wrote down something that came to him at times like this, something Doy had told him in one of his low moments: "You haven't lost until you give up."

Skip couldn't have said for sure when the bad vibes had started, but they had ruined life at the farm. Maybe they dated all the way back to the morning Murray had used the main bathroom to move his bowels, forgetting to flush. Howell wasn't exactly laid-back about such things; after a hectic week and a stressful drive from midtown Manhattan, the sight of a turd in the toilet bowl nearly made him gag. When Howell had raised the matter, Murray had apologized and, dumbfounded by such pettiness, vowed not to use the facilities again. He used a bucket in the trailer, or the latrine he'd dug in the woods. It might well have been Skip's turd, but why complicate things? The turd wasn't the problem, merely indicative of it.

Perhaps it was Murray's insensitivity to the rights of nonsmokers—a cause that Howell, whose mother had died of lung cancer, vigorously championed. Maybe it was his habit of frying bacon at high heat, spattering grease, then running a paper towel across the stove and figuring it was clean—Howell was a Windex man. Or maybe it was simply that his two-week visit had lasted almost three years and his plight seemed no closer to resolution than ever. He talked endlessly about legal strategies, letters to the governor, third-party buyouts. His daughter Robin, who made inquiries on his behalf, didn't know where he

was and had no way of phoning him, an arrangement that en-
sured their mutual protection but meant that even the simplest
communication seemed to take forever.

Weeding his cannabis patch, Skip shook his head and smiled
at Murray's headstrong ways. Crusty little fellow, no doubt
about it, blunt and ornery, with a gift for rubbing people the
wrong way. Mother Teresa would have done well to put up with
him for three years. Who could blame Howell for losing patience?

Then again, Howell could be a supreme jerk—Skip had told
Murray as much the first month he and the girls were there—
and he'd brought a good amount of Murray's bad feeling on
himself. One Friday evening he'd shown up with a young secretary from the office, ostensibly to work. Veronica happened to
be away that weekend, and the secretary's presumed skills at
shorthand were put to use, day and night, in the master suite.
When Veronica turned up unexpectedly on Sunday, almost
catching her beloved in flagrante delicto, Howell sought Skip's
and Murray's backing for his implausible claim that the secretary had just stopped by to pick up an urgent report. There was
an awkward moment by her rusty Chevette, which wouldn't
start; Murray got the car running, then beat a hasty retreat,
later telling Skip, "I got nothing against a piece of tail, but if
that motherfucker thinks I'm going to lie to save his ass . . ."

Or the business of the Camel cigarettes, which had so rankled
Murray. Howell had returned from shopping one Saturday
with Murray's groceries but no smokes, telling him the store
had been out of Camels. "What about another brand?" said
Murray. "You shouldn't be smoking anyway," said Howell, who
could have given seminars on how to infuriate people.

After going cold turkey on the weekend, Murray had walked
to town Monday morning. At the store he had found a whole
rack of Camels. "You ran out on the weekend, did you?" "What
do you mean?" said the clerk. "We always stock Camels." It had
aggravated Murray no end, fueling his contempt for Howell.
"If he lies about things like that," he said to Skip, "how can I
believe a single thing he says?"

Murray had also caught Howell in outright dishonesty. At Howell's behest, Murray had done a welding job for one of the neighbors. The labor was gratis; the neighbor had merely to reimburse Howell for materials, which were added to Howell's order at the hardware store. By accident Murray discovered that Howell had stuck the neighbor for the cost of all the materials—his own as well as his neighbor's.

"He bullshits me about what's going on with the lawyers," he told Skip, "he bullshits Veronica about his other women, and he bullshits his neighbor—who's supposed to be a friend—over a lousy sixty-five bucks. He's a liar."

True, Howell was an odd combination of generosity and stinginess, principle and deceit. The real problem, though, to Skip's way of thinking, was that both men tended to harbor grudges rather than deal with their feelings. Howell wasn't the type to voice displeasure. He kept his anger on low heat, quietly simmering. His expression tended to be indirect: a sigh as he climbed the stairs; an offhand remark to Skip, meant to be passed along to Murray; or, if he and Murray happened to cross paths, a curt nod, neutral as an iceberg.

Skip, who hated ego politics, found himself the unwitting medium of bile. For somebody who'd come to the farm precisely to escape life's petty intrigues, it was a bad scene. Skip had once been Howell's friend-in-residence, a combination guest and caretaker. After Murray's arrival, though, the dynamic had been altered. Howell's and Veronica's disenchantment with Murray had clouded their relations with Skip. Howell had come to treat him more as an employee than a friend, and Veronica virtually ignored him, viewing him as Murray's co-conspirator. Skip wondered if she also resented his long friendship with Howell—a friendship, he sensed with regret, now irreparably harmed.

Howell, too, regretted what had happened and believed the deterioration was a result of Murray's presence. It was a variation on the Stockholm syndrome: keep a guy too long in the same place and he starts identifying with the wrong side. It was why banks transferred their loan officers, and inspectors were rotated among toxic-waste sites. Skip spent so much time with Murray and the elephants, Howell felt, he'd come to sympathize with them completely.

Caught between adversaries, Skip would have been glum indeed if major changes had not been at hand. The year before, he and Roger and Peggy had done so well growing pot that they'd expanded the operation. This year's crop had come along nicely—unbelievably, in fact. The tough, spiky plants were gargantuan. The patch that Roger and Peggy were tending got more sunshine and was even further along. Roger had found somebody who wanted to buy as many kilos as they could supply, which would save them hassle and risk. If all went smoothly, they'd make serious money before long. Skip would pocket enough not only to travel the world, but also—if nothing came together for Murray before then—to help him and the girls out of their fix.

All the arrows pointed the same way. The time had come for Skip to leave the farm and begin a new phase of his life; in the process he'd enable Murray to do the same.

9

UNDECLARED WAR

Mexico would be the perfect climate for the girls if I could find a way to get there. I got to think it through, because it would probably mean we could never come back.
—Murray Hill, in his journal, 1987

▼ ▼ ▼ ▼ ▼ ▼ ▼ ▼ ▼ ▼ ▼ ▼ ▼

"I met Murray Hill when he did a fall tour for me across Canada," Ian Garden recalled over lunch in Toronto. A circus producer for most of his life, he wore a tan windbreaker, white sideburns, and two-tone shoes. "We went right across the country in the early seventies, ending up in the Maritimes and Newfoundland. Murray had a nice little act at that time, three young elephants plus the chimp he'd trained to work with them.

"Usually, if you have prima donnas in a 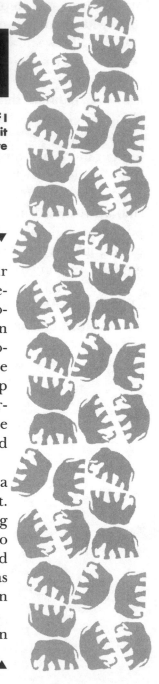 circus, you'll find them in the elephant act. They're the guys who always have the big threat over the producer—'If we can't do it my way, we'll put them in the truck and go home.' Murray wasn't like that. He was reliable, his animals were clean and in good shape, and he didn't agitate me.

"One day he called me. I knew he was in

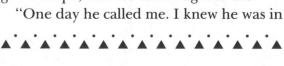

hiding with his elephants—everybody in the business knew about it—but I hadn't seen him or spoken to him in years. He said he heard through the grapevine the Drakes were getting tired of chasing him and were running out of money, so maybe the elephants could be bought at a reasonable price. I'd sold my own elephants and this would give me some control, as there was a shortage of elephant acts at that time. I was also interested in helping Murray.

"His proposition was that I should offer to buy the two elephants. The idea was that Murray would actually own them and gradually work off the money by playing dates with Garden Brothers Circus, doing a two-act. Part of the deal would be that Drake had to drop all charges.

"I'd heard of Drake but never met him. When I called him in California, he told me he was in no way interested in selling the elephants or accepting any money. Matter of fact, he offered me a reward if I'd tell him where Murray was. I didn't know where he was. When he first called, I joked that I'd heard he was hiding in Vancouver, at the zoo. Was that true? Murray laughed and said it was close enough. I thought it was a miracle that he'd managed to hide the elephants for so long. They're a lot of work and it never stops. I don't know how you'd do it. Unbelievable. Me, I wouldn't have persevered, but then I'm not Jewish.

"When Murray called me back, a couple of weeks later, I told him what Drake had said. He was a little disappointed, but I wouldn't say he sounded surprised. I wished him luck, and later I got a letter from him with a little package. He'd taken a goose egg, cut it in half, and fitted out the pieces as nightlights. Apparently he was selling these handicrafts. I don't know how long it took to make them or what he got for them, but I'll tell you this. You'd have to sell a hell of a lot of them to feed two elephants."

Yesterday the girls went to Water Hole #2 (the one that started out as a footprint filling with water), then Mud Hole #2. They threw mud on themselves for a while, then went to Water Hole #3. Then they changed direction and headed for the swamp. They browsed as they slowly made their way downhill. When they reached the swamp, they threw mud on themselves and Tory mudded down good.

When I was ready to bring them in, I started Dutchess toward the trail. Usually I start Tory, and Dutchess comes on her own. I wanted to reverse the process and see what Tory's reaction would be. I figured she'd just ignore us. I didn't command her, just told her we were going in. She turned in the other direction, wasn't the least bit interested. I had to command her.

Next day, as soon as they were turned loose, they headed for Water Hole #2. They threw a little mud, then headed north to the swamp. They watered a little and then browsed. When I was ready to come in, Tory and Dutchess were a good 150 yards apart in heavy woods. I told Tory (hand signals, no voice) that we were going back. I was sure Dutchess didn't know we had left. We were out of sight, it was still raining and the ground was soft.

I got Tory back to the chain-up and waited for a reaction. She didn't do anything for ten minutes, then she trumpeted. There was no answer. She trumpeted again, and this time Dutchess squeaked (way off in the distance). Tory kept trumpeting and Dutchess kept answering with squeaks, louder each time. It was about eight minutes from the first time Tory trumpeted until Dutchess appeared out of the woods, moving hell-bent for leather toward the chain-up.

Tory's foot seems to be completely healed so I have discontinued treatment. But Dutchess's feet are bad and need trimming. It will be a long process, but I'll just have to do a little on them every day. I worked on them for a short time today but had to stop because of my back problem.

For the past week I've been worried about Dutchess's drinking. She starts off normal, but after six or seven trunkfuls she twists her trunk around, putting it into her mouth and playing with the water as it goes in. On occasion she also pats the inside of her mouth, like me when my teeth are bothering me. She's taking her normal amount of food, and from what I can see she seems to be chewing properly. I can't tell if she has a tooth problem or if she's just playing with her water in a new way.

Yesterday the girls were grazing about thirty feet apart when Dutchess suddenly stopped. Her ears went straight out and her eyes bulged. She froze. Not a muscle moved for many seconds. Then she turned and hurried to Tory, squeaking all the way. A deer had moved to within about fifteen feet of where Dutchess had been. It stood, not moving, for a couple of minutes, then bounded away.

At the big pond, after Tory drinks for a few minutes, she plays. She opens her mouth wide, drops her head, and lets the water fill her mouth and spill out. Sometimes she shakes her head when her mouth is full of water. It reminds me of how the kids used to play in the bathtub when they were little. She's been doing this for the last few days and obviously enjoys it very much. I don't think I've ever seen her having so much fun.

"Lox?" said Veronica, reading the grocery list she'd snatched from Howell. "Cream cheese? Bagels? Wait a minute—he forgot capers. Surely he wants capers, too."

"Come on," said Howell. "He's got a right to eat what he likes. As long as he doesn't eat my stuff, I don't care."

"Think he ate lox and bagels before he moved in here?"

For three years, ever since Dutchess had eaten his clothes and his wallet, Murray had been without a driver's license. Howell bought groceries for him every Saturday. At the start Murray had requested what he called jungle—jam, cookies, bread, peanut butter—but his list had steadily grown, and he had indeed developed a fondness for costlier items. Still, Murray's mother was sending a money order each month to a post-office box in Manhattan, and it seemed petty of Veronica to quibble. Howell found himself in the odd position of defending Murray while wishing he and his elephants could be made to disappear into thin air.

" 'Chun King TV dinners,' " said Veronica. "You can pick up frozen Chinese dinners for less than two dollars, but he wants the kind that cost three."

"A lot of what he likes, nobody else eats," Howell pointed out. "That raspberry sherbet crap? That's on there. Great, let him have it. If I came out and found he'd eaten all my Asiago, I'd really be pissed off."

"Look at this. 'Camels, plain.' He expects us to pick up his cigarettes for him!"

"I don't like him smoking either," said Howell—not the point she was making, but an opportunity to get his digs in. "Maybe you could talk to him about it. As one smoker to another."

"I can't talk to him!" Veronica said under her breath. They were having cappuccino at a little place in town. It was a lovely autumn morning and the café was teeming with the Ralph Lauren and L. L. Bean crowd. Heads had swiveled their way. Veronica drew a calming breath and spoke in a whisper. "He gets completely irrational. Say anything the least bit critical and he gets so bloody defensive there's just no point."

"He's preoccupied these days. I understand Dutchess has a bad tooth. Apparently he found a piece of tooth and he's worried that she's got an infection or something. She's not drinking properly. So Skip tells me."

Unlike a human tooth, which is covered with enamel, an elephant's tooth—the crown is about the size of a waffle iron—has transverse ridges of enamel embedded in the dentine, ridges capable of reducing branches to pulp. An Asian elephant is born with two such teeth in each jaw. When the elephant is about four years old, a new tooth emerges at the rear of the jaw and gradually moves forward, displacing the front tooth, which usually breaks into pieces but sometimes gets spat out whole. When the elephant is about eight, a fourth tooth appears, slowly displacing the previous teeth and occupying the entire jaw. In its twenties the elephant gets a fifth tooth in each jaw, which gradually displaces the fourth; in its forties, a sixth and final tooth displaces the fifth. These final four teeth—one in each jaw—see the elephant through the rest of its life; in the wild, it will starve to death when it loses them.

Ever since he'd fled with the girls, Murray had feared a tooth problem, since he had no way of treating it. He couldn't get a vet without risking exposure, and he couldn't work in Dutchess's mouth himself. Start poking around in there, touch a nerve, and you might lose an arm. All he could do was monitor her closely and hope the problem corrected itself.

"Always some excuse," said Veronica. "I haven't been able to talk to him for ages. Imagine living on the same property for three years and we can't even have a conversation. Ridiculous."

"What do you want me to do?" said Howell, making to leave. Veronica was heating up and things were bound to get ugly.

"It's your farm. You have a right to make him aware that you have certain minimum expectations about his behavior."

"I don't know why the onus falls on me. You're the one who asked if he could stay here—" He let the sentence complete itself in her cerebral cortex: "—for a couple of weeks."

And off they went, trading accusations and recriminations, attacking Murray and defending him. The battle got going in earnest on the main street, raged in Howell's Range Rover, and finally burned out as they turned into the driveway. It ended, as it often did, in the master bedroom, with a reaffirmation of their commitment to the elephants and with Howell, full of beans, preparing to mount his beloved—a pleasure she withheld until he had promised to take action.

"I don't care how you do it," she whispered in his ear. "But we've got to get him out. I don't know how much more of him I can stand. Please, darling."

Against a background of bird song and insects in an Oklahoma meadow, the click of a pump-action shotgun is unmistakable. Dick Drake froze, thinking of his family and of all the things he had never got around to doing. But for the thumping of his heart, the whole world seemed to have fallen silent. Even the birds had stopped. He wondered whether you actually heard a blast, or felt anything, or whether it was like a flicked switch: on, off.

Slowly Dick turned, hands well out from his body, and found himself squinted at by a skinny fair-haired kid whose goofy expression and tattered overalls were straight out of *Deliverance*. The boy had fuzzy sideburns and missing teeth. Dick wasn't sure whether to feel relieved or alarmed.

Alarmed. The boy raised the old Remington just enough

that, if it discharged, Dick would have been demolished below the waist.

"How are you today?"

The boy said nothing.

Dick rubbed his neck. "I seen them camels out there and I said to myself, 'Look at that—camels.' "

The boy said nothing.

"You got llamas too, I see, plus the elephant, of course, which reminds me a bit of—"

"People been shot."

Dick laughed. "You know, my dad boarded all kinds of hoof stock when we were growing up in New Jersey, and people were always—"

"How'd you get in here?"

"I drove and then I walked up the trail—left my pickup back on the dirt road. I got directions from a fellow at the gas station in Broken Arrow."

The boy said nothing.

"I didn't realize you had this red clay in Oklahoma, you see a lot of it over Texas way and down—"

"Who you work for?"

Suddenly Dick understood. This was not a herd the USDA or USDI or any other regulatory agency knew about. If Dick had been a federal agent, the owners would have had problems; if he'd been a thief, they would have had no legal recourse. The camels were worth $25,000 each, the llamas $75,000. The elephant, tethered to a tree, might have been worth $50,000. Dick was standing between a million bucks' worth of stock and a moronic kid who'd been told to guard it with his life.

"Hey"—Dick shrugged, showing his palms—"I don't work for nobody but me. I'm looking for my elephants is all. Somebody stole 'em. I heard there was an elephant in here and I wanted to make sure it wasn't mine. Mine are females, too. One's got a split in the tip of her trunk—it sort of flops."

The boy sucked his teeth, contemplating.

"You might have seen it on TV or in the paper. There was

something in the paper just the other day. I'm from California and I'm checking out every lead I can."

The boy said nothing.

"Look, I'm real sorry if I'm trespassing."

To Dick's inestimable relief, the boy lowered the barrel.

"Don't tell nobody what you seen."

"Count on it," said Dick. He checked his watch and assumed an air of regrettable urgency, the old pal who'd love to chat but really must run. "Well, been good talking to you. Better be on my way. Have a nice day."

Hiking back to the pickup, Dick felt the adrenaline wear off, exposing the bedrock fatigue. Man, what a week. He'd been tipped off to check Bobby Moore's herd, which was playing the Detroit Convention Center with Ian Garden's circus. Many of the tips he got were farfetched, but this one added up. Garden was the Toronto producer who'd tried to buy the elephants, and he was an old friend of Murray's. Dick had driven like a crazy man from California, hit Detroit at the same time as a snowstorm, slept in his truck, and nearly froze. It had been tricky as hell getting downstairs to see the elephants—he had to get up close to identify them—but he finally managed to lie his way past security. There were several female Asians in the herd, but no Tory or Dutchess.

At the Convention Center he got chatting to circus people who told him Bobby Moore also had elephants at the Shrine in Tulsa. Dick had barrel-assed down to Oklahoma nonstop, reaching Tulsa at two in the morning. He checked in with the police to say he'd be sleeping in his pickup in the parking lot. The cops had offered him a cell, and he'd spent a not-very-restful night among the winos and hookers.

During the Shrine show, Dick had managed to get right next to the elephants—more female Asians, but no luck. Still, he had a feeling he was getting close. Sure enough, some show people told him Murray himself had been spotted pulling out with stock headed for winter quarters in Muskogee.

Before leaving Tulsa, Dick helped an older fellow in a motor home with Indian stickers on his windshield; he was trying to fix the suspension and Dick gave him a hand. Turned out the fellow was in town with the arts-and-crafts show—he sold Indian jewelry.

"Well, I'll be darned," said Dick, "I'm from Tehachapi, California, and—"

"They got a powwow out there," said the old fellow. "I go every year. I know the people who put it on—Dick and Doy Drake. They're friends of mine."

This was getting surreal. Dick said he knew them too and would say hello. Spacey from exhaustion, he got on the road to Muskogee and stopped for gas at Broken Arrow, where he'd learned of the exotic animals on a remote property outside town—the place he'd been caught snooping by the Okie kid with his shotgun. By then he'd been going hard for a week.

That night, when he got pulled over by a state trooper for erratic driving, he realized he'd almost fallen asleep at the wheel. Thank you, Lord—if I have to get stopped, let it happen when the blood-alcohol count is 0.00.

"How are you tonight?" said Dick.

"Step out of the truck, sir."

Once the trooper realized Dick wasn't drunk, he warmed up a little. "You're a long ways from home," he said, checking Dick's registration and license. "What brings you down here?"

"This is going to sound funny," said Dick, "but I'm looking for my elephants."

"Really? You're the guy can't find his elephants? I seen something about that on TV, didn't I?"

"That's me."

"How do you lose two elephants?"

"You know, you're not the first person who's asked me that. It's a long story. Let's just say it starts when you put your trust in the wrong people."

"I know what you mean. Well, sir, good luck finding them."

"Appreciate it," said Dick, putting the pickup in gear.

"Just one thing," said the trooper. "My wife isn't going to believe I stopped the guy we just seen on TV. Would you mind autographing my ticket book?"

The property next to Howell's in New Jersey—a gracious estate that belonged to a businessman and former diplomat—was unoccupied most of the year. Every so often groundskeepers could be seen trimming shrubbery, cleaning leaves from the gutter, or painting the trim. Now and then the diplomat and his wife came out for the weekend. Nobody saw them, but everybody seemed to know when they were around. Once or twice a season they threw a party and the place came to life.

On such occasions Murray lay low. Once, during his fourth year at Howell's, he was caught off guard by a network television crew doing a remote from the diplomat's house. They were beaming a segment of a morning show from the front lawn, and if they'd turned the camera 180 degrees and used the zoom, they could have broadcast live pictures of America's most wanted elephants, as well as America's heartiest cannabis patch.

One fall weekend it was clear something big was up. Word was that George Shultz and Zbigniew Brzezinski were on the way; whoever the guests of honor were, they got VIP treatment. People in town noticed an unusual number of late-model sedans bearing men who spoke to their lapels and had little plugs in their ears. One entrance to the property was sealed off; at the other gate, a Bronco and a Wagoneer were parked in a way that seemed random but made cars stop before passing through. Invitations were checked carefully.

When two helicopters flew in over Howell's property, noisy as a Vietnam soundtrack, Murray was taken by surprise. He had the girls back at the big pond and didn't have enough warning to move them into the woods or the trailer. From the top of the hill, he could see the choppers touch down on the diplomat's back lawn, flattening the grass and making the women clutch their dresses and their hats; then rise again to hover above the grounds while beefy guys in outdoor gear scanned the surrounding country with binoculars.

When the helicopters flew back out, directly overhead, the girls trumpeted in confused agitation. From the air they would have been in full view. Murray, hurrying down to calm them, imagined lighthearted radio communication, perhaps a joke about Republicans, a computer kicking up the bench warrant. He thought of fleeing, but the truck, idle for more than three years, wasn't fit for travel. A hasty departure might arouse suspicion; and he was stone broke in any case. No, if anybody looked into the elephants, it was all over. He could only sit tight.

Skip, hurrying back to the house from a clearing deep in the woods, was also peering upward, and saying a little prayer. It centered on his cash crop, which was tropically lush and ready for harvesting.

Howell, working at his desk, also appeared concerned—more so, it seemed to Skip, than Murray himself. Fear of detection, or the renewal of old animosities? Howell and his neighbor had been at odds for years, ever since the diplomat's caretaker, knowing of Howell's financial background, had asked for help with his tax return. Howell found that the diplomat had been deducting New York state taxes even though the caretaker never left New Jersey. It might have been in the diplomat's interest to use his New York payroll—a tax advantage or medical-insurance benefit—but the caretaker was paying $4,000 a year for which he wasn't liable. The man raised the matter with the diplomat, who was told of Howell's role, or surmised it.

Good fences had made even worse neighbors. When the diplomat had a chain-link fence erected along the property line without consulting Howell, and put in a gate that locked only on one side, Howell had Murray frame a second gate and wire the two gates together. The diplomat made an irate call. What was the meaning of this? It was pleasant to walk along the stream. Howell said he didn't want anyone down by the stream without his knowledge. The diplomat was incredulous. Are you saying I'm supposed to ask permission to take a walk? Yes, said Howell, if you cross my property to get there. I do shooting out back and you're no more bulletproof than anybody else. Now look here, said the diplomat, do you realize who you're speaking to? Howell rarely lost his temper, but high-handed arrogance did the trick. Howell told the gentleman that his shit smelled as rank as anyone else's and slammed down the phone. Relations had been rather strained ever since.

Howell might have been harboring a fugitive and two stolen elephants, but that wasn't going to stop him from pursuing this vendetta. With the gall of blue blood, he called the Federal Aviation Administration to register a complaint. He kept animals, he said, and didn't want them disturbed by an invasion of the airspace above his property. The helicopters were in violation of state and municipal statutes; any further disturbance and Howell would have no choice but to seek legal recourse.

Howell proudly told Skip what he'd done. Skip mentioned it to Murray, who took it as final confirmation of what he'd long suspected. For all Howell's money and connections, his careful reasoning and book learning, the man was an idiot. When Murray had said, at the start, "I don't know how I'm going to be able to make it up to you," Howell had said, "When it's all over, I want to ride the elephants through town." Animal nuts were one thing; this guy was nuts, period. Did he really think he'd be viewed as a hero rather than thrown in jail as an accessory? Like Veronica, he was generous in ways Murray could never repay. Like her, he was also off his rocker.

Still, Murray had to admit, somebody next door apparently got the message. The following weekend there were more official goings-on at the diplomat's place; this time the helicopters came in from the opposite direction and stayed on the far side of the mansion.

At the big pond, where Murray was painting a goose-egg belt buckle and the girls were playing in the mud, the distant commotion was no more disturbing than it was half a mile away at the cannabis patch, where Skip was removing the last traces of the crop he and Roger had harvested beneath the autumn moon.

Very cold last night, another winter coming, our fourth on this farm. I loaded the girls in the truck and started them on grain. Dutchess is drinking normally again and I hope that's the end of the problem with her tooth. Tory's had a slight infection in her eye but she's prone to infections and it's clearing up nicely.

This afternoon we went to the little pond. Tory went west to the trail, Dutchess north toward the top of the hill. About a hundred feet up the hill, there is a sharp incline and she has worn paths on both sides of the large rock (about ten feet long and flat on top, about three feet jutting out). She was on the east side, going up, when the ground gave way under her feet. Some small rocks rolled down. She went down on her ankles, extended her left hind foot back into a slight depression in the ground, bent her right hind knee, dug her nails into the ground, and crawled until she reached solid footing. She was able to climb up on the flat rock.

Wanting to come back down, she used the heels of her front feet, stretching herself out so her knees were on the rock and her front feet heading downhill, the heels dug in. She felt that the ground was slick, so she backed up onto the rock again. She looked up the mountain and decided it would be easier to continue up to the top. She headed west and joined up with Tory on the trail. People don't realize how agile these animals are.

Howell is in one of his lousy moods, which is common. I know he wishes we weren't here, but I don't know what the hell I can do about it. I've had Robin make some phone calls to see if I could line up a ride out. The people she's spoken to say sure, I could help him out, but when the talk gets serious, they back off. They don't have a decent rig or the timing is wrong or some bullshit like that. I'm thinking of phoning Drake directly to see if he's interested in a third-party buyout.

Tomorrow I'm meeting two women from an animal-rights group. I got their name from K. and when I called them they sounded interested and wanted to meet me. I'm a little surprised they're taking it this far. When Nada called some people she figured might help, they backed off when they found out the girls were circus elephants. Humaniacs tar all circus and carnival people with the same brush.

Howell and Veronica bought me some socks and a shirt. I really appreciated it but I couldn't accept. My self-respect at this point is very low and things like that just make it worse. I started to sew patches on my jeans as they are very shabby. It took me about four hours to sew on *two patches, but at least I did a pretty good job, or so I thought. When I went to bed last night I discovered the jeans were sewed to my undershorts. I had to cut them loose and will start again today.*

When Murray walked into the Friendly's restaurant, he spotted them right off—two well-dressed, guarded-looking women in a corner booth. He was not optimistic about this meeting. Veronica, he knew, was dead set against it. Anything he did that was out of her and Howell's control they didn't like. Were they worried he might spill the beans? That was a joke—Howell was such a goddamn blabbermouth he'd told half the county he had elephants at his place. No, Veronica was worried these two women might help spring him. She wanted to keep him there because she figured sooner or later she'd end up with the girls.

After graining and watering Tory and Dutchess, Murray had got a lift with Skip, then caught the Greyhound. The women, it turned out, had chosen this restaurant—a couple of hours from Howell's farm, in upstate New York—because the manager was part of what they called "the movement." Murray was surprised by their youth. Belinda was a copy editor at a New York publishing house, Cecille some sort of management consultant. Over coffee Murray described his circumstances and explained why he had to get out of that part of the country. The women asked detailed questions about his legal situation, the girls, and his own background. They solicited his views on factory farms and veal crates, vivisection and genetic engineering, the use of leghold traps and the tethering of pregnant sows—things about which he knew little and cared even less. They excused themselves to confer in the manager's office, then returned to the booth.

"There's a place you could go and probably stay as long as you wanted," said Belinda. "But it's quite a distance from here, and we have no way of arranging transportation for the elephants."

"Whose place is it?"

Belinda glanced at Cecille.

"Someone in the movement," said Cecille.

"I need to talk to him."

Contacting Chuck turned out to be an exercise worthy of John le Carré. First, the women had to use the restaurant phone to call an intermediary. The intermediary called back for instructions, then got in touch with Chuck, who called in to the restaurant. It was all long distance and everything had to be billed to a safe number in New York. Finally, in the manager's office, Murray found himself on the line with a young man whose accent he associated with Texas.

"So, who's going to ask the questions?"

"There's things I need to know," said Murray. "You regulated by USDA and USDI?"

"Yes." Which meant Chuck handled endangered species of his own, and was therefore subject to regular inspections.

"How much room do you have at your place?"

"How much do elephants need, anyway?"

"Do you have a heated barn?"

"No, but down here you probably wouldn't need to keep them inside even in winter."

South Texas, then, if he had the accent right. Murray had been thinking about Mexico lately, moving the girls across the border. This sounded more promising.

"How often do you get inspectors on the property?"

"USDI comes out anytime they want. With USDA, it's usually twice a year."

"Have you ever had any violations?"

"Never."

"What about papers for the girls?"

"Fair-sized piece of land here. We could keep them on the far end of the property where they won't be seen."

"If you've got two full-grown elephants on your land—anywhere on your land—somebody'll find out sooner or later."

"We could forge the papers."

"Let me ask you something, Chuck. How come you're willing to help somebody you don't even know?"

"It'd be cool having elephants here."

Chuck sounded like a decent kid, college age maybe, with the confidence that family money gives some people. Good intentions but not a lot of practical sense.

The sight of the women huddled over their ice cream only reinforced Murray's misgivings. Maybe they could help him, with money and legal assistance and a place for the girls. At what price? Belinda hadn't quite managed to keep a neutral tone when she asked why he'd gone into the animal business in the first place. Cecille had mentioned experiments done at the University of New Mexico establishing that animals in captivity had elevated stress levels. Their conversation was full of references to the Endangered Species Act and the Health Research Extension Act; they spoke of "multinational agribusiness" and "the holocaust of the animal kingdom." Did he feel there was a need to reevaluate the morality of keeping animals as pets? Did he support a bill of rights for animal experimentation? By small degrees they let him know they'd be more helpful, much more helpful, if he'd change his ways. Their hearts were in the right place; they wanted to help the girls. But they also wanted to make him see the error of his ways, renounce his past, and join in their fight to liberate animals.

How could he? He wasn't ashamed of the life he'd led. Not that animal people—himself included—hadn't made mistakes. Not that there hadn't been abuse and deprivation. But man had so fully imposed himself that the salvation of animals could be achieved only with his cooperation. To save the animals you had to know them. Elephants were still a mystery, and what knowledge we did have grew out of the efforts of people who— like himself—lived with them. The cause these women had embraced, for whatever reasons, was tied to the larger lesson Tory and Dutchess, in discovering their own essential natures, had taught him. He, too, had come to see that animals should be free to express themselves beyond the control and manipulation of man. But he had taken a different path toward that understanding, and they were disdainful of it—disdainful of the life he'd lived.

He and Howell generally steered clear of one another, but

Howell made a point, soon after Murray got back to the farm, of asking how the meeting had gone.

"It was friendly," said Murray, unchaining the girls to let them roam in the woods. "They want to help, but I don't think it'll go any further."

"We've turned up a lawyer in East Orange who does animal work. Veronica's had her checked out."

"Thanks for telling me."

Howell missed the irony. Again they'd gone ahead and acted without his approval or knowledge. "Isabelle Strauss. She may be receptive."

Sure. Another of their bogus contacts. Another part of their scheme to get the girls.

"I got my own irons in the fire," said Murray. "Move up, Dutchess. Let's get the hell out of here."

Tory has a new infection on the nail of her hind right foot. The infection is similar to last year (right rear foot, second nail from outside). I started treatment right away. I use soapy water or peroxide to clean it, also Betadine and penicillin.

Been having more trouble with the heater lately. It works for a minute or two and then shuts off. For the last week I've had to keep pushing the reset button all night. Most mornings everything is frozen solid, including the manure on the ground. It doesn't help when Dutchess tears down the board over the window. I fixed it and finally got it hot-lined. Tried to fix the heater several times but it still isn't working right. I was able to get better on-off control by covering the thermostat with a plastic bag, which gives the motor time to recover before coming on again. It started working better but it still throws the reset.

At six this morning it was minus two degrees. The wind was blustering all night. All the metal inside the truck is covered with a quarter-inch of ice from condensation. Any manure near a draft or against metal is frozen solid. All the drains are clogged. I was up all night again, keeping the heater running. It quits and each time I have to reset by hand.

It warmed up a little this morning. I unloaded at ten-thirty for twenty minutes to clean out the manure. They were both chilled but at least it wasn't a heavy uncontrollable shaking. They both drank from the outside tank and after a few minutes they stopped shaking. Dutchess played in the snow. (There's eight inches of snow.) The other stock (horse, cows, sheep, goats, geese, ducks) have taken to crowding around when the girls are loose for some hay, and Dutchess had a good time chasing them. She loves going after the geese and ducks like she's going to stomp them. They know she's only playing and come right back for more.

After shoveling out the trailer, I moved manure around to cut off as much draft as possible on the floor. But my back is bothering me and both arms give me trouble, which makes the work harder than it used to be. I can't help worrying about what would happen if I break down and can't look after the girls. I'm using seven or eight aspirin a day but they don't do much.

So far the heater is holding the truck at a bearable temperature but I've got to do something. Mexico would be the perfect climate for the girls if I could find a way to get there. I got to think it through, because it would probably mean we could never come back. But each winter here seems tougher than the last, and my spirits have never been lower. The cold wakes me every night and some mornings I can hardly feel my feet. It's a good half-hour before my hands work right. It's amazing the way the girls stand up to it, but I hate to think what it will be like if the temperature goes lower.

In the film version of a Carson McCullers novel, Isabelle Strauss would be cast as the schoolmarm who shares her rambling Southern house with cobwebs, cats, and dogs. As it happens, Strauss does share her rambling house—in East Orange, New Jersey—with cats and dogs, but also with the office machines and reference works that enable her to pursue her livelihood and one of her passions: the practice of law.

Her interest in law dates back to childhood; at four, she described anything she didn't like as unconstitutional, a word learned from her father. An attorney, he did immigration work and kept an office in Chinatown in lower Manhattan. Weekends he took his son and daughter with him to play while he gave counsel. After his death—from a heart attack at the New York Stock Exchange, where he was showing a high-school class around—Isabelle and her brother both decided to follow in his footsteps. She attended Rutgers University and then Rutgers Law School in Newark.

The roots of her other passion go back equally far. In the 1950s, walking to school in the Bronx, she used to take a circuitous path that allowed her to feed as many animals as possible. At Lebanon Hospital she joined the kitchen workers who fed scraps to the strays gathered at the service door. When her teacher ordered her to stop feeding newborn kittens by the school, she refused. To pay for the cat food, she began making pot holders and selling them door to door. She was nine years old.

At seventeen, Strauss became a vegetarian. During her college years there was little awareness of the animal cause and she was viewed as an oddity. Each year, though, she sensed a more widespread curiosity about the reasons behind her decision. She simply didn't believe in harming animals for food; she wore nothing made from animal products; and she whisked flies out the window rather than swatting them. To fellow law students she explained that her recognition of injustice, though not limited to animals, didn't exclude them either.

After graduating, Strauss rented space on the twenty-first floor of an office tower in Newark and decided she was in practice. For many years her mother worked with her. Though not an attorney—she had a master's degree in educational guidance—her mother probably knew more law at first than she did. They both loved pets. Strauss had once consulted an attorney who took his dog with him to the office, and the memory stayed with her. When she outgrew her high-rise space, she decided it made sense to purchase. East Orange might not have been an urban model—planners then referred to it, charitably, as a community in transition—but it was there that she found the house she wanted.

Bringing her life and her work together under one roof, sharing the house with a changing mix of pets, she paid the bills as a general practitioner while specializing in the nascent area of animal rights. She represented, among many other clients, the owner of a dog shot by police—the woman sued for deprivation of property without due process and won a settlement—and another woman charged with trespassing while picketing a pet store. Along the way she gained a reputation as a skilled if somewhat eccentric attorney. Other lawyers joked about the dog bones on the floor; and the cat that interrupted a deposition at her office became the stuff of legal legend.

In the 1980s, as animal rights moved higher on the public agenda, Strauss found herself increasingly in demand. One morning she got a call from Murray Hill, who said he was in hiding with two female Asian elephants. A warrant had been issued for his arrest, and he'd been on the lam for more than three years. Strauss took notes: "You said two of them." "Right, Tory and Dutchess." He had no money, he added, but wondered if she'd help them. She said she'd think it over.

In free moments, Strauss began researching the case. She tracked down the two veterinarians who had examined the elephants at Meadow Gate Farm five years earlier. She spoke to Murray's daughters, Robin, who'd moved to Manhattan, and Nada, who lived in Pennsylvania; she arranged to get transcripts of the trial.

When Murray phoned back a month later, Strauss was cordial but noncommittal. Before involving herself, she wanted to be sure he'd had legitimate concerns about the elephants' welfare. To satisfy herself of his credibility she needed more time.

Murray, looking out over snowy fields from the kitchen window, wondered why Howell had put him in touch with her. Cool and skeptical, she was giving him the runaround. More bullshit. Another of Howell's stalling tactics.

"All right," said Murray, "look, I'll call again in a couple of weeks."

"Phone collect if you like," said Strauss, raising her voice over the noise of dogs barking in the background.

"I'll pay for the calls. That way I don't have to worry about anybody turning me in."

"In the meantime, how are you and those elephants doing?"

"Dutchess has been off her water a couple of times, which bothers me, and Tory's had problems with infection in her foot, but she seems better now."

"Is Dutchess sick?"

"I can't see nothing, her stool's normal, but she usually drinks good in any weather. If it was Tory, it wouldn't bother me so much—she's the finicky one. When Dutchess goes off her water, I start worrying."

"Dutchess is from Thailand and Tory's the smaller one? From Burma?"

"You got a good memory."

"Lawyers are like elephants," said Strauss. "They never forget."

"They're like elephants, all right," said Murray. "You're lucky to break even just keeping them fed."

One night Dutchess broke her front leg chain and bent the service door in back of her. I made her a makeshift chain harness and she snapped that. The weather's warmed up, and lately when I've let them out, they try to tear the tar shingles off the roof of the shed. I caught Tory eating shingles again and got her straightened out—so far she hasn't returned for more.

With the better weather they're both getting anxious. They can't wait to get outside. Dutchess goes chasing after the sheep, and they both start heading to the pond to water, instead of the tank. I think they want to get back out in the woods again. I know I do.

Yesterday after I'd hayed the girls I saw somebody talking to Howell in the driveway. Howell had to leave, and A. and his wife introduced themselves and we had a conversation. It turned out he's an attorney, and I remembered when I first came here Howell said he'd talk to this attorney friend of his named A. who would help with my appeal. Howell later told me he'd talked to A. but he was too busy to take on my case. Yesterday I asked if Howell had ever mentioned my situation to him, and he said no. So Howell lied about that, too. This Isabelle seems like another phony. Anybody who comes recommended by him is automatically suspicious in my book.

These days Howell's either dripping sugar he's so goddamn friendly or else he's in such a lousy mood it ain't worth saying hello. The other day he tore a strip off me about the garage and the bathroom, how dirty they were. Then he started telling me how the paper towel has to go in the holder a certain way and why couldn't I do it that way? I let him run off at the mouth before telling him I never put the paper towels on the roller. The lying son of a bitch is getting on me at every opportunity. Skip says he's got a new girlfriend, and I wonder if he's trying to force me out so he can break up with Veronica. That's the impression I get from little things he's said, the blowups we've had, etc. She's the one who's attached to the girls—Howell's just interested because he thinks he can get them cheap, so if me and the girls were gone he'd have an easier time dumping her.

Thinking back over the period with Bunny, it's very evident that what she really wanted was the girls. The signs were there all along and I'm annoyed that I followed my heart instead of my head. I wanted so much to believe it would work out for us that I ignored the obvious things—saying she couldn't find the divorce papers when I told her I wanted to see them, getting me to sign over the girls, etc. I figure she had it planned from the start. She never really cared about me. All she wanted was to spice up her life and wind up with two elephants she could get around. I don't understand how I could have been so stupid.

"That you, Dick?" said the patrolman, knocking on the door. "Still looking for those elephants?"

"It's open, Charley."

Dick Drake and a partner had rented office space next to the Best Western in Tehachapi. The patrolman, seeing lights burning at one in the morning, had decided to do a check. That was his excuse, anyway; he enjoyed chewing the fat with Dick, who'd become something of a local celebrity. The *Tehachapi News* and the *Bakersfield Californian* ran stories from time to time about his heroic efforts to find the elephants stolen by a treacherous con man in the East.

Dick and his partner had started a business called Back Country Log Homes. California had prospered in the junk boom of the 1980s; the real-estate market was hot, and they figured to cash in building log homes for all the people who'd bought pieces of the high desert. The area north of Los Angeles was growing by leaps and bounds. Arnold Schwarzenegger was said to own half of Palmdale. Every time Dick drove past Louis Goebel's old place, he kicked himself for not buying it when he'd had the chance. He could have had it for $125,000. Today it was worth a million, easy.

With Dick's construction background and gift of gab, and Joe's resources and contacts, the partnership was a natural. The business hadn't clicked yet—they hadn't actually made a sale, in fact—but they'd only been open a few months and they'd had calls for estimates. In any case, Dick hadn't put up any money and he found it handy to have an office. He'd accumulated two suitcases of material during his years of searching for Murray, and it was nice to have a filing cabinet.

Many nights he worked late, firing off letters to anybody he could think of, from a reporter with the Associated Press to a producer on the television show *America's Most Wanted*. He had to do something; the New Jersey police seemed to have given up entirely. Sergeant Zupko had been transferred out of the Allenwood barracks, and nobody else had really picked up the case. When Dick had called at New Year's to ask them to check out a rumor he'd heard about Murray's whereabouts, a trooper had hung up in his ear. When Murray himself, frustrated at delays and increasingly desperate, phoned Tehachapi to see whether a settlement could be negotiated—"Murray! Good to hear from you! Where you calling from?"—Dick hadn't even bothered to alert the police. What was the point?

He wrote to Richard Lyng, the Secretary of Agriculture. He wrote to Secretary of State George Shultz, and Secretary of the Interior Donald Hodel, and U.S. Fish and Wildlife Director Frank Dunkle. He wrote to John Kaye, the prosecutor for Monmouth County, and California Attorney General John Van de-Camp, and Senator Alan Cranston, and U.S. Attorney General

Richard Thornburgh. Then he figured what the heck, why stop there?

"Dear President Reagan," he pecked out on his Royal portable, "I am writing to you because I have failed to get any response or help from State or Federal agencies." Dick explained his problem and asked the President to light a fire under someone in authority. "I am not going to pretend I am not being selfish taking your time away from so many worldly problems you have daily. But this problem is major not only to myself and my family but to all animals, endangered or not, in the United States of America. We need to set an example so this may never happen again."

Dick stripped the letter out of the typewriter, read it, then rolled it back into the machine. "P.S. I am the person who removed your horses from your ranch in Agoura, California, and took them to Westlake Equestrian Center, which I was managing, during the fire of 1969."

Dick was bone-weary from running a bulldozer at Indian Hill. Now that the good weather had come, he was doing all he could before June. In its third year the powwow had drawn twenty thousand visitors, and Doy was expecting even more this summer. She did the phoning and organizing and paperwork; Dick worked dawn to dusk on the property, ate supper, then spent hours at the office. He was desperate for sleep, but stayed long enough after chatting with the patrolman to type one last letter. It was a poem he'd made up for his sister and brother-in-law in New Jersey.

> *Dear Dot and Bill:*
> *Here is the latest on the Elephant Caper*
> *Take it to the bathroom for toilet paper*
> *No one will do anything like they did in the past*
> *So at least get some use from it and wipe your ass*
> *The letters I write lay somewhere on the side*
> *With no one looking, Murray doesn't have to hide*
> *I'm Bitter and Mad and a hole lot Upset*
> *But I won't give up, cause I'll get Murray yet*

If the law won't get him the Drakes and Wilkies will
If Alex gets ahold of him goodbye Murray Hill!

Spread out on the bed, viewed through a thin haze of smoke, $45,000 looked to Skip like money enough to live on for years. Having just returned from a celebratory dinner at Roger's and Peggy's place with a shopping bag full of cash, Skip was giddy with anticipation. Roger had given him his cut in used fifty- and hundred-dollar bills, along with a reminder to keep any bank deposits under $10,000.

Skip had never seen so much money. This was what led people to connive and cheat and kill one another. It's what corrupted politicians and policemen. It's what made the world go round. Wave untraceable loot at a dozen so-called honest citizens and it was amazing how many of them would grab it. You never knew. Even the sturdiest folks, people like Roger and Peggy . . .

Wait a minute, what was he thinking? Talk about paranoia. Roger and Peggy were no more materialistic than he was. Money hadn't even been their real motivation. It was the camaraderie of conspiracy, the nostalgic trip of winning the establishment game. Still, Skip thought, using a clip to suction the last quick hits off his joint, it was a lot of cash and he should have monitored the deal. Roger and Peggy could easily have talked themselves into thinking they deserved a bigger piece for handling the money. You could rationalize it so beautifully you wouldn't even feel guilty ripping off a friend.

Skip broke the $45,000 into parcels of $9,000. Handling the cash felt so good he mixed it up and broke it down again. He'd give one parcel to Murray. After all, he was the one who'd dreamed of turning elephant turds into money; Skip had, in a sense, taken his fantasy and brought it to life. Nine thousand would be a bonanza to him, and Skip would still be ahead of the game. Murray had said he wanted no part of it, but what would he do on finding the envelope? Throw it away? Skip would leave it in the fifth wheel while Murray was out with the girls.

That, at least, was the plan. Trouble was, breaking $45,000

into five equal parts oddly diminished the total. And when Skip, firing up another joint, began to consider exactly what the final $9,000 represented, he had second thoughts. The debts dating back to his divorce had to be retired. The cost of airline tickets had gone way up since he'd last traveled abroad. Bed and breakfast in London, rail passes on the Continent—man, he'd been blown away by the prices the agent had quoted. He'd been out of touch so long that everything seemed to have quadrupled. That fifth envelope meant more than money; it meant months of freedom in Asia.

It was Skip who'd had the idea for the venture. It was he and Roger who'd taken the risks. They hadn't needed the elephant manure; bumper crop, sure, but who could say regular fertilizer wouldn't have done as well? Besides, Murray's plight no longer seemed desperate. He'd been in good spirits lately; he was in touch with somebody about smuggling the girls out of the country, and he'd made contact with a woman lawyer who was interested in his case though she knew he had no money. After almost four years of bitter despondency, he was again talking about a retrial, vindication, legal right to Tory and Dutchess. Things were looking up.

Early next morning, Skip hefted his duffel bag, left a farewell note for Howell in the kitchen, and headed over to the rig to say good-bye. He was in a rush, needing to open several bank accounts before catching his flight to Gatwick. He hugged Murray, told him what a fantastic experience it had been, and hurried off.

It was best this way. What if there were complications? Suppose Roger and Peggy got busted, and fingered Skip. Murray might be questioned under oath, and he wouldn't have been credible denying knowledge of an enterprise that had gone on under his nose. Knowing about it was one thing; profiting from it was something else. No, Skip wouldn't have been able to live with himself if he'd implicated Murray. Cutting him in would have placed the poor guy in even greater jeopardy than he was already in. What kind of friend would do that?

Researching the elephant case, Isabelle Strauss had found that Murray's story stood up surprisingly well. The trial in Monmouth County really had taken a bizarre turn, and the judge's sympathies shone through the transcript.

Most instructive were the vets who had examined the elephants at Meadow Gate Farm the day after Murray had repossessed them. The hook boils had been serious, Tory's hernia had indeed been exacerbated, and both men commented on the animals' nervousness. The mistreatment had been significant enough that, more than five years later, they both recalled the elephants and their own concern. One even volunteered to testify if it came to that. In the past, Strauss had had difficulty getting veterinarians to testify in abuse cases. This fellow's willingness seemed telling.

In idle moments she found herself imagining what Tory and Dutchess were like and wondering how, as a fugitive, you could possibly maintain and care for them. Hadn't she read somewhere that a single elephant consumed two hundred pounds of feed every day and produced 150 pounds of droppings? She pulled out the encyclopedia, visited the zoo, and made a point of catching elephant documentaries on television.

And she immersed herself in the case. Reviewing the transcript, learning more about Murray himself, she became convinced that Judge Thomas had regarded the matter as nothing more than a petty fight over a tractor-trailer that should never have made it to trial. In retrospect, Gerry Martin had erred by failing to raise the abuse, but he could hardly be faulted—the original dispute had clearly centered on ownership of the rig. The case should have encompassed not only the financial warranties the Drakes had made but also their obligation to keep the elephants "in a fit and healthy condition" and not to "mistreat, neglect, or in any other manner harm, damage, or injure" them.

By the time Murray phoned her back, two months after their last talk, Strauss had come to feel that, if the issue of abuse had been litigated, the court would have seen the case in a different light. Almost everyone who lost at trial felt cheated, but few people had grievances as valid as his.

"Have you had a chance to look into the case?"

"I've spent quite a bit of time on it."

Here comes the pitch, Murray thought. Send money. "And what do you think?"

"I think we're fighting an uphill battle."

Because he had fled, thumbing his nose at the judicial system rather than going through the appellate process, the courts were unlikely to review the case with sympathy. He was also long past the limit for the filing of an appeal or a post-trial motion. And now, of course, he was burdened with criminal charges.

"I have to ask this," said Strauss. "It would simplify things. Would you be willing to turn yourself in?"

"Only if I get a guarantee the girls won't be returned to the Drakes."

It appealed to her that he seemed less concerned with himself than with the elephants. "I don't see how that's going to be possible," she said. "We're not in a position to bargain."

"Then I ain't coming in. Why do you think I took off in the first place? To keep the girls away from them bastards. Excuse the language."

"I appreciate your feelings. It's just that, from the legal point of view, it complicates things."

"Well, then, I guess that's that." Murray, lighting a cigarette, castigated himself for having got his hopes up and waited for the kiss-off. "You think I'm a crazy old elephant man."

"Not at all. If we can get anybody to actually look at the law, I think we've got a good case."

"We?" said Murray. "You said 'we.' "

10

ON THE
ROAD AGAIN

I don't know how long I've got before I can't care for them anymore.
    —Murray Hill, in his journal, 1988

▼ ˙ ▼ ˙ ▼ ˙ ▼ ˙ ▼ ˙ ▼ ˙ ▼ ˙ ▼ ˙ ▼ ˙ ▼ ˙ ▼

"Murray wanted to get to Mexico with his elephants, but he didn't know how to do it," recalled Albert Rix, showing a visitor the thirty-six bears in his compound. A cheery, gentle, white-haired man in his early seventies, Albert for many years handled the animals for Ringling Brothers. Today, in New York State, he breeds Kodiak, European brown, and polar bears, keeping these species genetically strong for the day, which he thinks not far off, when the human population declines and bears again take their rightful place in the world.

"Murray stayed in touch with me while he was in hiding. I didn't know where he was, but he used to phone me sometimes. One day he asked if I wanted to come out to see him, and I drove to the farm where he was staying. He was all by himself with

▲ ˙ ▲ ˙ ▲ ˙ ▲ ˙ ▲ ˙ ▲ ˙ ▲ ˙ ▲ ˙ ▲ ˙ ▲ ˙ ▲

the animals at this place. His hair had gone gray, it was long and wild, and he had a long gray beard. In a few years he'd got ten years older. He gave me such a big hug I thought he'd never let me loose. I brought him a pie, strawberry. I asked him, 'Do you need money?' 'Hell, no,' he said. Murray wouldn't like to admit he needed money. I knew his kids, they're good kids, and I thought maybe they were helping him.

"When I saw him he wasn't in good spirits. He was just trying to keep himself happy. He'd take the elephants out in the woods, and while they were roaming around he'd study the trees, peel the fungus off, make little knickknacks. It was a way of staying busy, maybe selling a few things to make some money. He also took care of the farm animals—ducks, geese, sheep.

"It was a beautiful place, but he'd been there a long time and he was desperate to get out. He had this idea of slipping into Mexico. I know guys in Mexico, circus people, and I made inquiries through somebody who was down there at that time. I knew it would be difficult, you'd have to give bribes and ship the elephants in somebody else's name, but I thought you might be able to get them across.

"When Murray decides to do something, you're not going to talk him out of it. Just ask the people he's worked for. He always fought for his animals—as long as I've known him he's done that. We used to play the Shrine circuses together—that's where I met him. I had my bears and he had the Mitie Mites, the two female elephants and the male. We traveled together, we always used to barbecue steak. Me being German and him Jewish, people wondered. Each year, we played the same dates. When he was in the East he'd stay here with his elephants, and I'd stay at his place in Wisconsin with my bears.

"Murray always had animals at his place, he used to buy them and sell them, every kind of animal. One time he bought a couple of bears, tough ones, out of a zoo. He phoned me and said, 'I'll sell them to you real cheap.' I never buy stuff like that, most zoo bears are idiots. I said, 'What are they like?' He said,

'They're both trained.' I said, 'Really? What can they do?' Murray said, 'They can do an iron jaw on your hand.'

"He liked to joke around like that. I remember one time I wanted to go up to Canada—Churchill, the polar bears come right into the town. I told Murray, wouldn't it be nice to get some of those cubs? He said, 'We could do it, Albert, I'll help you.' I thought he was kidding. I said, 'How we going to get polar bear cubs across the border?' He said, 'Get six black cubs and bleach them. We'll ship them into Canada as polar bears. Up there we release them, catch six real polar bear cubs, and bring them back under the same papers.'

"He's strong-minded, Murray. He was one of the first pioneers to fight for his animals. Sometimes the producers didn't care if you had a proper place for the animals. If they didn't have everything they'd agreed on, Murray would make a fuss. If the hay wasn't good enough, he'd send it back. He told them many times he wasn't going to unload until they fixed things. He complained about lack of heat, the feed, the quarters for the elephants. He never left his elephants, and I never left my bears. We used to put a couple of bales of hay together and sleep with our animals.

"My friend tried to make some kind of deal to get him and the elephants into Mexico. In the end nothing came of it, and Murray had to stay where he was. But he didn't regret taking the elephants back from those people, even when he'd been stuck at this place for so long. He said he'd do it again. He was sorry he couldn't see his kids anymore, and couldn't work. His boys were young men and they were growing up without him. But he thought the court shouldn't have given the elephants to those people, not when they stopped paying and didn't look after them.

"And if you want to know the truth, I can't say I disagreed with him. I might do the same thing if someone did that to my bears. If they just thought about money, if they didn't care about the animals and treat them properly, I don't blame him for taking them back. I really like my bears, and Murray really likes those elephants."

Stopped for a red light, Dick Drake glanced at the truck beside
him. What do you know? Big John Strong and his wife! Dick
had known them for years—Big John had had his own circus
and owned property near Jungleland in Thousand Oaks. Dick
hit the horn and waved. Big John signaled to follow him out to
the lot.

Dick was doing a tour of Maine—four circuses were playing
the state at the same time—before checking out a circus touring
the Maritime Provinces of Canada. Like everybody in the circus
world, Big John knew the story and had a theory about where
the elephants were. They traded gossip; by the time Dick left, it
was evening. With a night to kill before the circus opened, he
scouted out the best motel in town—best suited, that is, to his
own rather specialized needs. He wasn't planning to rent a
room, merely to sleep in the parking lot. Motels were ideal.
Sleep in the lot at a shopping mall and you found yourself
jolted awake by the beam of a high-powered searchlight. The
law cruised the malls, and out-of-state plates meant you got
checked for sure. Besides, you never knew what lunatic might
be wandering the asphalt at four in the morning.

At a motel, you were just another out-of-state guest, and
there was no security. Dick decided on a two-story motor inn
done up in fake Colonial style, with white pillars, manicured
lawns, and a new restaurant. The place was large enough that
no one would notice an extra vehicle. Parking was around back,
out of sight of the office. Dick pulled into the farthest corner of
the lot and crawled into his sleeping bag.

At sunup, he was awakened by the concussive thud of car
doors. An elderly couple was checking out. The old fellow put
their suitcases in the trunk of their Lincoln Town Car. He made
his way upstairs for a final check of the room, and off they went.

Dick sniffed his armpits. He bared his teeth in the rearview
mirror. Grabbing his shaving kit, he headed upstairs and didn't
even have to force the door—it hadn't been pulled fast. Hesitantly, he went in. The room gave him a queer feeling—the

▲ 233

unmade bed, the steamed-up mirror, the wet towels heaped on the toilet. He let the TV play while he showered, shaved, and put on clean clothes. By the time he'd made himself instant coffee he felt at home. He stretched out on the bed, watching cable news, and was half asleep when he heard a key in the lock. Damn. Hadn't the maid noticed the DO NOT DISTURB sign?

When the old fellow opened the door, both men nearly jumped out of their skins.

"I'm terribly sorry. I must have made a mistake."

"Maybe not," said Dick, getting to his feet. "Is this your room?"

"I thought so," said the old fellow, confused, looking back and forth between his key and the door number.

"My brother's with the circus and he told me I could use his room to wash up. Said he'd leave it open for me, second door from the end."

"This is the third door, isn't it?"

"Well, isn't that the craziest thing," said Dick, gathering his stuff, needing to get the hell out before the old fellow got any ideas. "I'm real sorry to disturb you."

"Well, look, finish your coffee. I certainly didn't—"

"That's all right," said Dick, closing the door behind him. By the time the old fellow opened the door again to offer assistance, Dick had made his way around the motel. He climbed in his truck and roared off.

Dick lingered over breakfast, got an oil change, scouted the town. It was still early, and when he came on a Holiday Inn he turned into the lot. The sun was already fierce; it was going to be another scorcher. He noticed that the marquee advertised a swimming pool, and that exit doors were spaced along the exterior hallways. Hot and bored, he pulled on his shorts and T-shirt and got to one of the exits as a young family was emerging with their bags. "Here, let me get that for you."

Inside, he grabbed a clean towel off the maid's cart. Farther down the hall another maid had set out three cans of warm beer and a newspaper. The next housekeeping cart had a plastic ice bucket; the ice machine was around the corner on the way to the pool. In theory you needed a room key, but the pool area was being mopped and the door had been propped open. There was nobody around but the maintenance man. Dick said good morning, iced the beer, pulled up a lounge chair, and opened the paper.

Other people began showing up for a morning swim, and before long Dick was fast friends with two young couples on vacation. One of the guys was in the mood for a Bloody Mary.

"How about you, Dick?"

"That's kind of you, but I really should make a phone call."

"Hey! Tell room service we need some drinks, will you? And Dick here needs a phone."

In Tehachapi, Doy was getting ready to wait tables at the café.
"Hi, honey," she said. "Having any luck?"

"There's a circus opening today I want to check out."

"Everybody's fine here. Eddie and Julie and the kids have gone back up to Oregon."

"Running crane with that same outfit?"

"Right. Julie's pregnant again. Like to have died when she found out it's twins."

"Isn't that great," said Dick. "Listen, Doy, get the new *Circus Report* yet? Can you give me the routes?"

"Didn't come yet. Where are you, honey? Haven't heard from you for a few days."

"Bangor, Maine."

"Have you found out anything?"

"Not about what I came for," said Dick—he nodded thanks for the drink—"but I might write a book about how to see the United States on fifty cents a day."

"Tell me something," said Murray, pulling a tattered blanket over himself in the stifling, fetid darkness. "How come we always hook up with screwballs?"

The girls fussed and caressed each other in preparation for sleep. Murray tried to make himself comfortable, but the foam rubber made him sweat, bugs were eating him, and arthritis pained him terribly. He chewed aspirin and swatted a mosquito. How to figure it? Bunny and Leonard, Charles the Vietnam vet, Howell and Veronica—he always seemed to find himself among nut cases.

In Skip's absence, Murray's relations with Howell and Veronica had gone from bad to intolerable. Veronica now spent most of her time at the farm, and there was no escaping her blabbermouth, meddlesome ways, and misguided sympathies. If he'd had lingering doubts about her mental health, or lack of it, the coyote incident had dispelled them.

Murray often heard coyotes at night and noticed them on the property. Attracted by the sheep, they grew bolder, ignoring him and the girls. Veronica adored them until they took a lamb. A few nights later they took another. Now she wanted a way of keeping them out. One idea was a 220-volt fence, but Howell objected, she said, because it would cost $60,000 to do the whole property.

"How would you stop them from coming back?" she asked.

"Shoot the motherfuckers," said Murray. "They won't come back."

The suggestion appalled her; that, of course, was the idea. Howell hated losing sheep, though, and Murray knew he wouldn't hesitate to shoot if Veronica could be finessed. One Saturday morning, while she was in town, Murray came up to the house and told him, "That coyote's out there again."

Knowing Veronica might return at any moment, Howell hurriedly unracked his .303 Browning. He took aim from the living-room window and squeezed off a shot. The coyote, two hundred yards distant, went straight up in the air. Howell fired again; the coyote made it as far as the marshy area before it died.

"Damn fine shooting," said Murray.

While they were inspecting the dead animal, Veronica, sensing what had happened, came running down from her car. At the sight of the carcass she flew into rage. "You murderous fools! That's not even a coyote, it's a German shepherd!"

Like hell. Murray had bred coyotes; he knew what they

looked like. Instead of reassuring her, he shrugged and said, "What's the difference? You been losing sheep to him."

"You killed a shepherd in cold blood!"

Howell returned to the house for his hunting knife, cut off the ears and tail, and put them in a plastic bag. "I'll take these in," he said, "let the environment officers do an identification. Maybe that'll cool her out."

Quite the opposite. When Veronica came back with a spade and saw the disfigurement, she pounded Howell's chest. "Can't you let it rest in peace? You're getting as bad as he is!" She fetched needle and thread, retrieved the bag from the freezer, and headed back to the marsh. Murray thought this hysterical —was she really going to sew the severed parts back on?

Toward supper, looking like a madwoman—covered in dirt, hands raw from shoveling—she found Murray back in the woods with the girls.

"Get him buried all right?"

"You'll never find his grave, you bastard."

Murray rolled over in the dark, trying to find a position that didn't hurt. "We got to get out of here," he told the girls. "These idiots are driving me insane."

The girls made gentle blowing sounds, caressing each other and moving in their slow, primordial way, side to side, rocking the trailer so that it almost seemed to be afloat. Murray had come to depend on this lulling rhythm to drop off. Many nights, if he wasn't in deep sleep, he woke again when the racking ceased. Wide awake in the heavy-smelling dark—his left brain, the Ministry of Rationalization, shut down for the night —oh, the dreadful clarity right then. How he longed for freedom! How he missed his kids!

Phoning the children, hearing of changes in their lives, only deepened his isolation. Seasons, whole years, were flying by. He was becoming an old man. Both twins were now working, Allan as an elephant keeper at the zoo in Springfield, Adam on the road. Robin's boy, Ian, his first grandchild, was not a baby any longer but a redheaded kid with a goofy grin Murray knew mostly from pictures. Robin had remarried, and Nada had married her boyfriend, Ron. What kind of father was he, missing his daughters' weddings? Nada now worked as a booking agent. All the kids were doing him proud. Denise, too, had far more strength than he'd given her credit for—she'd landed a job at a microfilm place in Springfield, working an eight-hour shift and spending four or five nights a week with her support group. She was flourishing without him. Could he have been the cause of her unhappiness all along?

Isabelle Strauss, whom Murray had come to trust, felt that publicity might aid her effort to reopen the case. Publicity carried the risk of exposure—someone who'd seen the elephants or knew Howell was bound to put two and two together—but it might also pressure the Drakes to settle, especially when they learned of Isabelle's maneuvers and realized they'd have to incur more legal fees. A car dealer in Vermont, to whom Murray had sold an elephant years earlier, had offered to buy the girls for $50,000. Isabelle reported that Bunce Atkinson was recommending that the Drakes accept. Maybe, just maybe, a resolution was at hand.

Meanwhile, Murray and Robin were discreetly seeking a new spot for the girls to hide out. They also needed transportation: Bunny's old rig had long since fallen into disrepair. Bucky Steele, an elephant man in Texas, had invited Murray down to his place—a few hundred miles from Mexico—and even offered to haul the girls. Next time they spoke, however, he changed his tune. He couldn't free up a rig after all. Murray and Robin had called at least a dozen animal people, trying to line up a tractor-trailer; most supported Murray and hoped his saga would have a happy outcome but wouldn't put themselves on the line. Robin did find somebody in California, Jack T., with a tractor-trailer suitable for elephants. He was willing to rent it out, but Murray didn't know the man well and feared he'd tip off the Drakes.

Robin had also arranged for her father to speak to some media people, including a CNN producer, a Canadian Broadcasting Corporation interviewer, and a reporter on *The New York Times.* The resulting coverage, including the *Times* article— "In Custody Case, Hiding Elephants Is the Easy Part"—had brought a deluge of inquiries. She'd set up more phone interviews with her father but none of the other writers, television producers, or movie people wanted to know about the bogus trial or the abuse. It bugged Murray that they all skipped the heart of the matter—the reasons behind his improbable odyssey —in favor of the same dumb question: "How do you hide two elephants?"

One reporter had complimented him profusely on his commitment, calling him a courageous man who'd turned his back to shore over a matter of principle. Was he? Or was he a fool who'd misread the tide and waded in over his head? At the time he'd taken off with the girls, he never imagined the fix he'd find himself in. Like anyone close on sixty, he'd had his share of woe —the back operation that set him down for six months, his father's mysterious death from an inner-ear tumor, the pain of dealing with Denise in her blotto years—but nothing had prepared him for the exquisite torture of hiding with two elephants who, in four years on the lam, had become both the object of his deepest affections and a seven-ton ball and chain.

For all his troubles, though, the girls had never been more playful, and their carefree spirits made these bleak moments bearable. They chirped back and forth in the darkness and voided themselves noisily, thickening the rank air of the trailer. Then they resumed their gentle rocking, allowing him sleep.

United States Department of the Interior
Fish and Wildlife Service
One Gateway Center, Suite 700
Newton Corner, Massachusetts 02158

Dear Mr. Drake:
Thank you for your recent letter advising us of the case entitled "State of New Jersey vs. Arlan Seidon aka Murray Hill." Director Dunkle has requested I respond to your inquiry. A member of my staff, Assistant

*Regional Director of Law Enforcement A. Eugene Hester, has apprised
me of his discussion with you concerning this case.*

*As related to you by Mr. Hester, in order to take action we would need
specific information concerning where the elephants might be located and
positive identification of them by you. This is essential information which
we must have in order to investigate the allegation that the endangered
animals may have been moved interstate illegally in the course of a commercial activity. When you have information that may allow us to pursue
this investigation, please advise Mr. Hester by telephone. . . .*

One of the worst snowstorms in New Jersey's recent history
happened to fall on the day Isabelle Strauss was scheduled to
present her motion for a new trial for Murray Hill—January 8,
1988. Seeking a postponement, she called Bunce Atkinson.

Though Atkinson and his partner had moved their offices
from Colts Neck to Red Bank, New Jersey, and though the
Drakes owed Atkinson fees in five figures, he had continued to
represent them diligently. For four years he had been sending
statements to Tehachapi; the tone of his covering letters had
evolved from cool professionalism ("Enclosed please find a
statement of account for legal services rendered to date") to
agreeable flexibility ("I would appreciate if you would contact
my office to arrange a payment schedule") to outright pleading
("Dick, I, like you, am a businessman, with overhead and
monthly obligations that must be met"). And for four years Dick
had been assuring him he'd done a great job and they'd square
things as soon as they could.

Atkinson had urged Dick to accept the buyout offer from the
fellow in Vermont, but Dick figured the elephants were worth a
good deal more than $50,000; and his motivation, Atkinson
sensed, had changed. No longer did he merely want to recover
the elephants; he wanted revenge. A buyout would let Murray
off the hook, and when the charges of abuse had turned up in
the newspapers, Dick had vowed that Murray would regret
what he'd said. Much as Dick needed money, he'd rather have
seen Murray go to prison. Atkinson was throwing good money
after bad, but he had to oppose Strauss's motion. The last thing

he wanted was a new trial. His only hope of getting paid was to see the elephants returned to the Drakes, to be sold off or put to work.

"The roads are bad," Isabelle Strauss said on the phone. "What do you want to do?"

"Courts are open down here," said Atkinson.

Strauss closed up her office in East Orange and pointed her ten-year-old Chevy into the storm. From a legal standpoint, she knew, her strategy was tenuous. All she could do was argue that the trial had been unjust and hope that, in person, she could make an insightful judge comprehend what had happened. The trip to Freehold, normally an hour, took three. The courtroom was empty but for Strauss, Atkinson, Judge Michael Farren, the clerk, and a security guard.

"Two ninety-nine on the list," the clerk droned. "Drake versus Seidon."

"There is a judgment rendered against your client," said Judge Farren, stifling a yawn.

"Yes," said Strauss.

"With regard to money damages. And the jury also awarded the plaintiff two elephants?"

"That's correct, Your Honor."

"Have the money damages been paid?"

"No," said Strauss.

"Have the elephants been turned over to the plaintiff?"

"They have not."

"Which indicates your client was dissatisfied with the verdict. I'm sure he took an appeal to the Appellate Division, did he not?"

Strauss knew where this was going. Your client's a fugitive, under indictment, and in contempt of court. You're asking us to exercise discretion? He won't play the game but wants us to play on his behalf?

What frustrated Strauss was the court's emphasis on the defendant; the animals were excluded from consideration. If only there were a way to represent Tory and Dutchess, a mechanism to have them viewed as anything more precious and deserving than stereo speakers or farm equipment. Strauss ran up against this systemic failure of empathy time and again. In family law, when a father and mother fight over an infant, the baby's welfare is not only taken into account, it's often the deciding factor. Animals, however, are mere property.

Not that Judge Farren was unable to appreciate the unique nature of the case. "I don't know how one secretes two Asian elephants," he said, doing a Carson-like doubletake. "I don't know where you'd hide them."

Strauss said patiently, "I don't know how you hide two elephants, Your Honor."

Smiles in the courtroom. Each time Strauss tried to argue that a key issue, abuse, had not been scrutinized in the original proceedings only because, at the outset, rightful possession of the elephants had not even been—

"Maybe in Lakehurst or something?" said the judge, cocking an eyebrow at Bunce Atkinson. Judge Farren smiled indulgently at Strauss and shook his head. "I do take my hat off to your client. How he can hide two elephants is beyond me."

And so it went. Driving home through the pelting snow, with Judge Farren's last words echoing in her ears—"No reason whatsoever why this judgment should be set aside. The motion is denied"—Strauss fumed. She'd literally been laughed out of court.

But that, as she told Murray when he phoned, was only strike one. She didn't want to be overly optimistic. This wasn't going to be easy. Still, public sentiment was mounting—people who'd seen the newspaper stories or heard the radio interviews were asking how they could help Tory and Dutchess—and further means of legal recourse were available. She had already begun, in free moments, preparing to appeal Judge Farren's denial of her motion.

The legal argument behind her appeal was threefold. One, because of the plaintiffs' admission that the elephants had been rightfully repossessed, the defendant had had no opportunity to litigate the crucial issue of whether the Drakes had abused Tory and Dutchess and so violated the security agreement. Two,

New Jersey's long-standing policy of preventing cruelty to animals, together with the unique living nature of the collateral, underscored the importance of the court's failure to litigate the abuse issue. Three, Judge Farren's emphasis on Murray's fugitive status prevented him from properly considering the merits of her motion for a new trial, which constituted an abuse of judicial discretion. Six weeks after the original motion, she filed the appeal.

Nice swing, said the appellate court. Strike two.

Yesterday morning I was down in the dumps, feeling real sorry for myself after talking to Isabelle. It was foggy and chilly. I went out in the woods by myself, same way I used to in Burlington, or at the farm in Missouri when I needed to cool out. I kept walking deeper and deeper into the woods. I got off the trail and started feeling better mentally. After a while I came across four deer, all females, grazing on the edge of a clearing. It was an area with no trees but a lot of tall grass and ferns. Two of the deer were in the woods, two were out in the clearing.

None of them even picked up their head when I got to the clearing. Somewhere I'd heard you could sneak right up on a deer if you worked at it, so I figured I may as well give it a try. I wet my finger to see which direction the wind was coming from, but there was hardly any breeze. I got down on all fours and started crawling toward the closest doe. I was maybe a hundred feet away from her when I started. The leaves were damp enough that they didn't crunch. She had her white ass toward me. The two in the woods were facing me, and the one off to the side also had her ass to me.

I crawled slowly on all fours. Now and then one picked up her head to look, and I froze, staying in position until she went back to grazing. My knees and elbows started hurting and I wondered what the hell I was doing. I went down flat on the ground, using my elbows to drag myself along, going as slow as necessary not to alarm them. After an hour I'd covered maybe half the distance. I was getting real sore and my back was killing me, but I wanted to see how close I could get.

I must have spent two hours crawling along, freezing when they looked up, inching closer when they went back to grazing. Finally I got right up close. There was her white ass right above me, I was practically underneath her. I could have grabbed her hind legs. I thought to myself great, you made it. What now? I reached up and patted her ass. That white tail shot up like a flag and just like that she was gone, along with the others.

The way I figure it, deer probably can't see worth a damn, they function more by sound and smell. If the smell is familiar, it doesn't bother them. They've never been afraid of the girls—right from the start they would all graze together. At first the girls were more concerned about the deer than vice versa. Sometimes I'd take my whip along, and when we spotted deer I'd stay out of sight and watch for a while. The deer mixed in with the girls, and if I cracked my whip, they looked up at the noise but didn't bother taking off. As long as they were with the girls, they didn't get spooked. Then I'd step out to where they could see me, and right away they took off.

That sure says a lot about the human race. They'll accept an animal they've never seen but they won't accept man, same as the chipmunk that comes around when I grain the girls. They let him share their grain and he accepts the girls. Soon as I show up, the chipmunk takes off. How did that start, the distrust between the wild animal and the supposedly civilized animal?

I don't object to hunting with a purpose. In Burlington I used to shoot chipmunks that came in the barn. They were destroying the feed supply for my animals. I kept shooting until they got it through their heads the barn was my territory and they weren't welcome there. But I never chased them outside and killed them on their territory. When Howell's doctor friend comes up here to hunt, that's never bothered me. He takes a deer and his son takes one. They eat the meat themselves or else they give it to family members for the freezer. I figure that's just nature at work. It's people who shoot animals for the hell of it that make me mad.

When I was sneaking up on those deer, the wind shifted several times. There's no way they didn't smell me. All I can figure is they smelled elephant on me and accepted that. Or else they accept my smell now. I don't know what the hell the whole thing accomplished, but it sure made me feel better.

When Dot Wilkie, at home in Far Hills, saw the item about Murray Hill on the evening news on WOR-TV, she hollered. Alex was working on his weapons collection; he bounded downstairs wondering what had happened. Bill lumbered out from his spot at the kitchen table.

"There they are! Dick's elephants!"

As soon as the clip ended, Dot called her brother in California. The item had included footage of the elephants in the woods and at a large pond; Murray wasn't seen or heard, but he was again quoted as saying he'd hidden them to prevent them from being abused.

To Dick, the news item was salt in the wound. Murray had been spouting off all over the place, and reporters were swallowing his version of the story. Bunce Atkinson had said Murray's new lawyer was some animal-rights nut who was also ranting on about abuse. Taking off with the elephants was one thing; smearing Dick's name was something else again. Dick still had ties to the animal industry, and that kind of talk stuck to you. Murray had stolen the elephants and was now trying to justify what he'd done. What other explanation could there be? If he really thought they'd been abused, he would have brought it out at trial.

Playing the tape over, Dick felt his anger congeal into hatred. The little prick. He'd outsmarted himself this time. Dick would find out what cameraman shot the film and get him to reveal Murray's whereabouts. No, Murray wouldn't have been that careless. The film was an amateur job. The tape had likely been sent to the station, the interview done by phone.

Still, there must have been enough to nail him. They could convict murderers from a speck of blood. With satellite photographs they could count bullets in an ammunition belt. Think they couldn't take a piece of film and figure out where it had been shot? If you calculated time of day from the shadows, identified the ground vegetation and the trees, their age and grouping and such, biologists could identify the general area right off—the Northeast, by the looks of it, not so different from the country around Dot's place—and with some analysis they could pinpoint his location.

Maybe Dick could rouse the New Jersey State Police once more. The last time he'd called, a trooper named Gerry Barbato seemed to have inherited the case. Dick had told him that, through Isabelle Strauss, somebody in Vermont had offered to buy the elephants. Barbato had phoned Strauss, who said she had no means of contacting Murray and no knowledge of where he was. Barbato had also, at Dick's urging, called the owner of African Lion Safari in Cambridge, Ontario, a fellow knowledgeable about the animal trade between the United States and Canada.

When Dick phoned Barbato after the news item, however, he was told that Barbato had been transferred. How many cops was that who'd passed the torch? Five? Six? Dick was put in touch with Detective Glenn Miller. Unfortunately, Miller said, he doubted they could locate Murray from a videotape, but he would run a new fifty-state driver's-license check. Miller also called Isabelle Strauss. She said the proposed sale to a third party had fallen through because the Drakes would not agree to terms. And she repeated that, although Murray sometimes phoned, she had no idea where he was.

Strauss, meantime, was also getting calls from the Monmouth County Prosecutor's Office, which was feeling the heat of the publicity. The prosecutor's office was being made to look foolish—four years and they still hadn't found the elephants? Their insinuation that she knew where the girls were, was perhaps even hiding them, made her laugh aloud. "I live in East Orange. Do you think I've got them in my basement?"

Dick felt he had no choice but to drive East yet again. He'd heard from several people that Murray was trying to line up transportation, and his gut told him the elephants were in Canada or the northeastern United States. If Murray was indeed preparing to move, it was worth investigating anybody with elephants or a rig to transport them.

Dick set up shop at Dot's place in Far Hills and headed up

the Hudson Valley. He spent an afternoon poking around the Catskill Game Farm, then checked out some people who ran a small circus out of Windham, New York. Al Vidbel had Asian elephants, and over the years he'd done business with Bunny and Leonard, Ian Garden, and many other people Murray knew.

Dick located the Vidbel place, a hilly acreage outside the town, easily enough. The house was on one side of the road, the barn on the other. There was no stock in the field, but somehow he knew there were elephants in the barn. He drove past a couple of times. Not wanting to arouse suspicion with his California tags, he left the truck in town and walked back out. He was wearing shorts and tennis shoes; he'd pass himself off as a jogger. He'd left his glasses behind and put on one of the wigs he kept in the truck.

Dick jogged back up the road toward Vidbel's. He got to the property just in time to see somebody with a limp enter the barn. Dick sneaked through the orchard and came around back, waiting for the keeper to leave so he could get a look inside. Hiding in the long grass, he felt so drowsy, and the sun was so warm, that he allowed his eyes to close . . .

. . . and woke with a start, unsure how long he'd been asleep and whether he'd dreamed the swishing sound. Dream, hell. There were three Asians no more than fifty feet away; the keeper was chaining them, and the elephants—females, but no Tory or Dutchess—were all facing Dick's way, knowing he was there. At any moment they'd tip off the keeper. Dick was trapped. He couldn't go back the way he'd come. The keeper was no kid, and his limp was pronounced, so Dick broke cover and took off for the road. Startled, the keeper hollered after him and the elephants trumpeted.

Fueled by adrenaline, Dick chugged along until he was out of sight. Luckily it was downhill all the way into town. Even so, he'd nearly split a gut by the time he reached the main street. Panting, he stopped into the first spot he came to. It was a yuppie haven, the sort of place where they put foam on the coffee and cloth bonnets on the jars of preserves. Still short of breath, he lit a smoke and ordered a soda.

When he took a seat outside, a girl on the patio giggled. A whole table of kids burst into laughter. It wasn't until Dick turned, curious, that he realized what they were laughing at: the gray-haired old fart with a potbelly, sweating like a hippo, wearing yellow shorts and a brown wig that was too small for his head.

This morning when I was ready to bring the girls in, they'd drifted off so far in back I had to track them for half an hour. When I finally caught up to them I heard voices coming our way. I headed in the direction of the voices and saw two men walking through the woods, a couple of hundred yards from the girls. I hid behind a bush. When Dutchess started chirping and Tory started rumbling, the men's eyes popped. The men looked at each other without saying a word, turned around and headed back the way they came. They weren't running but they were sure taking long strides.

Robin's getting pissed off with all the people calling her for interviews —CBS morning show, National Public Radio, A Current Affair, New York Daily News, etc. I'm afraid with the publicity it's only a matter of time before I get picked up. Somebody in the area will see something on TV and realize I'm a fugitive. Also, the more press, the worse the cops look for not finding me, which means they might get serious. I don't think they could have been looking too hard up to now.

Robin told me Drake was on TV last night. He said they had information about where I am, they almost caught me a few times but I slipped away. His story is that I'm crazy and I'm in Canada and they're worried that it's too cold there for the girls. I'll bet they're real worried about the girls. I spoke to those bastards three different times when I was trying to negotiate directly and they didn't mention the girls once, never even asked if they were dead or alive.

Spoke to Isabelle, who said somebody else has offered to buy the girls. The reason I never felt good about the Vermont offer was because the girls would be ride animals again. I've decided I'm not interested in any buyout that would put them back to work. They shouldn't be working, they should be free to do what they like. A third-party buyout would mean Drake gets money out of this, which I'm opposed to after the way they treated them and tried to cheat me. But I could live with it if the girls ended up in a good situation. But a buyout where Drake got money and the girls went back to work isn't something I'll even consider anymore. After all this, I want to see them end up someplace they'll be happy.

I don't know how long I've got before I can't care for them anymore. Last night was very bad as I had severe cramps in my left calf and my rectum, plus pain in my back. I was up for four or five hours, coughing, dry heaves and phlegm. I've got to get off the cigs—my coughing is worse than ever. At present the leg has a lot of pain when I walk and it's stove up. My back is also worse than it has been. I'm on six aspirins a day and some days eight. They help a little but not much. I need my cane to get going in the morning and to get back to the truck at night.

A few weeks ago Howell asked me to make one of my canes for an older woman at his office who hurt herself. I made one and burned in the initials he gave me. I don't know why, but I felt he wasn't telling the truth, which is normal. Sure enough, he hid the cane in his gun room (so Veronica wouldn't see it) and the other day when I picked up the mail right there on top was a postcard from his new girlfriend thanking him for the cane. The lying puke. I don't know how Veronica can stand him, but I don't know how he can stand her either. The older I get and the more I see of people, the less I trust anybody.

Better go now and work on Dutchess's nail. She's developed a crack down the middle of one nail on her right foot and I'm having a hell of a time trying to get it healed. I used some epoxy material which joins it for a while but then it opens up again. She also has a hole and a sore spot in her left rear foot (I've been medicating that) and now she's developed an infection in her tail (ingrown hair). If it doesn't clear up soon I'll have to deal with that also.

Howell Phillips IV put down the newspaper and rubbed his bony skull in despair. Of all the dumb stunts—"Elephant trainer stays on the lam for 4 years with 2 trunks, 7 tons." Page one. Wasn't it just like him to yack to the press even though

Veronica had told him how strongly she opposed the idea? The egotistical little idiot. Why didn't he just give the reporter directions to the farm? Veronica was going to have conniptions. Howell himself was ready for a shouting match but Murray, no fool, had taken the girls into the woods.

Murray, too, was distressed. By coincidence, a reporter on the local weekly had contacted Howell to ask about the elephants. Howell told Murray he'd taken the young woman into his confidence. The elephants were involved in a legal problem that would soon be sorted out, he'd explained, at which time he'd happily cooperate. For now, though, they'd prefer no publicity. Murray figured Howell had been trying to get into her pants. Even so, he couldn't believe Howell's stupidity—why even allude to the legal situation? Why not just say the girls were recuperating? He feared he'd be picked up imminently.

Other incidents had heightened his paranoia. Earlier in the week, while he was alone at the farm, a phone repairman had shown up, saying there were problems on the line and he needed access to the house. Murray stuck to him as he went from room to room checking the phones, but next day, speaking with Robin, he heard a distinct click. Robin heard it, too, and they cut short their conversation. Could the repairman have been a fake who'd installed a bug? If so, at whose behest? The police? Howell? Had Howell been taping his calls all along? What for? To safeguard himself? Or to blackmail him into turning over the girls?

Murray and the girls were again in the woods when a state trooper turned in the driveway. Veronica, upset by the newspaper article and in daily contact with her attorney, figured this was it. Oh, her poor mother, in frail health to begin with. The humiliation! The disgrace! HEIRESS IMPLICATED IN ELEPHANT THEFT. Fighting back anxiety, Veronica asked the trooper to wait while she fetched Howell from the barn. The instant Howell saw her expression he knew. His shrug of resignation was pure bravado —panic rippled his bowel. INVESTMENT BANKER PLEADS GUILTY TO CONSPIRACY. He drew himself up, imagining the horror of jail, the jokes among his friends on Wall Street.

"Are you the owner of this property, sir?"

Howell swallowed hard and took the offensive. "Why do you ask? What seems to be the trouble?"

It turned out the trooper only wanted to notify them of a rash of burglaries. A place down the road had been hit the night before and the police were asking everyone in the area to keep an eye out for a blue van. Veronica was so relieved she sent the trooper off with an armload of dahlias from the cutting garden.

Next morning, after Howell and Veronica had returned to the city, Murray and the girls went back into the woods. He wanted to remain as inconspicuous as possible, and had found a new way to pass the time. Whenever hay was delivered to the farm he saved the baling string to braid into belts, ropes, and harnesses for the girls. While they wandered off, browsing and stripping bark, he sat on a log in the sunshine and worked on Tory's harness. Next time he looked up, the girls had vanished.

An hour later, with the phantom grace of ghosts, they emerged from the woods near the stream. Dutchess squeaked in greeting, and they began making their way up the hill. They were more than halfway to the summit when faint voices, carried on the breeze, came wafting from the far side of the hill. The girls froze, looking to Murray for direction.

Hikers who'd strayed off the Appalachian Trail? He could only hope so. By the sound of it they, too, were near the summit. There was no time. Quietly, using hand signals, Murray had the girls lie down. Dutchess usually squeaked when she did a laydown, but this once she made no sound. She and Tory settled into position just as the hikers came into view.

The hikers, two men and a woman, made themselves comfortable on a rock outcrop and ate some chocolate. One of the men had binoculars, which he passed around. The hilltop commanded a panoramic view and each hiker in turn gazed out in every direction. They spent a good ten minutes not two hundred feet from the girls. The hill was dotted with big boulders; the girls stayed so still and blended in so well, the hikers never noticed them.

Murray spent those ten minutes with his heart in his throat.

How much more could he take? The hikers, the trooper, the repairman, the click on the line—was he getting paranoid or were these all signs to go while he still could? As soon as it was safe, he moved the girls back to the trailer; that evening, when the cheap rates kicked in, he phoned Bucky Steele in Texas.

Bucky had worked elephants in Mexico; he'd also told Murray he was selling his six-horse liberty act to some Mexicans— exactly the contacts Murray needed. Murray asked how hard it would be to get elephants across the border. He spoke no Spanish, he said, and he was flat broke—he'd need work right away. Bucky figured there were one or two Mexican shows he might be able to join.

"Everything's pay, pay, pay. That's how things get done."

"I'm a long way from Mexico right now and it's hard setting anything up. But I got to move the girls soon."

"Bring 'em down here," said Bucky. "I told you before. I got plenty of land, and the barn's almost finished."

"Sure you got room enough for my two?"

"Hell, yes. I got two out right now, one in Canada and one in Guam. If anybody asks, your two are mine come back home."

"I can't pay feed, room and board, nothing," said Murray. "Ain't got a cent."

"Don't worry, we'll work it out. You can help around here."

Bucky had a reputation as a drinker, but his wife had said he was off the booze completely, and he'd sounded perfectly sober each time Murray had phoned. As for getting down there, Murray wished he had a more reliable ride. But now was the time and Jack T.'s rig, risky or not, was the ticket. If Jack T. sold him out to Drake . . . well, it was a chance Murray had to take. He told Bucky he'd almost firmed up transportation and expected to be in Texas in a week.

U.S. Department of Justice
Washington, D.C.

Dear Mr. Drake:
Attorney General Thornburgh has asked this office to respond to your

letter. Unfortunately, the U.S. Department of Justice can neither offer legal advice to, nor conduct an investigation for, a private citizen. As an arm of the Executive Branch of the Federal Government, the Department of Justice is charged with representing the United States, its agencies and personnel of the Executive Branch in legal matters. You may wish to consult with an attorney to discuss the legal options open to you. Your local Legal Aid Society (listed in the phone book) may be able to help you locate an attorney. . . .

Murray spent his last days at Howell's in a state of suppressed excitement, which the girls seemed to share. They set off eagerly each morning, chirping back and forth, as if aware that four years of bliss was soon to end; they stripped trees, frolicked at the pond, played hide-and-seek in the woods. Murray worked on their feet and was glad to see improvement in Dutchess's nail, though it was so slow to heal he was beginning to think the condition was chronic.

During his discussions with Jack T. about money (the trip would cost $3,000 cash, which Murray's mother provided), permits (Murray told him what states they'd pass through, plus a couple they wouldn't, to keep his destination secret), and the truck itself (a forty-five-foot Peterbilt rigged for elephants), Jack T. had been helpful and straightforward. But it could have been a setup. Jack T. could have figured out the identity of the elephants and been planning to collect the reward Drake was said to be offering.

Howell and Veronica were ignorant of Murray's plans until the Saturday morning the rig was due. They had come up from Manhattan late Friday night; Murray broke the news as they made coffee in the morning. He was glad he'd waited. Veronica, as expected, jumped up and down like a chimp, and Howell, at the kitchen table, glared at him with unconcealed hatred.

"You selfish bastard," said Veronica. "Where are we going to find someone to stay here on such short notice?"

Howell, morosely rubbing his bald spot, said, "Don't forget to leave the key to the back gate."

They both feared that, if caught, Murray would implicate

them. At the same time, the media attention had caused them no end of anxiety. Despite the risks involved in transporting the girls, it would be a monumental relief to be rid of the little tyrant.

"Here," said Veronica, pressing money into his hand. "You'll need this for the girls."

Her tears, withheld until Murray had limped across the yard for the last time, were prompted by the thought of losing Tory and Dutchess, whom she'd come to love. If only he'd get out of their lives but leave the girls behind . . .

Howell got up from the table. Ardor had restored his spirits, and Murray's departure was cause for celebration. "Shall we go upstairs?" She was wonderful in bed when she'd been crying.

"You foul bore."

"Hey, where did that come from?"

"Is that all you care about?" Veronica snapped. "Don't you understand a thing?"

Howell sat down again. "You know something?" he said, instantly deflated, sullenly staring at the table. "I am fucking sick of our so-called life together."

All the gear for the girls—chains, tools, and foot-trimming equipment—was piled by the gate, along with a dozen bales of hay and a sack of grain. Murray's things—clothes and toiletries, as well as his fungus, gourd, and eggshell handicrafts, carefully wrapped in newspaper—fit in a duffel bag and a cardboard carton. The truck, due at nine, showed up fifteen minutes early.

Jack T.'s son, Michael, the driver, turned out to be a stocky kid with an air of eager competence. The rig had one compartment for the elephants and one for equipment and supplies. They loaded the gear, and then Murray went for the girls. Before boarding them, he had them void themselves. Elephants often have to be coaxed into a new truck, but they climbed the ramp without hesitation. Playful and cooperative, they seemed as happy to be leaving as Murray was. He set their chains, secured the doors, and hopped into the cab beside Michael.

Free at last! He'd already made this trip a dozen times in his mind. They'd snake through New Jersey, picking up Interstate 80 in Pennsylvania, heading west and south, the wind whistling by the window. Finally! They had a tank of diesel and permits for every state they'd pass through. The girls had decent quarters and plenty to eat. Murray could have danced a jig—he felt the relief and anticipation of a man released from prison. What could go wrong? They'd travel all day and through the night, ducking the scales, using secondary roads to cross state lines, putting the nightmare of the past four years behind them. Mexico, here we come! With a stop at Bucky Steele's along the way.

In a slow grinding of gears, engine straining under the load, they made their way down Howell's driveway. When they turned onto the county road, Murray craned his neck for one last look at the house, where Howell and Veronica were now shouting at each other; and at the property, which he had come to cherish.

"Beautiful place," said Michael. "I'll bet you're sorry to leave it behind."

11

MEXICO OR BUST

I sometimes wonder, has it been worth it? Speaking for myself, the answer would have to be no. But when I see the girls under no stress, enjoying themselves, that's what makes it worthwhile.
—Murray Hill, in his journal, 1989

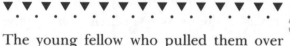

The young fellow who pulled them over didn't look old enough to shave. An illusion brought on by age, Murray wondered, or were children now performing most of the world's duties? Was this kid old enough to be an Indiana state trooper?

Murray kept his eyes front while Michael, fumbling with his wallet, produced his papers for the trooper's inspection. They'd be all right unless the trooper wanted Murray's ID as well, but why would he? Michael would check out fine and so would the rig. They'd be on their way in no time. Murray tried to keep the thought of arrest out of mind. To consider the possibility, it seemed, would invite it.

Tory and Dutchess had been good the whole trip. Now, wanting to be unloaded, they began rhythmically jolting the rig. The trooper, taking Michael's ID to the

cruiser, stopped to regard the truck with an air of deliberation, like the weight-guesser on a midway. A drumming noise started up inside the trailer. Urine began percolating through the floor, dripping onto the shoulder of the interstate.

"What are you hauling today?" said the trooper.

Michael, who'd figured out which elephants these were, was ready to panic.

"Elephants," said Murray.

The trooper paused for indications of humor. "You got elephants in that trailer?"

"Two of them," said Murray. "Shirley and . . . Princess."

"My uncle fought in Burma in World War Two," said the trooper. "He brought back pictures I still have. They used them in the jungle over there, building roads and carrying supplies. They were fighting the Japs."

"You want to see these ones?" said Murray, opening his door and hopping down.

"I'm crazy about elephants," said the trooper. He came around the front of the cab to the passenger side. The cruiser had its flashers on; drivers slowed as they passed, hoping for a glimpse of misfortune.

"These ones from Africa, or where?"

"They're Asians. One's from Burma, the other's from Thailand."

"Had them very long?"

"Twenty-five years," said Murray, opening the gates on the side of the trailer. "Pretty well their whole lives."

"Man, what a smell."

"Essence of pachyderm," said Murray.

Tory, curious about the trooper, snaked her trunk out leisurely. The trooper took a cautious step back.

"She's okay. Stay on that side, though. The other one, you don't want to get too close to her. She might take a swing at you."

Tory began sniffing the trooper. He submitted stiffly, like a kid in a funhouse. "Ever hear about that guy hiding his elephants?" he said, trying to pet Tory's trunk while she checked his pockets. "There was something in the paper, two, three years ago must have been. New Jersey, I think it was."

"Sure I did," said Murray, fishing for a Camel and turning away, as if from the turbulence of the traffic. His hand shook and he needed a few tries to strike a match. Thank God the rig had California tags.

"Everybody in the animal business heard about that guy," said Michael, who'd climbed down to join them.

"You wonder how you'd hide them," said the trooper as Tory gave him a going-over, sniffing his leather, checking his bulges.

"He was a Jew," said Michael. "Prolly put them funny little hats on them and pretended they were rabbis."

"Sure thing." The trooper chuckled. "If I remember, they disappeared into Mexico. Maybe they grew droopy mustaches and picked up a couple of sombreros."

"Big sombreros," said Michael. "Them ones people bring back that take up the whole wall in the rec room."

"I always wondered who those were for," said the trooper.

"You know the other thing he could have done? Paint them black and white and put them in a dairy herd."

"Imagine trying to milk one of these guys?" said the trooper.

"Girls," said Murray. "They're females."

"Well, excuse me, Shirley," the trooper said to Tory. "I hope they're not easily offended."

"You got an apple or some candy or something?" said Murray. "She's a mooch."

The trooper petted Tory's trunk. "Sorry, miss, nothing for you. I'm real crazy about elephants," he said. "My uncle used to tell us stories about them when we were kids. They cleared airstrips, moved artillery, you name it."

"These ones ain't war vets, but I could tell you a few stories myself."

The trooper took Michael's ID back to the cruiser. He seemed to spend an inordinately long time on the radio. Murray began telling himself it wouldn't be so bad. After living in the trailer with the girls for four years, a jail cell and three square meals had a certain appeal.

But what about the girls? What would happen to them?

To Murray's surprise, the trooper returned in the same light-hearted mood. He handed back the ID, took off his hat, and stood there inspecting the brim. His blond hair, cropped short, was already thinning on top. He seemed embarrassed.

"Hope I'm not out of line," he said, "but I'm just getting off shift and I only live six or seven miles from here and I wondered if you'd want to come out to the house. Wife'll make breakfast and my kids could see the elephants. They've only ever seen elephants on TV."

Murray raised his eyebrows at Michael, buying time.

Michael shrugged. "Guess we better go, huh? Otherwise he might arrest us."

Michael and the trooper shared a laugh.

"Appreciate the offer," said Murray, closing up the trailer. "We could use some breakfast, but we better keep going."

"Well, worth a try," said the trooper, putting his hat back on. "No harm done."

"Maybe next time we come through," said Murray.

"Nice of you to ask," said Michael.

"Take it easy now," said the trooper, making for his cruiser. He stopped. "Hey, the brake lights on your trailer? Fix them first chance you get, will you?"

While Murray was trucking southwest toward Texas, Dick Drake was heading northeast toward Canada. A friend had called him to report that two female Asians had crossed the Canadian border in odd circumstances. The friend, lining up animals for a Goldie Hawn picture, *Bird on a Wire*, had learned of a Canadian importer who knew how to bring exotics in without an inspection. The importer had apparently found two border crossings in Quebec where the authorities could be evaded.

Dick had earlier been convinced that the elephants were in Canada; he'd also heard rumors of two elephants having turned up mysteriously at the zoo in Bowmanville, Ontario; and he'd been told that Michael Hackenberger, the trainer at the Bowmanville zoo, had good contacts and knew everyone's business. Recently, word had also come through the grapevine that Hackenberger was one of the people who'd talked to Murray, or someone acting on Murray's behalf, about transporting the stolen elephants. Dick had a strong feeling that Murray and the elephants were in southern Ontario.

He would have asked the New Jersey State Police to alert the Canadian authorities, but lately they'd been totally useless. Dick was unaware that Detective Glenn Miller was about to file his last report on the case—"All attempts by the undersigned have been negative to locate the subject. For this reason the case will be placed in the station fugitive file and considered closed"— but the news would not have surprised him. The only offer of assistance he'd received in the past year had come from a trooper who'd said he had friends who might be able to find the elephants. They'd be working unofficially, of course, on their days off. Meaning, Dick assumed, that they couldn't be expected to work for nothing.

The only way to check out Bowmanville was in person. Which was fine, since there were other places in the area Dick wanted to see—African Lion Safari, Marineland in Niagara Falls, Rockton Game Farm, and the Metropolitan Toronto Zoo. Broke as ever, he borrowed money from friends and a credit card from Eddie's wife, kissed Doy good-bye, and set off across the continent. He'd lost track of the number of trips he'd made, but it was well over a dozen; he could almost have followed the interstates in his sleep. He drove straight through, stopping only for fuel and fast food and, when he nodded off at the wheel, an hour's snooze. At Dot's place in New Jersey he had a beer with Bill and Alex, climbed into bed, and slept for a day and a half. Then he got the Ranchero serviced and headed for the Canadian border.

"Welcome to Texas," said Bucky Steele. "Goddamn, I hardly would have recognized you. With that hair and beard, you look like Rip van Winkle."

"Feel like him, too," said Murray, shaking hands. "Good to be here, Bucky. Where do we spot the rig?"

"Put your stuff in that trailer and I'll show you around."

Bucky had eighty-one acres of sandy red soil and pine woods outside Jefferson in northeast Texas, near the Arkansas and Louisiana borders. He had moved from the Dallas area, and was building a log home for his family and a barn for his three Asian females. A legendary elephant man, he lived in a road-house trailer on the property with his latest wife, Bonnie, and her two kids.

Murray, delighted to be someplace new, full of energy and optimism, felt deeply grateful to Bucky and Bonnie. He gave them painted switch plates, a pigeon planter, and a fungus decorated with elephants. He bunked in a semi-trailer with a kid named Bill, who worked for Bucky. Not ideal, and the facilities were rudimentary—they washed in cold water from an outdoor spigot and built themselves an outhouse—but he didn't plan to stay long. The prospect of crossing into Mexico was invigoratingly real. With Bucky's help, he'd be gone by spring. Meantime, the winter was mild enough and his aches and pains seemed to have retreated.

Jefferson, seven miles away, had a sleepy quality that belied its history. Before the Civil War, a blockage in the Red River had backed water up into Cypress Bayou, enabling steamboats to navigate all the way up to Jefferson. The town thrived as an important commercial center, boasting a population in its heyday of more than 25,000 people. Cotton from Louisiana, southwestern Arkansas, and East Texas passed through its scales. Jefferson became home to the first artificial-ice plant in the United States, and the first sitting of a federal court in Texas.

The removal of the natural dam on the Red River started the town's demise. Without the river commerce, it shrank to half its former size. An oil boom in the 1930s briefly revived its fortunes, but it wasn't until the Corps of Engineers built Lake of the Pines in the 1960s that Jefferson found its present identity as a collection of bed-and-breakfasts and antique stores, a thriving little tourist trap in a county that's two-thirds black and mostly poor.

Given the tourist trade, Murray thought he might have some luck selling his knickknacks. Meantime, he gave Bucky a hand finishing the barn, and they moved all the girls inside—Tory and Dutchess, Zola, Chang, and Lulu—before turning their attention to the log home. Each morning Murray watered, fed, and shoveled up after the girls, then worked on the house alongside the contractors and the help. Bonnie sent lunch and supper down to the trailer; seemed like circus winter quarters all over again. Bucky had a couple of beers in the evening but seemed to be in control.

Murray was happier than he'd been in years, especially after arranging to have his own little Starcraft trailer brought from Missouri. Too derelict to be towed, it was trucked on a flatbed. Bucky wanted it spotted on the slope by the barn; the front end wound up higher than the back, and Murray spent an afternoon getting it blocked and leveled. It was a mess—Robin's ex-husband had rolled it ten years earlier—but he set to work with gusto. He got the gas, water, and electricity hooked up, applied roof topping, caulked the joints, and began evicting insects and rodents. A thorough cleanup and he'd be ready to move into "the mansion."

The trailer had sat in a field for years; it was full of garbage, newspapers, and printed junk. Murray came upon reams of yellowed letterhead that carried a drawing of a chimp's face and the words "Murray Hill Enterprises." There were brochures, schedules, and mimeographed photos of acts he'd worked over the years. Many of the flyers showed the girls with Onyx when they were the Mitie Mites; one shot had been taken after Tory split her trunk. Twenty-some years—he remembered the blood and the panic as if it were yesterday . . .

Heading out of Detroit after a show, he'd stopped for fuel, opened the trailer to check the elephants, and found a scene out of a horror film. Tory's trunk was split like a heron's opened bill, the trailer awash in blood. She often stuck her trunk in Dutchess's mouth; Dutchess must have bitten it.

An elephant's trunk is, in effect, an elongated upper lip that also incorporates the nostrils. It contains sixty thousand different muscles and is used in almost everything the elephant does, as vital as hands to a human. An acute sense of smell helps the elephant determine whether an object is edible. The little "finger" at the tip of the trunk (an African has two such fingers, top and bottom) is highly sensitive and gauges the size, shape, temperature, and texture of the object. The finger, combined with controlled suction, enables the elephant to grasp the object and bring it to its mouth. An elephant can pick up a penny or a half-ton log. In the wild, an injured trunk usually means death by starvation.

Murray had to do something fast. He jumped in the cab and drove 280 miles in less than five hours, white towel ready to signal a medical emergency. Barrel-assing through Chicago at eighty-five miles an hour with an eight-ton load, think he could attract a cop? When he hit the Wisconsin line, thirty miles from the farm, he pulled into a rest area and called Denise. By the time he got home, the local vet, Ralph Smith, was in the barn. Ralph examined the wound while Murray soothed Tory.

"What do you think? Going to have to cut some of it off?"

"We'll sew it up and see what we can save. We can always cut a new finger on the tip if it comes to that."

The bottom fourteen inches had been slit. First they had to clean the wound of hay and dirt and congealed blood. Ralph injected Tory with novocaine, then sewed her trunk while Murray held it. She didn't resist, perhaps understanding that it was for her own good. When they finished stitching, they wrapped her trunk in stretch bandage.

"That ain't going to hold," said Murray. "Soon as she feels better she'll start using it again."

"I know. What do we do?"

Murray stayed with her all night. When she began making tentative use of her trunk, he could only watch helplessly as the bandage turned crimson. In the morning he got Ralph out to sew her again while he called the best elephant people he knew —Les Fisher at Lincoln Park Zoo in Chicago, Dr. Marlo Dittebrant at the Portland zoo, Dr. Ted Reed at the National Zoo in Washington. How do you immobilize the trunk? No one could tell him.

Murray made some diagrams, then began fashioning electrical conduit into a long, narrow cone. Using a headpiecelike harness to keep the contraption in place, he fitted Tory out that night. The thing seemed to restrict her trunk; he went to bed relieved and pleased with himself, but woke to more blood. She'd got out of the sleeve, reopening the wound. Ralph had to sew her a third time.

Everybody helped care for her. Nada got the job of feeding and watering by hand. In the meantime, Murray was busy modifying the sleeve. The new headpiece was solid; if Tory raised her head, her trunk moved with it but not independent of it. He welded eyes to the tip of the sleeve so her trunk could be chained to her feet. It worked well, limiting her range of movement; but they had to unchain her each day so the muscles of her neck wouldn't stiffen or atrophy, and in those few minutes she reopened the wound.

Ralph sewed her again and again, running out of good tissue but gaining half an inch each time. Nada fed and watered her faithfully, keeping her weight up. Finally, after a month, the trunk had healed as much as it would. It still flopped open at the tip, but they'd avoided amputation and Tory was as dextrous as ever. Talk about round-the-clock care. To think of all the hours . . .

But that was then. Here in Texas, the less evidence he kept of his life the better. Retired circus folk lived nearby, people he'd crossed paths with over the years. One of them—Red Hartman, once a lion trainer on Beatty Cole—had already made the connection. "Well, goddamn," Bucky had said to Red, "now that you mention it I do see the resemblance. If you shaved off that beard and subtracted a few years, he would look a bit like Murray Hill." That had seemed to satisfy Red, but a few weeks later Red's son-in-law, who was helping build the log home, said to Bucky, "Is Rip the fella who's hiding his elephants?"

Rip he was now—Van Ripley, when he needed a full name—

and hints of his past only put him and the girls at risk. One evening he made a bonfire behind the mansion and fed the flyers and old photos into the flames, a handful at a time, watching them blacken and curl.

So far things are working out pretty good. Bucky treats me like one of the help and introduces me that way to anyone who asks. He takes care of his girls pretty much the same as I take care of mine, but he keeps his a little warmer than I do. He mixes his own grain, oats, salt, soybean, corn, and bran, and his girls look real good. I think it's better than the prepared grain I've used.

Tory gets along fine with Bucky's girls, but Dutchess doesn't get along too good with the middle one, Chang. I told him she'd try to establish dominance and suggested putting her next to Chang in the barn (they're about the same size), letting them straighten it out between them. But Bucky said no, he couldn't change his line. He likes to do things a certain way, and if you suggest something different he automatically rejects it. When I told him I thought we should have the girls out exercising more, he turned it down. A week later, he said we should take the girls out and run them and work them every day, like it was his idea.

Two days ago I worked on Dutchess's nail again. I removed all the epoxy and it was growing solid near the coronary band. I've got it this far before but always lose it about five-eighths of an inch from the band. The epoxy cracks within twenty-four hours. This time I put a piece of fiberglass cloth across the nail and epoxied it. If this doesn't hold I don't have the slightest idea what to do. But so far so good. It's been forty-eight hours and the epoxy has held.

I've never had so much trouble with the girls' feet. Ever since I took them back from Drakes there's been constant problems with their nails and pads. I wonder what the hell they did in less than a year to affect them so. It looks like this is going to be a lifelong situation.

Bucky Steele's grandfather, an Ohio farmer, used to buy hackney horses in Canada, break them, then sell them to the Amish, who used them for churchgoing on Sunday. Bucky's father, also a horseman, worked on rodeos, put together a liberty act, and wound up on the circus. His mother, an aerialist in her younger days, was looking after the elephants on Russell Brothers Circus when his father met her. Bucky was delivered by his dad in his grandfather's primitive cabin.

As a child, Bucky loved the farm animals and the smell when you took off a saddle, the good clean odor of a sweaty horse. As a teenager, he drove stock trucks and worked in a slaughter-house, where the smells weren't so pleasant. Summers he toured with his dad's Wild West show, mastering the hardscrab-ble arts of roping, sharpshooting, bareback riding, and chuckwagon racing. Each winter his father took Frontier Days to the Philippines; one year he returned from Manila with a young Asian elephant named Stormy.

Bucky had been around elephants before, but Stormy was the first he'd trained. He had a knack, and other owners hired him on. Working elephants, you start hankering for one of your own. Bucky had put together a bear act that he booked on fairs and amusement parks; along the way he kept an eye out for an elephant. His first, Priscilla, he bought from a petting zoo.

Before long he was making his living as an elephant man. He had a real gift for handling touchy animals and he cut some good deals. He bought an unwanted elephant from the zoo in London, Ontario. When a big female Asian killed somebody in Quebec City, he picked her up cheap. An African female caus-ing problems at the Toronto zoo, he bought for a dollar. Over the years he'd had close to a hundred elephants, and he re-membered every one.

Start shooting the breeze with Bucky and he might tell you about the time the new hand—the one nobody liked—got talked into putting iodine on an elephant's wound and was killed on the spot. Or the time a female Asian had a stroke in the rig Bucky was driving: an elephant eight feet tall in a trailer seven feet nine inches wide. Or the time . . .

Like all elephant men, Bucky'd had such a wealth of uncom-mon experiences that people kept telling him he should write a book. He figured it might be a good way to set the record straight—much of what he himself had read about elephants was "boolshit"—and in the 1970s he started work on *Everything You Wanted to Know About an Elephant But Were Afraid to Ask.* Every few years he dug out the manuscript.

"This Iain Douglas-Hamilton book?" he'd say to a visitor, putting on his glasses, wetting his lips with his gums, and paging through a well-thumbed typescript. Bucky's articulation wasn't the best, with those gaps in his teeth, but his voice was deep and resonant. "You ever seen that? I correct some of the boolshit in that one. Here's the part about penises.

" 'The information is surely instilled by the author,' " Bucky would intone, quoting himself, " 'when he states that the bull's penis when chasing the female was four feet eight inches— that's four feet longer than normal. If zero inches were normal in this case, then four foot is slightly above the average. So he must get an awesome thought as to the full measurement of this magnificent bull. Two different passages in the same book refer to the pleasure moans of the bull elephant while in copulation. In over fifty occasions where I worked within arm's length of my breeding bull, the only sounds I heard was the passing of gas, due to lack of manners. He also mentions a seventeen-inch erect clitoris in the same passage in an eight-year-old. In an eight-year-old I've measured only two and three-quarter inches and as a sixteen-year-old measured three and three-quarter inches. I know that at a distance of fifty to a hundred yards in the wild, sound can be distorted, and this type of sighting is something very few people will ever witness. The excitement would tend to stretch the yardstick so to speak in the ballooning eyeballs from accuracy. I'm sorry I had to mention these examples but I just could not stand for this type of exaggeration. I'm sure the female elephant couldn't either.' "

Murray, of course, had stories of his own, and the two men sometimes regaled one another while shoveling out the barn in the morning. Between them they'd worked just about every show and met just about every elephant man, and it was instructive to compare impressions and fill in the gaps. Bucky had been in many foreign countries. Murray had been off the continent only once, having worked briefly in Venezuela. Again he asked about Mexico and getting the girls across the border.

"We'll talk about that," said Bucky, rubbing his forearm, the one they'd set wrong after a winch snapped the bones. "Right now me and Bonnie need to go into town. When you finish spreading the manure, move some of them bales inside. Then put the battery back in the pickup and see if you can get her running."

"Yes, sir!"

United States Department of Agriculture
Animal and Plant Health Inspection Service
Federal Building
Hyattsville, Maryland 20782

Dear Mr. Drake:
Thank you for your letter concerning your loss of two elephants. Because our agency of the U.S. Department of Agriculture (USDA) enforces the Animal Welfare Act (AWA), your letter was referred to us for reply. We understand your desire to recover your animals, and we appreciate this opportunity to clarify the role of the AWA in preventing animal theft.

Although the Act discourages theft by requiring that dealers maintain records concerning the acquisition and disposition of animals, we have no specific authority in the area of animal thefts. From the information you have provided, it appears that this is a civil matter in which local law enforcement authorities have responsibility. . . .

At her house in East Orange, Isabelle Strauss was still fielding calls about her fugitive client—legal inquiries, referrals of other animal-related cases, and requests for interviews. One of the callers, she told Murray when he phoned from Texas, was an attorney in Newark, Mike Caulfield, who'd offered his services in the event of criminal proceedings. His firm, he'd said, encouraged its attorneys to work pro bono on worthy causes.

"Never thought of myself as a worthy cause," said Murray, perched in the kitchen of Bucky's house.

"Let's hope we don't get to that stage," said Strauss. "But it was good of him to call and I said we'd get back to him should the need arise. We go to court again next week."

"Wish there was something I could do."

"I understand from Robin you've changed your location. How are the girls liking their new surroundings?"

Tory and Dutchess were chained in the barn with Zola, Chang, and Lulu. The Rottweiler was scratching fleas; the cockatiels were fighting noisily; Bucky was snoring in front of the TV, beer in hand, while Bonnie gave Kelly and K.W. their lessons. The kids didn't go to school; she taught them at home. "I told you to pay attention. Now, where's the pronouns in this sentence?"

"Totally different setup," said Murray. "The girls are doing all right. I'll call next week to find out what happened."

In her petition to the Appellate Division of the Superior Court of New Jersey, Isabelle Strauss took a new tack, focusing on the issue of abuse and arguing that animals ought to be treated under a different set of rules than those governing inanimate property.

Again Bunce Atkinson appeared on behalf of the Drakes. He had little trouble persuading the court that Judge Farren's dismissal of Strauss's motion for a new trial ought to be upheld. There were no "exceptional and compelling circumstances," he argued, to justify the defendant's failure to appeal the original decision, or else move for a new trial, within a reasonable time. As for Strauss's contention that Murray's attorney had been unaware that ownership of the elephants was at issue—a claim of excusable neglect—here, too, the time limit for the filing of such a motion (one year) had long since passed with no exceptional and compelling circumstances to explain why. Moreover, Atkinson argued, during the trial the question of whether Murray had wrongfully repossessed the elephants had indeed been at issue.

No evidence had been adduced in the original trial to corroborate the claims of abuse; the Appellate Division found no reason for reopening the case on those grounds. As for Strauss's broader argument about the need to view animals in a new way, this amounted to a plea to change the law, an undertaking beyond the power of the court. In its decision, the Appellate Division concluded: "If Seidon was dissatisfied with the result of the trial, he had a right to appeal. Certainly, he had no right to ignore the direction of the court and to abscond with the elephants. Thus, we are in accord with the trial judge that Seidon does not present himself as a fit person for this extraordinary relief, while at the same time being in contempt of court and a fugitive from justice."

Strike three.

Bucky and Bonnie have gone out to do the Gatti show for three weeks, not leaving enough decent hay for the girls. Frank (the carpenter) dropped by to see how I was doing, which I appreciated. He brought me some cigarettes and I gave him one of the nite lights. I showed him my other handicrafts and he said I'd probably sell quite a few at the flea market. Helen (Frank's ex) gave me a bicycle so I don't have to walk every time I go to the store (three miles) or town (seven miles). It needs some work and a new tire but I should be able to get it running.

I've been comparing this place to Howell's. I'm sure happy to be away from those people but there are some things I miss. I miss every once in a while sleeping out in the woods with the girls, I really enjoyed that. I also miss taking them out at night to practice escape routes, so we could find our way in the dark if discovered by the police.

The thing about Howell's was that it was so beautiful. We had an unrestricted area because of the Appalachian Trail. With advance warning we could have got away, with luck maybe even made it all the way to Georgia. At least winter is milder here, and spring came that much sooner. Bucky's hundred acres (approx.) is fenced in. In decent weather I let the girls loose three or four hours a day to eat and roam as they please, but it isn't the same. They don't have the same freedom and there isn't the variety of natural foods there was in New Jersey. I can't feed them properly right now and they can't make it up with their browsing. They've lost weight.

I have, too, I can tell from how my clothes fit. I don't know if it's from not eating or from being sick. The pain on my left side (especially arm and hand) is getting worse. My bad tooth is acting up so I can't chew. Yesterday all I had was a can of soup. My other physical problems are about the same.

The past two nights I haven't got much sleep. Two nights ago I had cramps in my leg all night, last night I had them several times, real bad ones. Also cramps in my rectum. There was quite a storm and I was concerned the mansion would blow over, so I went in the barn with the girls. The heavy winds only lasted about an hour but they kept me up a long time. We lost our electricity. It's been out at least seven hours, which gives me a problem watering. Without the electricity there is no water. The girls won't drink out of the pond, not that I blame them, mucky as it is. I'm getting concerned. They haven't had water for a day and a half now.

The weather lately has been so bad I've had to keep the girls in the barn. When the lightning lets up, I run them out to eat. The hay's lousy (mold, etc.) and I only have about five bales left. I've got to get more hay in here. Turning them loose for a few hours doesn't seem to be enough. I don't know if they're still losing weight, but they're sure not gaining any. We had tornado warnings all yesterday and now it's flash-flood warnings.

If my situation wasn't serious, it would be laughable. I have no money to buy hay for the girls or feed myself. Bucky told me we'd work something out before I came down here, as I did not mislead him about my situation. But when I tried to talk to him, he kept ducking me until he left to go on the road. Same when I tried to pin him down about Mexico. I've been trying to get hold of J. to ask him about Mexico, but I get no answer.

Last week the fridge went out. I tried to get the propane lit with no success. I went to change the area where the girls were (I only give them one and a half bales now) and I lost one of the clevises. Then I started to take down one of the deer stands on the property. I went up to the top, slipped and landed on my left leg, so I'm limping again. When I fell, I got bit by something (possibly fire ants). Now I have little pus swellings on my left hand. The ticks are also out and I have no protection from them.

Last week I also got a package from Nada. I'd forgot my birthday was

coming up. She sent some cash, underwear, a card, and some N. Yorker
mags. I don't know why, but I cried for a while.

Tomorrow is May 4, 1989, five years since I went into hiding. I
sometimes wonder, has it been worth it? I don't mean not having money
or my physical problems. You learn quick in my situation that all you
need is a roof and enough food to survive. The hard part is missing my
sons' graduation, my daughters' weddings, not seeing Ian grow up, not
having contact with people who mean something to me. Speaking for
myself, the answer would have to be no, it hasn't been worth it. But
when I see the girls under no stress, enjoying themselves, that's what
makes it worthwhile.

But lately they're feeling the strain, too. They're down a fair amount
of weight. I've had nothing but trouble with their feet, and Tory's had an
infection in her eye. Dutchess's nail finally seems to be doing better. It is
now about a third solid. I can't see the bottom two-thirds as the epoxy
covers the nail. I think the fiberglass across the crack is doing the trick,
at least I hope so.

One morning soon after Bucky and his family got back, Kelly
came running over to the mansion, where Murray was painting
elephant heads on a pair of eggshell earrings. A lovely little girl,
with Bonnie's blond hair and clear skin, she banged on the
door, red-eyed and sobbing.

"Rip! Come quick! There's a fire!"

The kids had found an old lighter in the grass and shown it
to him. Unable to make it spark, he'd given it back. It turned
out they'd started a fire in the pine needles. A black circle on
the ground, edged in red, was slowly expanding, and Murray
set the kids to work, fetching gunnysacks and a shovel. He
smothered the fire with the gunnysacks while they dug a
trench. To teach them a lesson, he worked them hard. When
the fire was out, he told them Bucky would notice and they'd
best go tell him what had happened.

Kelly was terrified. "Do we have to?"

Poor kids. Bucky was strict as hell with them, treating them
the way he himself had been raised. His father had shipped him

off to military school in Virginia and had run the household along similarly rigid lines. Some things you could do; some things you got your hide whipped for doing. Slip down in a hog pen full of sows and you might get eaten—that's why you got a butt-paddling for going near the pen. As a kid, Bucky took orders. Now he gave them, and expected obedience. When he wanted something done, he wanted it done now. He called K.W., who was four, "boy." Both children addressed him as "sir."

And Murray's children figured he'd been tough? Hell, he'd been a pussycat by comparison. Kelly and K.W. were real sweet kids, but Bucky rode them constantly, expecting them to act like adults. No wonder they were fearful of telling him about the fire. He was certain to chew them out, or worse, and what could Murray do? Not a damn thing. He had no right to comment on the way Bucky treated the children; but that didn't mean he had to like it.

He didn't like Bucky's drinking, either. Bonnie had misled him, or else Bucky's good intentions hadn't amounted to much. From what Murray could see, when Bucky felt pressured he got drunk, and when he got drunk he turned mean. All Murray could do was pick his spots and let Bucky set the tone. If he was moody and withdrawn, best stay out of his way. If he wanted to talk, fine. If he insisted on treating Murray as nothing more than hired help, that was his privilege. It made the atmosphere at the farm unpleasant, though, and Murray figured it was time to get out.

When he again raised the subject of Mexico, Bucky was evasive and discouraging. Even since the CITES (Convention on International Trade in Endangered Species of Wild Fauna and Flora) agreement came in, restricting the movement of elephants and endangered species, he said, everything had been tightened. You had U.S. authorities giving you a hard time at the border, and now the Mexicans shook you down as well, doing an inspection every time you crossed. Naw, he said, Mexico wasn't a good idea.

What the hell, that wasn't what he'd been saying when Murray and the girls were in New Jersey. On the phone Bucky had made it sound like it was just a matter of a bribe here and there. Could things have changed that much in six months, or was it Bucky's story that had changed? He had a reputation for picking up reject elephants and making something of them, selling at a handsome profit. Murray couldn't help wondering why he'd been invited down. Had Bucky, too, figured on ending up with the girls?

A few days later, shoveling out the barn, Bucky asked if Murray would be interested in going to Israel. Bucky knew somebody who was building a park in Israel and wanted to put in elephant rides. Murray said he might consider it if there was a way of getting the girls safely out of the country. Bucky said it could probably be arranged, which Murray found baffling. Good luck getting them to Mexico, but no problem making it to Israel? Bucky's stories didn't add up, and Murray's attitude was turning from gratitude to hostile skepticism.

Since learning of the appellate court's decision—and understanding, finally, that the legal system was never going to help him—Murray had been toying with a scheme of his own. What about hiding the girls in transit, building a partition in the fifth wheel and hauling them across the Mexican border with a load of horses? If you piled bales of hay against the partition it would look like the whole front of the trailer was filled with hay.

Bucky said it wouldn't work. Blocking off so much space would look fishy, and the weight would tip them off. Besides, how would you keep them from racking? Drug 'em? Naw, that plan was boolshit, but Bucky had an idea for making some money. He'd been working his own girls on Reid Brothers the past few years. Maybe the Reids would pay an extra five hundred a week to add two elephants to his three. Maybe they'd like a five-act.

Murray was in no mood to go on the road, fearing he'd be recognized, and he'd prefer that the girls not work. But Bucky treated his elephants well—Tory and Dutchess would be cared for—and the money would certainly be useful. Murray could look after their place while they were away. Sure, he said, find out what they think of a five-act; Bucky said he would.

And that was the end of it. Murray waited, but Bucky never raised the matter again. The man could be downright infuriating. He'd mentioned an attorney in Dallas who might be of help, promising to put Murray in touch. It had been months before he came across with the name, and the attorney in question was a district attorney! Did Bucky not understand? Didn't he realize that Murray might just as well turn himself in?

Or was that the idea?

U.S. Department of Justice
Federal Bureau of Investigation
Washington, D.C. 20535

Dear Mr. Drake:
Your correspondence to President Reagan regarding the theft of your two elephants has been referred to FBI Headquarters. Unfortunately we are unable to determine from a review of your letter and enclosures whether your concern falls within the investigative jurisdiction of the FBI . . .

Before going out with Reid Brothers, Bucky holed up in the house and tried to sort out the mess he'd got himself into. Murray's labor in return for room and board had seemed like a good idea—Murray knew how to do a lot of things, and Bucky had things needing to be done. But the little guy was turning out to be more trouble than he was worth. Bucky's son from a previous marriage, Bobby, had said there was a rumor going around Florida that Murray was at Bucky's place. Meanwhile, Murray takes his girls down to the lake and they tear up the willow trees Bucky's dad had planted on his last visit. And he gives the kids a cigarette lighter to play with! How dumb can you get? Lucky they didn't burn the barn down. What the hell, when you open your home to somebody, you figure at least they'll respect it. You're paying for his electric and groceries and propane, you're feeding his elephants, and he's down there burning initials into walking sticks and making elephant-head coat hangers and watching the little color TV you give 'im . . .

Plus you got new worries. Helen down the road calls to say the USDA inspector has been asking directions to Bucky's. Sure enough, the inspector shows up and Bucky has to keep her busy in the house while Murray hustles Tory and Dutchess into the woods, hays them and chains them and sneaks back into the mansion to hide out. The inspector hangs around all afternoon. Finally she goes to the barn to look at Zola, Chang, and Lulu. There's no problem, she's reasonable enough, not like some you get, but this cloak-and-dagger boolshit, who needs it?

With Murray around, there's all kinds of funny stuff going on. Fresh tire tracks in the driveway—somebody's come right through the gate, past the NO TRESPASSING sign and up to the house before turning around and heading out again. Kelly answers the phone one night and somebody asks, "Is there a Murray Hill there?" Kelly knows him only as Rip, and she gives the phone to Bonnie. The caller, whoever the hell it is, hangs up.

Meanwhile Murray's all depressed because the court told him to screw off and his latest buyout deal fell through. He finds a place in Jefferson willing to sell his handicrafts and spends hours in the mansion working on his stuff, but if he's making any money he sure ain't saying nothing about it. He wants an extension phone in the mansion and he's out of propane and he wouldn't mind a ride next time you're heading into town and you know he's about to hit you up again and it's enough to make you grab a six-pack and turn on the TV and wish to hell the problem would go away. . . .

One evening Bonnie walked down to the mansion and knocked on the door. Murray was doing his wood-burning artwork. They were heading out in a couple of days, she said, and wondered if he'd mind looking after her cockatiels. And Tillie, of course, the stray mutt she'd taken in. And the kids' turtles. Murray could hardly refuse, though he was already looking after Robert's trained bear, and Greta the Rottweiler, as well as Bucky's cattle, horses, and mules, to say nothing of Tory and Dutchess.

"We sure would appreciate it."

"Hell, I could almost put together my own show."

And by the way, Murray, Bucky wondered if you could take down the rest of the deer stands on the property and put new spark plugs in the pickup and fix the cattle guard and . . .

Bonnie told me Bucky would phone every Monday night at seven o'clock so I could let him know what's going on. Last night I waited outside the house until eight and he never called—that's three weeks in a row. I sure don't understand people. I'll take the company of elephants anytime.

My potatoes are beginning to rot, so I cut them up and planted them. As I was putting bedding hay around them, something in the hay stung me. I've been stung by all different types of insects, but never this one, whatever it was. The pain was severe for an hour and persisted for seven or eight hours. Then there was numbness. This morning it feels normal. There never was any swelling.

Yesterday I started having trouble with my remaining teeth again. I rely on the aspirin to kill the pain. It helps up to a point. I couldn't chew so all I had yesterday was some soup. I took eight aspirin but by the time I went to bed they didn't help at all. I dozed off for maybe forty-five minutes last night but the rest of the time I was up. Today I've tried to nap but no sooner do I drop off than the pain wakes me. It has now moved into my left ear also. This past week I have also broken out in sores on my back, plus none of my other problems have lessened.

Tillie's got fleas, so I'm scratching like crazy. She's a good dog but I sure don't need anything else to get attached to right now. I clean the cockatiels' cage and the turtles' aquarium every other day. Yesterday, as I usually do, I put the turtles in a mud hole while cleaning the aquarium. When I went to put them back, one was missing and I haven't been able to find it. I dug a hole a foot deeper than the mud and couldn't find it anywhere. I gave up searching after an hour. I feel real bad because it's the kids' turtle.

I've got to build a fence around the well house, as the girls have eaten the shingles off the roof. I notice when I turn them loose they go eat at the same spot every day, same time of day, until the supply is exhausted. Then they roam until they find a new spot for that particular time of day. I also notice that they dig for the roots of certain trees.

I continue to treat Dutchess's toenail which is slowly improving. I've put a piece of wire across the crack (baling wire, about an inch long) plus the fiberglass cloth, like a bridge, then a heavy layer of epoxy over that. The epoxy adheres to the nail for several weeks before breaking away in sections. I'm now more than halfway down the nail with no signs of cracking, the best I've been able to do with that nail so far.

I planted gourds and cucumbers out back and they're really coming along. I use old manure, at least a foot thick on top of hard red clay. I don't have to tend it at all. So far I've harvested ten cucumbers weighing about a pound each. I'm giving them away to Frank and anyone else who wants them as there's no way I could eat that many. I'm going to have bushels of them. That elephant shit sure does wonders.

Playing circus dates, you work so goddamn hard—unloading, setting up, doing the show, keeping an eye peeled for accidents and trouble and idiots who want to pet the elephants—you don't have time to think. Then you tear down and load up and set off and it's late and everybody else is sleeping and you keep that white line on your left and there's nothing to do *but* think . . .

Here they'd been trying to get the fence finished before leaving and not only does the little son of a bitch make himself scarce when there's heavy work to be done—bad back, some boolshit like that—he blabs away to everybody who's being paid cash. Murray's supposed to be putting the wire clips on the fence, Frank's supposed to be doing the carpentry, and where does Bucky find them? Sitting on the step, having a smoke and laughing at some goddamn story about the time Murray upstaged Johnny Carson on *The Tonight Show*. Half a dozen butts underfoot and they're still gabbing like Greek widows. Oh, he's great with the stories; next time Bucky walks by he's telling Frank about the time he talked a Shriner into putting six inches of fresh elephant manure on his lawn. Anybody around here remember who's paying the freight? Anybody understand the significance of the term "hourly wage"?

And them goddamn girls of his, knocking down the trees and

tearing shingles off the well house and bothering Bucky's girls every chance they get. In all his years Bucky had never seen an elephant that couldn't be made compatible with another herd. He'd mixed herds many times—once put three together, fifteen elephants in all, and it wasn't two days before they'd worked out where they stood in relation to each other, dominant or accepting domination.

Not Dutchess, no sir; nine months on the property and she was still as cantankerous as Murray himself. She was so goddamn sneaky she had the other girls permanently riled. She'd already got one tail and it must have been her who munched Tory's ear, poor little thing, trunk tore up and half her goddamn ear missing. Even after the five of them had spent all that time together, Dutchess was still the instigator, taking shots at Chang. Physically she couldn't do shit—she was underfed and scrawny, though at least she wasn't as pathetic as Tory, who hobbled like a crippled old lady—and yet she sneaked around biting tails and ears every chance she got. Hell, she was going to get hurt if she kept it up, any fool could see that, and of course Murray'd lay the blame at somebody else's doorstep being as how he himself had never been wrong about a goddamn thing in his life. Man oh man, Bucky could just see it coming. . . .

Sure enough, one day Dutchess pulled that shit on Zola and old Zola put the hammer on her, turned her over. Things were getting a little rough. Just dumb luck Bucky was around, otherwise Zola would have downed her and browned her, no doubt about it. Bucky didn't call her off, exactly, he told her don't go breaking no goddamn leg or nothing, just pop her a couple good ones. Zola's got to have a thousand pounds on her, gives her a pretty good whack and what does Dutchess do? Comes right back and bites her tail again! Just what Bucky needed, a goddamn war on his hands. Murray's elephants were getting as crazy as he was.

Why in hell should Bucky have to worry about somebody else's animals when he had his hands full with his own? "Tell you this much," he said to Bonnie, who'd woken up to check the children as Bucky wheeled the semi through the Idaho night. "Once we get back home, the boolshit is going to stop right smartly or there's going to be some changes made."

The fifth annual Indian Hill Powwow, at the end of June, had been a roaring success. The weather had been ideal and Doy had put together a magical weekend of native crafts, dances, stories, and music. In five years the event had grown into a major tourist attraction for Tehachapi: the 1989 powwow had raised money for five charities and attracted more than twenty thousand people to the site at Indian Hill.

What a site it was—1,200 acres with five lakes, a beaver pond, and panoramic vistas. Autumn days were hot and dry, nights crisp and lit by great frozen whorls of stars. The people who'd been running the campground weren't very industrious; when their lease came up, the owner, impressed by the powwow, asked if Dick and Doy wanted to manage the property full-time. If they did so well in summer, maybe they could get the place humming year round. He offered to lease them the whole works, house included, for five years, with an option for another five, at five hundred a month plus a percentage of revenue over $150,000.

The deal would give Dick and Doy a gorgeous spot to live with abundant room for their horses and spectacular country for riding. They both enjoyed having family around and they could see the day when the kids would move trailers onto the property. One day, Dick was sure, they'd get Tory and Dutchess back, and there were ideal spots for a barn and a corral. Dick's log-home business was going nowhere; every month was the same old juggling act. Bunce Atkinson still hadn't been paid and he'd racked up more hours fighting Isabelle Strauss. Meanwhile, the finance company that held the second mortgage on Cameron Canyon was again threatening to foreclose.

Here was a chance to make good money in return for hard work and imagination. They'd be their own bosses. They still had time to get the house in shape for winter; then Dick could start upgrading the roads, adding more campsites and RV hookups, and exploiting their powwow mailing list. The military used the property for war games; perhaps other organizations could be brought in. Dick was a thirty-second-degree Mason and the Masonic order was a great source of contacts. He could run the grader and the backhoe, get the water system working and the place in shape; Doy was marvelous at organizing and managing, and she'd learned to use a computer. Their youngest, Donna, who lived at home, could answer the phone and greet people who pulled in; and Doy's nephew Bobby, whom they'd raised as their own, was handy in a dozen ways. Kenny and his family could stay on at Cameron, and Doy could continue to wait tables until the campground gave them adequate income.

"What do you say?" said Dick. "Shall we give it a shot?"

"Let's go for it, honey."

Lately I've had more thoughts of turning myself in. I sure could use medical and dental attention. The problem is the girls. I just can't see giving up and returning them to Drakes, but I've got to find some way to feed them properly. Bucky didn't leave me enough hay and now I've stopped graining them, money's getting too short. They're underweight but still not too bad. I'm down to my last hundred dollars in the safety money I was hoping I wouldn't have to touch.

Yesterday I was out with them all afternoon. They played and had some fun, but they're not as happy here as they were in New Jersey. At one point they headed for the lake, so I ran them over to the pond (which they don't like). As we went past the lake I saw the little turtle that escaped a couple of months ago. As soon as it saw me it dove deep. It made me feel good that it was free and surviving on its own.

I've started rationing my food (eat once a day) and I'm real tired of peanut butter and jam. Friday morning I was cycling to the convenience store for a loaf of bread when R. drove by and said he was going to the flea market. I went back to Bucky's, put out hay for the cattle, and chained the girls in the woods in case anyone came on the property, then R. picked me up.

The flea market is about seven miles down the road. We were set up by

11:30 A.M. and stayed until 5 P.M., sweating in the hot sun. We were the only ones outside, everyone else had a spot inside. It's an old barn and the spots are separated by chicken wire. The whole time I was there I only saw one person and didn't sell a thing. The place has only been open a month and everybody said it was a Saturday and Sunday spot. I had to dip into the safety money again to get something to eat.

I can hold out until Bucky gets back, but then I'm going to need a lot of things and unless something changes he's not coming up with anything. I feel like I'm getting pressure from him and I still don't understand why he invited me down unless he was figuring on getting the girls cheap. He knew my situation all along. He knows I can't just pack up and leave. If I could just make a little something on the side I'd be all right. I'll go back to the flea market and try again today.

Heading home with Bonnie and the kids, burned out from the road, Bucky wondered how the hell he'd got himself into such a fix. If he'd known the situation was going to stretch out so long, he never would have invited Murray down. Helping out had been the thing to do—Murray would have done the same, elephant men had to hang together—but this was ridiculous. The weather had changed, October was here and winter was coming. The feed bill kept growing, and all the talk about selling to a third party or getting the whole deal back in court, well, it amounted to so much hot air. Murray kept bringing up the Mexico boolshit and Bucky kept telling him things ain't what they used to be and somehow a friendly gesture had turned Murray's problem into Bucky's problem.

"I'm supposed to keep on with the handouts while his own goddamn kids, all of 'em got jobs . . ."

"A ten-dollar bill every week wouldn't hurt," Bonnie agreed.

"But nobody says nothing about that, no sir. Good old Bucky'll bail him out."

"I don't know why you should be the one."

And what does Murray do? Makes all these trinkets and crap —they're nice, really, and Bucky's proud to have them in his circus room along with his collection of memorabilia and huge plywood cutouts of Canada, the U.S., and Mexico showing all the dates he's ever played—but they don't bring in enough for the goddamn worm medicine, never mind keeping the elephants fed. Murray had explained he was broke, sure, but how was Bucky to know he'd be content to stay that way indefinitely?

"You can help somebody for a while, but when it's coming up a year . . ."

"How much responsibility can you take for someone else?" Bonnie agreed.

What about all the money him and Drake must have pissed away on lawyers? Hell, they could have used that money to settle things. This wasn't a dispute over two elephants no more, this was a vendetta they'd carry on all their lives.

Bucky was fifty years old now, and he found the road more taxing every time out. Coming home was something he used to look forward to; the idea of finding the little guy still there, still mooching, still miserable—shee-it, it was too depressing to contemplate. Some people, give them a hand and you end up losing an arm. Enough of this goodwill boolshit. Something had to be done, that's all there was to it.

I went back to the flea market yesterday and set up about thirty feet from the building where I could be seen from the road (the only outside exhibitor again), but the sun was miserable and the change of location didn't help at all. I was there five hours and didn't sell a thing. I used up the last of my safety money to get something to eat.

When I got back home the little dog (Tillie) was gone and I haven't seen her since. I'm not sorry, as I'm still scratching from her but I didn't have the heart to kick her out.

I got up at 2:15 A.M. to urinate (still urinating four or five times a nite) and noticed that Bucky and the others had just pulled in. When I saw him and Bonnie this morning I asked if his insurance company got ahold of him, as they had called here the other day. Seems Texas has a new law that you have to keep your insurance up even if you're not using your tractor. Boy, if that isn't a bureaucratic shakedown.

That's all that was said, so I left. Bonnie didn't even offer me a cup

*of coffee. Whenever I saw them today I got the feeling there was a bigger
wall between us than before. Any conversation that occurred was initi-
ated by me. I told Bucky I'd been watering my girls back by the elephant
corral and they were drinking very well, but he didn't say anything and
he brought his girls into the barn to water last night. Mostly he avoids
me and obviously prefers having no communication at all.*

*Kelly came down here to ask me about my gourds, and I got the
feeling they sent her down to check on me, see what I was doing. I also
notice Bonnie didn't make supper for me. I can't see this situation continuing under the present conditions. I sure hope I'm not getting paranoid. . . .*

"Indian Hill Campground."

"Dick there?"

"You know, I'm not sure if he's left yet," said Doy. "Who's
calling?"

"A friend with some information."

"I'll see if he's still here."

Dick, four feet away, eating supper, lifted his eyebrows. Doy
shrugged. Dick set down his knife and fork and took the receiver.

"Dick Drake."

"You don't know me, Dick, but let's suppose somebody could
tell you where those two elephants are at. Would that be useful
information to you?"

Dick had lost track of all the calls he'd had over the years—
people who knew where they were, people wanting to buy them
for thirty cents on the dollar, people who'd spotted Murray on
a carnival in Quebec. People who wondered about a finder's
fee, people who said Murray'd had plastic surgery, people
who'd heard the elephants were dead. Still, there was something about this young fellow's voice. He sounded nervous and
tentative and ashamed. Dick signaled his daughter—something
to write on.

"Yes, sir, sure would be useful."

"I was just wondering, what sort of value would that have?"

"Tell you what," said Dick, "I couldn't say off the top of my head, this being kind of sudden and all, my son and I, he's up in Oregon right now, they're really his elephants, we'd have to give it some thought and get back to you on that. Where can I reach you?"

"Don't let's get ahead of ourselves. Now, suppose those elephants were on somebody's property. Would there be a way for you to take them back, protecting the person?"

"Well," said Dick, "I think we could probably work out something along those lines. . . ."

"I'd have to know the person who owned the place wouldn't get involved."

"Like I said, probably work that out."

"Not probably, definitely."

"It wouldn't be a problem," said Dick.

"Now, from what I've read, I understand you've spent a lot of time looking for your elephants."

"Drove all across the country many, many times. I've been as far as Miami, Florida, and Sydney, Nova Scotia. You know where that's at?"

"It'd be real helpful if somebody could tell you where to look."

"Provided we got 'em back, safe and sound."

"They'd be saving you a lot of trouble and worry—"

"Be a load off our mind, all right."

"—and money."

"Well, now," said Dick, with his nervous laugh, "I tell you, if you want to know the truth, things are a little tight around here this month, being as how we've already sunk so much into this thing."

"I mean, when you read in the paper where somebody lost their pet and you find it for them, you generally get something for your trouble. Isn't that the way it works?"

12

BLESS THE BEASTS

Like immortal flowers they have drifted down to us on the ocean of time, and their strangeness and beauty bring to our imaginations a dream and a picture of that unknown world, immeasurably far removed, where man was not. . . .

W. H. Hudson

▼ ▼ ▼ ▼ ▼ ▼ ▼ ▼ ▼ ▼ ▼ ▼ ▼ ▼

The sheriff was a pale-eyed, lumbering fellow near retirement age, good two hundred and forty pounds, with neatly trimmed white hair showing under his Stetson. Maybe quicker than he looked, but he couldn't have had much endurance. The deputies were both heavyset men over six feet. The older one had a beer belly and an air of being impossible to amuse. In a sprint, his age and size would have offset his determination in no time. The younger one might have gone straight from high-school football to law enforcement—solid as a medicine ball, straining the seams of his uniform. They waited at Bucky's front gate, impassive men in tan uniforms and cowboy boots.

If Murray made for the woods, ran flat out, he'd have a chance. If his bad leg held . . . if he stayed on his feet . . . if

▲ ▲ ▲ ▲ ▲ ▲ ▲ ▲ ▲ ▲ ▲ ▲ ▲ ▲

they didn't shoot him . . . if the young one didn't take him in the first hundred yards . . .

Sheriff Walter Thomas and deputies Eugene Tefteller and Ed Baird watched the approach of the blond woman and the little man. He was a wild-looking character, skinny as a goose neck, with straggly white hair and beard. They'd talked it through in the car, always did before an arrest. What if he goes? Sixty years old, according to the warrant. No Carl Lewis, but he didn't have an ounce of fat. He'd head south and wind up in Big Cypress Bayou, where Ed Baird had done a lot of fishing and squirrel hunting. Might make it in, but he wouldn't make it out. Use dogs, if it came to that. . . .

Murray tried not to limp, matching his pace to Bonnie's. His leg pained him terribly. He'd reach the woods before they could even get on the radio. The one on the right, that was the one he'd have to beat.

Sheriff Thomas took off his Stetson as they approached, squinted through steel-rimmed glasses in a grandfatherly way. The idea was to minimize the people's anxiety.

If his leg held—now was the time—if he made it to the woods . . . *What are you waiting for? Go!*

What was he thinking? He didn't know the area like they did. All he knew was Bucky's property. Even if he made it into the bayou, where would he head? What of the girls? What would be the point? These five years had been for Tory and Dutchess. He'd done what he could. An ancient voice came to him, Denise's. *Don't do anything stupid, Murray.*

"Is your name Arlan Seidon?"

He looked at Bonnie, who'd fetched him from the mansion. She was the one who seemed nervous. She wiped her hands on her jeans, looked anxiously about for her children.

"My name's Van Ripley."

There was a moment of awkwardness. Bonnie started up the drive. Sheriff Thomas waited until she was out of earshot.

"Do you know Murray Hill?"

"I know him, all right."

"Ever been in New Jersey?"

"Sure. I've also been in Arizona and Montana and pretty near every other state."

"Do you have identification?"

"Not since Dutchess ate it."

Sheriff Thomas and Deputy Baird exchanged glances. "Would you mind coming with us? We'll need to confirm your identity."

"You make it sound like I got a choice."

When the sheriff asked me to go to town, I figured the Drakes must be around. Sure enough, when I got to the jail in Jefferson (Marion County), they were waiting in a pickup. Dick asked how I was doing as they took me inside. "Just fine," I said with disgust, and turned my back on them.

I told the sheriff who I was. I said Bucky and Bonnie didn't know what was going on and I wanted to keep it that way. After I went through the paperwork, mugshots, etc. I was given one of the prisoner uniforms (orange jumpsuit) and taken upstairs. My cell is part of a unit with five cells. There are four other prisoners here. The four young men all seem very nice and we've been getting along fine. I feel like a father to them. The one they call Big Mike asked me why I was here. When I told him about the elephants, he wasn't sure if I was putting him on.

The food is not too bad. In the morning they bring a muffin, fried egg, sausage, and coffee. For lunch they get a meal (not big, but adequate) from the local restaurant. Supper consists of a heated TV dinner. Even being a small man in stature, I don't believe the supper is sufficient in volume. The exercise program is very poor. Really it's just a break from the cell to have a cigarette, but this is only allowed three times a week. What I really miss is fresh air (got a bad headache right now). Now I know what my chimps used to feel like in their cages.

For me, it's a relief to be caught. I was at the end of the line. I did what I could. But it tears me up, thinking of the girls going back to the Drakes. I don't know what I can do to prevent it. Now that I found out the justice system ain't worth shit, where do I turn to get justice? Without the girls I have no bargaining power. They have it all.

I wasn't here long when they brought me downstairs for a phone call from WOR-TV, New Jersey. The woman started with the normal stupid questions, so I cut it short. I understand they didn't use it right away. A big earthquake hit San Francisco and all the coverage is out there right now. Next morning I also did a TV interview with Ch. 12. The gal who did that interview was young but she didn't come up with questions that make me look like an idiot. They shot about twenty minutes of tape and I'm at their mercy. The way they edit it will be important to the way I come across.

The other inmates tell me the food has gotten better since the TV people started nosing around. I guess politics never stops. This morning when the dispatcher came up to check the inmates, I asked if it was possible to get a haircut as I hadn't cut my hair or beard for over two years. It wasn't twenty minutes later they took me off to the barber. I got my hair and beard off and almost felt like a human being.

Bonnie came to visit and ask what I need, as I had locked the mansion before I left. All I could think of was my glasses. I also gave her Robin's number in New York and the number at the farm. So far I haven't heard of anyone asking Bucky about aiding and abetting me. I know for sure someone turned me in, not to the sheriff but to Drake. Several people around here knew my real identity and could have tipped off Drake. But who did it?

When Bonnie visited, her main concern was what I thought as to how the sheriff got onto me. I told her there had been rumors about my location. I asked if she thought it was Bucky's father. She said no, he'd never do anything to hurt Bucky. Since Bucky and Bonnie got back off the road, Bucky went out of his way to avoid me, and the few times we did speak, he wouldn't make eye contact. It was three days before he showed up here. When he came to visit he left a pack of smokes for me and twenty dollars, but when we were talking (glass between us, phone on each side) he at no time looked me in the eye. Not normal for him. Bonnie also acts strange. I can't say for sure, but I get the feeling he's the one.

More badminton; time for some new attorneys to take up their rackets and hit the shuttlecock back and forth. Dick found a lawyer not two blocks from the jail—Jesse M. DeWare IV, known as Duke to his friends. The DeWares were one of Jefferson's leading families and had seen the town's fortunes wax and wane over the years. Duke, a fifth-generation Jeffersonian and the son of a doctor, had gone to college at The Citadel, in Charleston, South Carolina, moved on to law school at Southern Methodist University, then returned home to hang out his shingle. These days he does a good deal of business law and counts among his clients a number of Swedish and Asian investors. A handsome fellow, smartly tailored, with a fine house west of town and a boutique office on Vale Street, he's the nearest thing to a yuppie you'll find in Jefferson. Dick and Eddie Drake are the furthest things from yuppies that you'll find, but then law, like politics, makes strange bedfellows.

Over in Dallas, meanwhile, an attorney named Mike Aranson had had a call from Isabelle Strauss in New Jersey. Though not an animal-rightist, Aranson was an activist lawyer who had represented some unpopular causes and clients over the years—gay rights, adult theaters, head shops, First Amendment cases. Five minutes into talking with Isabelle Strauss, he figured Murray Hill was somebody he wanted to meet. Murray's bond hearing at the Marion County Courthouse gave him the opportunity.

Most of the people Mike Aranson represented were—well, you wouldn't have them to dinner, put it that way. Murray, now, he was one of a kind—charming little guy, full of stories, fun to shoot the breeze with. There was even a personal connection, sort of. Aranson was from a small town in Oklahoma, and Murray knew the owner of a carnival that used to play the town. The more Aranson learned about Murray's case, the more he was intrigued. The idea of taking off with two elephants? Hiding out with them for five years? With no monetary gain? It blew his mind. Murray was either a great human being —a genuine folk hero—or else a complete nut. Either way, it was bound to be fun.

Murray was broke, of course, but Isabelle Strauss wired down a $2,500 retainer. She also contacted Mike Caulfield, the Newark attorney who, the previous year, had offered his services in the event of criminal proceedings and who turned out to be a remarkable fellow. If all attorneys had been like Mike Caulfield, lawyer jokes would not have been invented. Educated at Jesuit schools in New Jersey, he had considered becoming a priest and done graduate studies in theology in Austria. Along the way, however, he had fallen in love. He wanted to marry and have children, and couldn't reconcile himself to the Catholic demand of celibacy.

Caulfield returned to the United States with his master's degree in pastoral theology. The logical vocation was social work. In New Jersey's Corrections Department, where he spent three years, he enjoyed himself but lacked independence and barely eked out a living. About to turn thirty, he decided to attend law school at Loyola in Chicago. To support his studies he worked nights as a hotel doorman, attending classes by day. When that became too taxing he clerked in a law firm and went to school at night. On graduation in 1984—the year Murray fled with the girls—he returned to New Jersey to work briefly as a prosecutor before joining Meyner & Landis in Newark.

Founded by Robert Meyner, a former New Jersey governor, Meyner & Landis is a small, highly regarded firm that specializes in litigation work for such blue-chip clients as National Westminster Bank, Sealand Corporation, Englehard Chemicals, and Litton Industries. The New Jersey Bar Association encourages its members to do pro bono work; Caulfield filled his calendar with a mixture of lucrative advocacy and benevolent concern. He acted for the Commission for the Blind, the Humane Society, and the New York Rotary Club; he pursued his interest in environmental law and taught evening courses in problem resolution.

And he took on another charitable cause. In tandem with Mike Aranson in Dallas and Isabelle Strauss in East Orange, he began to negotiate on Murray's behalf with the Monmouth County Prosecutor's Office. Caulfield admired people who acted out of deeply held moral conviction; he took it upon himself to find a way to keep Murray from going to prison.

FBI agents with a minimum twenty years' service can retire at age fifty. At age fifty-two, Special Agent George Kieny planned to keep working until mandatory retirement at fifty-seven. Kieny sometimes wore a hearing aid—he'd nearly deafened himself on the firing range—and he'd torn up his knee chasing a suspect, but such injuries were a small price to pay for work he enjoyed. As one of the dozen agents in the Tyler field office of the Dallas division of the FBI, he dealt mainly with personal crimes (kidnappings and extortion), theft (of cattle, tractor-trailers, oil-field equipment), and public corruption (county commissioners taking kickbacks, for example, from the manufacturers of heavy equipment).

Kieny liked the friendly atmosphere of Tyler, a college town of some seventy-five thousand souls. With many friends outside the law-enforcement community, he was less cynical and burnt out than some of his colleagues. Besides, he had unfinished business. In 1983, five people had been abducted from a Kentucky Fried Chicken outlet, taken into the oil fields, and shot in the head. The killers had made it look like robbery, but Kieny knew the murders had resulted from a dispute over a formula for making high-potency methamphetamine. He wanted to see convictions before packing in his career.

Like doctors and therapists, cops can't afford to take on the pain of the people they encounter. In this case, however, it was impossible not to. Three victims had been college freshmen; when Kieny went to interview one young widow, pregnant at the time of her husband's murder, the baby turned out to be the spitting image of the father. Kieny was the father of four kids, one a college freshman. The case made his heart ache. It made him realize he had work to do before retiring.

The frustrating part was that he knew who the killers were and figured he had put together a strong case. But some key physical evidence had prompted disagreement among the forensic experts and caused the local U.S. attorney to doubt whether they had a prosecutable case. Kieny became obsessed, conducting 550 interviews before being told to cease work on the investigation. He wasn't about to forget the case; he planned to see arrests. Perseverance was a quality he prided himself on and admired in others.

One afternoon in late 1989, Dick Drake phoned the Tyler office of the FBI and made an appointment. He brought along a briefcase full of documentation, which Kieny perused as he listened to Dick's story. Perseverance indeed: Dick had made twenty-two separate trips from California, he told Kieny, once putting fifteen thousand miles on the odometer on a single outing. Finally, after five years of looking for his elephants, an anonymous call had brought him to Texas. He and his son had spotted Murray in the Jefferson area, and Murray had been arrested by the sheriff of Marion County. Bail had been set at $100,000, but Mike Aranson had got it reduced to $20,000. A bail bondsman had put up the money less than a week after the arrest; Murray was now back at Bucky Steele's place. The Drakes had obtained a court order freezing the elephants on Bucky's property, but Dick feared Murray was about to take off again. Could the FBI help him get the elephants back?

Kieny called New Jersey. The prosecutor's office in Monmouth County verified Dick's story and forwarded some paperwork. There was certainly no problem construing this as a federal case, to justify FBI involvement. By law, interstate transport of stolen property worth more than $5,000 is a federal offense. In practice, the FBI didn't usually look at anything under $50,000; otherwise they'd be chasing every car thief in the country. The elephants, Kieny learned, had a value of more than $100,000.

Kieny liked the endless skies and fields of East Texas; he enjoyed the ninety-minute drive up to Bucky's place. Discreetly, from the red dirt road, he looked the property over. Bucky's driveway was secured with an orange pipe gate, and the entire eighty-one acres was fenced with barbed wire. Walking the perimeter, charting distances and noting exits, Kieny heard the unmistakable sound of elephants. He drove back to Tyler and began work on an affidavit—in effect, an application for a

search warrant that would enable the FBI to seize Tory and
Dutchess as evidence of a violation of the section of the United
States Code that deals with interstate transport.

Holed up in his log home, Bucky Steele wondered when the
goddamn circus was going to end. Phone ringing off the hook,
idiots with dumb questions, strange vehicles prowling around.
Seemed the whole world had found out where Murray had got
arrested, and they all wanted something for nothing. Is Murray
Hill there? Could I please speak to Rip? I have a person-to-
person long-distance call for Mr. Arlan Seidon. Talk about your
media maggots, shee-it, the place was crawling with them. People asked Bonnie leading questions, wanted in the barn to take
pictures of the elephants, even followed the kids around—
Bucky, slamming down the phone for the umpteenth time, was
about ready to bite some goddamn heads off.

And then some walking hairdo from Shreveport opened the
gate, strode past the NO TRESPASSING sign up the driveway to the
house, checked herself in the window, and knocked confidently
on the front door. Bucky asked what the hell she wanted. Why,
to put the elephants on the news. Big smile, like they're doing
you a goddamn favor and you're supposed to be grateful! Do
these dumbbells not understand a thing? Why not just put the
elephants in a police lineup so the Drakes can study them and
say, yeah, that one on the left, and this one here. Like the sheriff said, before they can take the elephants they got to be able to
prove which is which.

"Going to put them on TV, are you?"

"News at six."

"I know what that racket's all about," said Bucky. "Hell, I've
made a few movies. Generally I get paid for it, if you see what
I'm driving at."

"But this is news."

"It's television, ain't it? Don't people get paid in television?"

"We won't disturb you. A few minutes is all."

"You know what liability insurance runs? What do you think they'll say if some idiot cameraman gets his head took off?"

"We'll be careful, Mr. Steele. Now, if we may, we'll take the crew down to the barn?"

"Get the hell out. And don't come back."

The smile was fading fast—the walking hairdo was going to have some explaining to do back at the station. "Mr. Steele," she said, trying to keep it light but unable to prevent deep furrows of frustration from creasing her unnaturally pretty face, "has anyone ever told you you're a very uncooperative person?"

"This is private property. You got two minutes to get off of it."

The walking hairdo let it be known that Bucky was unstable —go near the place and you risked getting run off with a twelve-gauge. Still the media horde kept coming, phoning at all hours of day and night, pleading, cajoling, camping beyond the fence line with telephoto lenses. The most persistent one of all, the Steeles sent on a wild-goose chase down to Marshall. You'll find Murray at the auction tonight, they told her, can't miss him, he's wearing a safari suit. That got rid of her, and Bucky figured they might finally get some peace and quiet. Next morning, when he went out to see what the commotion was all about, he found a goddamn helicopter buzzing the place! Sick of the whole deal, wanting Murray and the elephants out of his hair, he phoned the sheriff.

"Look, Walter, you got your man. Why don't you take the elephants while you're at it?"

"Take them where?" said Sheriff Thomas. "We're not talking about a stolen car I can lock up in the pound."

"You'll need 'em for evidence."

"Long as I know where they are, we know where to go when we need them."

"I've got a mind to tie them off to the parking meters in front of your office."

"I wouldn't do that. Your barn's plenty big enough."

"I'm supposed to feed the goddamn things while the court

figures out what to do with them? Just like I been doing for the last year? There's a few people getting suckered on this thing, Walter, know that?"

"Think I'm going to hire extra deputies just to change their diapers? The elephants stay right there."

On his résumé, C. B. Wiley describes himself as, among other things, past director of the Boy Scouts of America; past president of the Van Zandt County (Texas) Cancer Society; past president of the Canton First Monday 100-Year Centennial Corporation; member of the American Potbellied Pig Association, Texas Longhorn Breeders Association, Ankola Watusi International Breeders Association, and Exotic Wildlife Association; founder and head trainer of the Van Zandt County Bloodhound Team; private investigator; Texas longhorn cattle rancher; former federal class three machine-gun dealer; ex-candidate for sheriff; gunsmith; ex–clinical researcher for the use of succinylcholine chloride; ex-instructor for firearms safety; graduate of four Dale Carnegie schools; holder of a state trapping license; author of the only complete training video on the ABCs of animal tranquilization; instructor in the use of cannon nets, wing nets, and drop nets; licensed peace officer; ex–U.S. Army paratrooper; and notary public.

It was his proprietorship of the C. B. Wiley and Son Exotic Animal Ranch, however, that prompted Dick Drake to call him. The FBI had been authorized to seize the elephants, Kieny had told Dick, but they needed a suitable rig and somewhere to lodge them pending disposition of the Texas court case. Kieny had worked with Wiley in the past and knew he had an exotic-animal compound next to his gun shop near Canton.

When Dick called to ask about boarding elephants, Wiley said he could put them up, all right, but had no way of transporting them. Dick worked the phone, calling contacts in the animal business, then prospects in the Yellow Pages. Tell you what, we've got these two elephants to move to California? Do the haul free and we'll make sure you get all kinds of publicity. Why, I got a list of media contacts. . . .

He finally found someone in Texarkana with a North American Van Lines rig. The fellow said he'd make the haul for a thousand dollars. The rig had seen better days but was sound enough to do the run and, if necessary, serve as winter housing for the elephants back in California. Dick, with financial backing from a friend in California, arranged to buy it for $3,000. All that remained was to move on Bucky's place.

Early one November morning, everybody gathered in Marshall—Dick and Eddie; C. B. Wiley and his son, Cash; George Kieny and other FBI agents. While the Drakes and the Wileys reinforced the floors and walls of the trailer, the FBI prepared with military precision, going over and over the plan. Dick loved the nylon FBI jackets and walkie-talkies and automatic weapons—couldn't wait to see the look on Murray's face.

Six vehicles accompanied the rig as it made its way up to Jefferson, then west toward Bucky's. When they got to the intersection three miles from the property, who should they spot coming out of the convenience store, short-haired and clean-shaven, looking preoccupied and opening a pack of Camels?

Murray wished to hell he could quit smoking. Sometimes he coughed so much his belly hurt. No point worrying—he had more important things to worry about. The hearing into custody of the girls was set for that afternoon. No use even trying to get off the weed when your guts were churning. If the hearing blew up in his face, well, the Mexican border was only two hours away. So long as he planned it carefully . . .

Climbing on his bicycle, he noticed a North American Van Lines rig turn into the gas station. When three cars followed, he knew something was amiss—the cars were clean and anonymous, and they had antennas. He set down his bike and started for the pay phone but a casually dressed fellow got out, intercepting him, to ask if he knew a certain family in the area.

"I don't, but try the lady in the store."

When Murray picked up the receiver, Eddie stepped out of another car. Before Murray could finish dialing, Eddie had grabbed his arm and twisted it behind his back.

"I'll cripple you, motherfucker."

Murray broke free and went into the convenience store to call the sheriff's department. A deputy told him there was nothing they could do. He called Mike Aranson, who'd left for the Dallas–Fort Worth airport to fly in for the custody hearing. His secretary said she'd try him on the car phone; Murray had to wait around, pacing and smoking, while the FBI caravan headed off to Bucky's. When Aranson finally called back, he said he didn't understand how the FBI could move with a court date imminent; he tried to reassure Murray.

Out at Bucky's, meanwhile, the FBI team, brandishing weapons, stormed the place. It reminded Dick of those drug busts on TV, with screeching cars and armed agents yelling to each other. George Kieny informed Bucky they had a search warrant to see whether the Drakes' elephants were on the property; if so, they planned to remove them.

"Shee-it," said Bucky, rubbing his neck, "bust in like that, I'd hate for my children to be in that driveway. Think we're goddamn criminals or something."

"We're here to execute the warrant, Mr. Steele."

"Yeah, well, I'm going back in the house."

"Can't let you. The warrant gives us complete authority."

"I know, I know," said Bucky. "You can do any goddamn thing you want. You can step on my kids and bugger my cattle, because you're the feds."

Once he calmed down, Bucky turned out to be cooperative enough. He led the Drakes and the FBI to the elephants, griping about how he never should have let him and them goddamn elephants come in the first place. Zola, Chang, and Lulu watched from the steel corral; Tory and Dutchess were back in the woods, chained to stakes. Bucky's three looked healthy and fit compared to Tory and Dutchess, who were noticeably underweight.

It was an emotional time for Dick, the culmination of a five-year search—it was all he could do to hold back tears of joy. "Listen to them, Ed, they remember us, see that? This one's Tory," he told George Kieny. "You can tell by the tip of the trunk here. See how it flops open?"

"They just like you remember them?" said Kieny.

"You never forget," said Dick. "They're part of the family. Look how skinny they've got—look at them ribs showing through. Look at Tory's ear. Half of it's missing, must have froze or something. And this is the guy telling everybody we abused them! Look at them. You tell me who didn't treat 'em right. Come on, Dutchess, we're going home."

Dick unchained the elephants and led them out. When they didn't move smartly enough, Eddie used his hook. In a jolly mood, he said to one of the agents, "You know where her sex organs are, don't you?"

"Can't say I do. Never gave it any thought."

"In her foot."

"You kidding me?"

"No, sir," said Eddie. "If she steps on you, you're fucked."

Tory and Dutchess were reluctant to enter the unfamiliar trailer, but Eddie, raising his voice and using his hook, got them loaded. Before they left, Kieny apologized to Bucky. It's not that they were expecting trouble, he said, but you never knew what the situation would be.

"Hate to think what it'd be like if you were expecting trouble," said Bucky.

"That's right," Bonnie agreed.

Two agents had been posted on the red dirt road to intercept Murray. When he'd showed up, pedaling for all he was worth, they'd told him he could go no farther. They listened to his story for a good half-hour, keeping him away from the property.

At Bucky's, everybody laughed and joked as they prepared to pull out with the elephants. Piece of cake—even the weather was perfect. The cavalcade proceeded along the dirt road, rounded a corner . . .

. . . and there was Murray, flagging them down. The operation so far couldn't have gone more smoothly; Kieny wondered if their luck had run out. Murray had been reasonable enough at the store. He was ludicrously outmanned, but you never knew. This was someone who, five years earlier, had decided his most promising option was to disappear with two elephants. Kieny and two other agents stepped out of their cars; the rest kept weapons at the ready.

"I need to know what's happening with the girls."

Inside the trailer, Dutchess chirped and Tory rumbled in response to Murray's voice; their trunks snaked out the trailer door, which had been left ajar for ventilation. Like twin periscopes, both trunks turned in the direction of his scent.

"They're on the way out," said Kieny. "We're authorized to repossess them."

"You can't," said Murray. "You can't. There's a court order. Nobody can move them before the hearing this afternoon."

"The FBI is a federal agency."

Dick, watching Murray talk and gesture and light one cigarette off the last, almost felt sorry for the little thief. That haunted face, that wasted little frame—it was amazing how he'd aged. For most people, their fifties are the last really fruitful decade. Murray had wasted those years, to say nothing of the time and energy he'd cost Dick. Here it was over and he still wouldn't let go, doing his damnedest to persuade George of something or other. Kieny listened and nodded patiently. What was Murray going on about?

Turned out he only wanted the leg chains, to remember the girls by.

Up all night, couldn't sleep at all. This morning I went and fed Bucky's girls and shoveled the shit. Bucky and Bonnie avoid me if they can. The atmosphere isn't good. Meanwhile I'm stuck here. Part of my bail is that I can't leave Marion County until this thing is sorted out.

I can't understand the so-called justice system in this country. FBI stands for Federal Bureau of Investigation and what did they investigate? Not a goddamn thing. They listened to one side of the story and moved on it. I'm totally disgusted. Why would the feds get involved at this point? Especially the timing the way it was—a few hours before the custody hearing. The whole thing stinks. Seems they can do whatever the hell they want.

Aranson thinks I should probably go back to New Jersey voluntarily, not make them go through the whole extradition. He said we could fight it, throw bricks in the road, but that will only delay things. I don't like lawyers and now I've got one in every goddamn city. Nobody knows what's going to happen. Mike Caulfield told me not to push too hard on the feds, it will only aggravate them. There's several charges they could nail me on. Aranson figures they'll go ahead with interstate transport of stolen property. Looks like I'll go to jail one way or the other. The feds could also go after Bucky for being an accessory. Why that son of a bitch would turn me in when he stands to get charged I don't know. Maybe he's just dumb.

I've always been willing to accept the consequences of my actions, figuring it was the only way to get justice. Now I know I'm never going to get justice. But I believe I did the right thing and if I had it to do over I'd do the same. But it eats me up that Drakes have the girls back. All I can do now is keep fighting in court. I'm never going to stop fighting.

I'm worried about the girls. I'm worried that if Dutchess steps out of line, they'll knock the shit out of her. The rig they took them out in isn't even roadworthy—no skylight, no ventilation. I can't see how Drakes could get permits to take them to California, but that won't stop them. I just hope the girls are all right. I don't even know where they are.

After trucking the elephants over to Canton and unloading them at C. B. Wiley's place, Dick suggested a group photo. It was a triumphant moment, a type of satisfaction he'd not often known, and he wanted it to last. Tory and Dutchess—bobbing and weaving nervously, adjusting to their new quarters—were more than stolen property he'd recovered. They were sweet vindication. For the first time, Dick had thrown himself into something and wound up a winner.

Everybody huddled together, smiling for the camera. Somebody realized that ten of the twelve FBI agents from the Tyler office had taken part in the operation. "Cheese," he said. "I sure hope nobody's robbing any banks right now."

A veterinarian came out the next day to examine the elephants. Dick delighted in pointing out what tough shape they were in; he was gratified when Travis Dean, who had worked for Wiley in the past, found Tory underweight and emaciated, suffering from low-grade anemia and low blood protein. (Tory had been anemic all her life.) In Dutchess the vet also found symptoms consistent with poor nutrition and internal parasitism. "Both animals were in a less than adequate nutritional state," his report concluded, "with low blood protein and mild internal parasitism. Skin damage was present on the ears of both elephants. The mental response in Dutchess was less than in Tory. Tory was in a worse physical condition than Dutchess. Both animals need routine worming and an improved high-protein balanced diet." Dick headed back to California to look into permits, leaving the elephants in the care of Eddie, who impressed the Wiley family with his diligence.

In the courts, meanwhile, the badminton game was heating up. Duke DeWare had followed up the Drakes' original petition —which named both Murray and Bucky Steele as defendants— with an amended petition for injunction. Bucky's lawyer had filed a counterclaim; in effect, Bucky wanted some board money before turning Tory and Dutchess over to anybody. This prompted DeWare to file a motion to dismiss Bucky's counterclaim. Meanwhile, Mike Aranson was in there swinging on Murray's behalf. The shuttlecock whizzed back and forth.

Three weeks after the FBI operation, on December 14, 1989, a U.S. district judge, "being advised of the inadequate temporary facilities now being used to house the two Indian elephants Tory and Dutchess," granted the Drakes permission to move them to Tehachapi, stipulating that they not be used for any commercial purpose until the civil action in Texas had been resolved.

By the terms of the Endangered Species Act, the Drakes needed a permit from the U.S. Fish and Wildlife Service before they could legally transport Tory and Dutchess interstate. Their old permit had lapsed after Murray repossessed the elephants; Dick had applied for a new one, but it hadn't been granted by the time, just before Christmas, he loaded the elephants, thanked C. B. Wiley and George Kieny for their help, and headed off to California. Shoot first, ask questions later.

The weather had turned cold, and the rig wasn't winterized. On the way home the Drakes encountered subzero temperatures. It was too cold to travel at night and in Albuquerque they got a motel. Eddie stayed in the truck with the elephants while Kenny and Dick shared a room. They'd brought along a propane heater; whenever the temperature in the trailer dipped into the forties Eddie fired it up. The frigid weather made for a long trip; Dick, who had tipped off the local paper, had never been happier to see the sign on Highway 58: TEHACHAPI, POPULATION 5,664."

The true population is more like twenty thousand these days. Real-estate prices have gone through the roof as people have moved out from Los Angeles. Jack Palance has a cattle ranch in the area, as does Chuck Connors, and Debbie Reynolds is rumored to be the money behind the new plaza in Old Town. Everywhere you look, parcels of fenced scrub have sprouted FOR SALE signs: AVAILABLE 12.4 ACRES. SIX-SCREEN MOVIE THEATER COMING SOON. NOW LEASING—NEW SHOPPING CENTER—RETAIL—FOOD—OFFICE. You can still pick up fried chicken gizzards and a fifth of Old Grand-Dad at the Texaco station, and Louis L'Amour still outsells Danielle Steel at Pay 'n' Save, but the signs are everywhere. Progress has come to Tehachapi.

Much else had changed in the seven years since the elephants were last in the high desert, including the lives of Dick and Eddie. They got home three days before Christmas and put the elephants in the barn at Cameron Canyon. Next morning Eddie took his kids out to see these mythical creatures they'd heard so much about; then he and Dick trucked them to the café where Doy waited tables. The Drakes and the elephants were local celebrities; so many people were asking to see Tory and Dutchess that Dick figured the easiest thing was to invite the whole town to a public celebration. Hundreds of people turned out to watch Tory and Dutchess eat a chocolate cake Doy had baked for them. Dick told the crowd it felt good to have the elephants again; it was like getting the family back together. The *Tehachapi News* ran a big picture on the front page with the caption "Elephants' odyssey ends."

It was such a hectic time, Christmas and all, and Dick was so tired from the trip, it wasn't until the elephants were back in the barn at Cameron Canyon and he was up at Indian Hill that he got a chance to reflect on a question that had begun gnawing at him on the way home. Looking for Tory and Dutchess had occupied a large part of his life for much of the 1980s. He'd become as fanatical about finding them as Murray had been about hiding them. Bringing them home was deeply satisfying, the best Christmas present he could have wished for. Only thing was, now that he'd got them back, what was he going to do with them?

Between working on a public-corruption case and buying Christmas presents for his family, George Kieny found himself wondering what would possess a man to do what Murray Hill had done. People's motives were usually simple enough— ninety-eight percent of the crime Kieny encountered grew out of greed or anger or lust. The elephant case was different, harder to reckon. This wasn't greed or anger or lust, it was pride and principle. Seemed a shame to ruin your life over a couple of animals, and it certainly looked like Murray's life was ruined. The assistant U.S. attorney was eager to prosecute the federal case, and New Jersey was pressing ahead with the extradition. Murray was done like dinner. The only question was whether he'd be incarcerated in Texas or New Jersey.

Kieny figured Murray must have cared deeply for the elephants and believed in what he was doing. Fair enough, Kieny could respect that. But how could you feel sorry for someone who'd flouted the law, brought his troubles on himself, and put others through trying times? Back East they were playing Murray up as some sort of hero, a renegade St. Francis. In California, of course, Dick was the hero and Murray the villain. The papers liked it that way—good guy and bad guy. Law enforcement taught you about the many stops in between.

Kieny was an upbeat fellow who appreciated the richness of life; he was always researching his wife's Spanish heritage—they'd traced her family all the way back to the time of Columbus—or planning a hiking and trout-fishing trip with his son. Sometimes, though, remembering the unsolved murders, he got down in the dumps. Like everyone in the Tyler office—in many FBI offices across the country—he also felt the growing weight of the savings-and-loan scandal. It was a bottomless pit; the Bureau's resources were being poured into it.

Multiple murder, billion-dollar fraud: every so often you needed a laugher to boost morale. Around the Tyler office, the elephant seizure was known as the EAT case (for Elephant Attack Team); at the Christmas party, the agents had a few drinks and reminisced. One of the wives had written a poem, and she recited it to the revelers. It was a takeoff on "The Night Before Christmas," and it ended:

> *The Dallas office may be known for a lot in the paper*
> *Now Tyler is known for the elephant caper.*
> *We wonder what special training these men must complete*
> *To pull off this rescue that they did so neat.*
> *I know we feel safer knowing they're around*
> *Criminals tremble when they come to town.*
> *They deal everyday with toil and strife,*
> *But they're proud to be agents in the circus of life!*

Mired at Bucky's place, broke and drained and disheartened, Murray was finding the holidays a good deal less festive. Another year stuck someplace he didn't want to be. Another Christmas he couldn't spend with his family, and now he didn't even have Tory and Dutchess for company. He couldn't help recalling the girls' nervousness and fear when he'd unloaded them at Bunny's place; couldn't help imagining Eddie wielding his hook. What an awful, helpless feeling. Nothing he could do but sit in the mansion, paint eggshell earrings, check the mail, and consult with his various lawyers.

The first question was whether to go back to New Jersey voluntarily. Extradition is an elaborate and costly procedure, particularly if contested. It would make life easier for everybody, Mike Caulfield and Isabelle Strauss believed, if Murray returned voluntarily. If he didn't, the prosecutor might well use his reluctance against him in the courtroom.

Murray agreed to return to Monmouth County and was released from Marion County on his own recognizance. The assistant U.S. attorney in Tyler, believing Murray would be vigorously prosecuted in New Jersey, backed off the federal charges. No point proceeding in both jurisdictions.

There are four degrees of indictable crime in New Jersey, and theft can be either second- or third-degree, depending on the value of the stolen goods. If the goods are worth more than $75,000, it's a second-degree crime; under $75,000, third-degree. Back in 1984, when the grand jury had indicted Murray, it had had to assign a value to Tory and Dutchess. To ascertain their value, someone in the prosecutor's office had called Dick Drake in California. Unaware of the significance of his answer, Dick had replied that the elephants were worth about $70,000. As a result, Murray had been indicted for theft in the third degree.

Had Dick said $80,000, Murray would have been indicted for second-degree theft. The distinction is critical. First- and second-degree crimes carry the presumption of incarceration. The second-degree sentencing range lies between five and ten years; the presumptive sentence is seven years. When someone is found guilty of a second-degree crime in New Jersey, by plea or by trial, the sentencing judge starts at seven years and then looks at mitigating or exacerbating factors. Does the defendant have a prior record? What's his work history? Educational background? Community involvement? If the answers create a favorable impression, the judge moves down from seven years; if they suggest a bad apple, he moves up.

Third- and fourth-degree crimes, by contrast, carry the presumption of a suspended or probationary sentence. Dick's off-hand answer, in other words, stood to mean the difference between a prison term for Murray and a slap on the wrist.

In early 1990, Monmouth County had five judges in the Criminal Division of Superior Court, only four of whom actually heard cases. In a typical week there might be a hundred cases listed for trial. Like other jurisdictions, Monmouth County disposes of as many cases as possible by plea negotiation and by diversionary programs such as pretrial intervention (PTI).

PTI enables nonviolent first offenders to avoid the criminal-justice procedure altogether, and helps the county to reduce its caseload. Accepted candidates are granted supervised release for a fixed time while performing community service. Upon successful completion of that service, and expiration of the probationary period, the indictment is dismissed; they're left with no criminal record.

At first Mike Caulfield sought to have the charges against Murray dropped altogether. He felt there were valid questions of jurisdiction—why had the case been heard in New Jersey in the first place? The sale of the elephants had taken place in Oregon; the contracting parties lived in Missouri and California; the elephants had been repossessed in Pennsylvania. The Monmouth County prosecutor was unwilling to drop the charges but he let Caulfield cut an excellent deal. If Murray presented himself for arraignment on the theft warrant, he'd be freed on bail of $10,000. While on bail, he'd be permitted to stay out of state, at Robin's apartment in Manhattan, and see his grandson. And if he was accepted into the PTI program, the prosecutor would not veto it.

Murray seemed to Caulfield a likely candidate for the PTI program. He'd committed a third-degree offense; his crime was nonviolent; he had no prior record. There were, however, two strikes against him. He'd been a fugitive for five years, and he had, by generating publicity for himself, held the prosecutor's office up to ridicule. Nonetheless, the PTI director found him to be a suitable candidate; the county prosecutor endorsed his admittance; and Murray headed off to perform his community service at a place called the Primate Foundation in Arizona.

Paul and Jo Fritz, old friends of Murray's from circus days, house unwanted chimps in a private complex in the desert near Phoenix. They provide a setting where chimps rejected by zoos, or dumped by owners who'd bought them as pets, live undisturbed in large colonies, as they do in the wild. When Murray told them of his legal plight and the requirement that he perform community service, they invited him down to help out.

In early 1990, while Murray was fulfilling the terms of his PTI by doing odd jobs at the chimp haven—welding, carpentry, trapping skunks—a district judge in Marshall, Texas, awarded Dick and Eddie permanent custody of the elephants. He ordered them to comply with "all federal and state regulations regarding care, maintenance, transport, and use of said animals." The Drakes, he ruled, were the "true and lawful owners" of Tory and Dutchess.

Animal stories are supposed to have happy endings. They're supposed to be heartwarming tales in which the connection between man and beast proves stronger than the forces of chaos and evil. The good guys, after their tribulations, are supposed to get their reward, the bad guys their comeuppance. Through it all the animals persevere; they overcome daunting adversity and find their way home to those who care most for them. This restoration returns the world to moral equilibrium; it renews our faith in sacrifice, fidelity, and love.

In the story of Murray Hill and the Drakes, and Tory and Dutchess, the happy ending is elusive. What ending, in fact, would be altogether happy? If the story were fiction, what conclusion would seem most appropriate? Which would the reader desire more keenly—a fitting end for the people involved, or for the elephants?

A number of people who appear in these pages were asked to suggest the ending they felt would be most satisfying. Some wanted to see the girls returned by the courts to Murray. Given events to date, and the shortcomings of the system by which we protect ourselves from one another, that's unlikely to happen. Someone suggested that the happiest ending would be for Murray to acquire an orphaned baby elephant from Asia, to start all over again knowing what he knows now. But endangered species may no longer be transported internationally, and such an ending fails to take Tory and Dutchess into account. Someone else envisioned a final scene in which Dick and Murray shook hands, admitted what stubborn fools they'd been, and swapped stories about their adventures. Given their personalities and the depth of bitterness between them, that's not going to happen either.

Someone with strong views about animal rights suggested that the happiest ending of all would have Tory and Dutchess airlifted back to Thailand or Burma, and set free. A herd of Asian elephants will accept newcomers, and Tory and Dutchess could certainly adapt to the wild, but the idea is hopelessly utopian. Human incursion has radically altered elephant habitats in every Asian country; there is precious little "wild" left. The girls can no more return to the lives they were born into than Murray can return to the New York of his youth, when he visited his grandparents on Coney Island and his cousins swam home across the sparkling waters of Sheepshead Bay.

Several people expressed the view that Murray and Dick both deserved their fates; that the real victims are the girls. Perhaps. But are they victims of an obsessive dispute? Of the limitations of the justice system? Or are they more properly victims of our shortsighted and despotic tendency to consider ourselves both separate from the animal kingdom and superior to it?

Our ancestors joined their fellow creatures in unions of mutual benefit. Domesticated wolves, with keen ears and noses, warned of danger in return for discarded bones and a place by the fire; they became dogs. Donkeys, with stubborn resilience, eased man's physical burden. Oxen, with plodding strength, drew water and enhanced the productivity of agricultural land. Camels, with their broad feet, provided a means of mastering the sands. Horses, with their unique combination of speed and endurance, made possible new ways of conducting husbandry and warfare. Asian elephants, with mighty finesse, facilitated, among other things, the teak industry.

Our ancestors' reliance on animals, and close contact with them, led to a veneration that post-industrial man reserved for the automobile—the horseless carriage—and that technological man now bestows on the eighty-megabyte hard drive. People adore their pets, of course, and old-style unions persist here and there. Seeing-eye dogs guide their blind masters in partnerships of profound intimacy. Elephants and their oozies, fewer each year, labor on in Thailand and Burma and Sri Lanka. The nose that scented a marauding bear now detects illegal drugs. No all-terrain vehicle can do the work of a cutting horse, and cats have proven to be remarkably therapeutic companions for the autistic and the senile.

In large measure, though, animals in the Western world have been relegated to ceremony, sport, or enslavement. Many species of livestock are nurtured with laced feed and raised in conditions of appalling deprivation, so that we may dine economically on meat. Thoroughbreds are saddled, booted, and whipped along a race course, so that we may bet on their order of finish. Broncos and Brahma bulls are spurred into displays of violent agitation, so that we may compare our talents of subjugation. Exotic animals, their natural habitats turned increasingly to human purposes, pace up and down in cages, imprisoned without trial so that we may point them out to our children and, perhaps, reassure ourselves that they exist. Our changing relation to other animals may be best symbolized by a patent granted in 1988 to Harvard University for its "oncomice," creatures genetically engineered to be susceptible to cancer for use by Du Pont Chemical.

To many urban children, wild animals are exotic fictions seen only on television and T-shirts, no more real than Teenage Mutant Ninja Turtles. Gradually we eradicate animals from our lives, banish them to the margins of our empathy. In the process we induce in ourselves a kind of schizophrenia. Capable we may be of grand scientific, technological, and artistic schemes. Stunningly complex instruments are maneuvered through the heavens, wealth is created out of copper futures, and Monet stirs in us the noblest sentiments. Yet we too are animals, with no choice but to eat and defecate, replenish the white cells in our blood, and prolong our survival through procreation. Evolution has placed us at one end of the natural continuum, but not removed us from it.

As the only animals able to argue our hegemony in nature, we point to the size of our brains, our repertoire of emotions, our written language and awareness of history. Yet man exercises his will in the natural world with the brutal disregard of the tyrant, and the achievements that would astonish and perplex our forebears are, after all, relative. Is the satellite dish any more marvelous than a dying salmon that returns to the pool in which it was spawned? Does an eighty-story office tower bespeak greater ingenuity than the termite mounds of the Serengeti? The deterioration of the planet under our stewardship may be proof enough that our assumption of superiority is self-delusion.

Ah, but there is hope! Each year, the moral fitness of protecting rather than exploiting other creatures is more widely argued, more deeply enshrined in legislation. Prison sentences have recently been imposed on people convicted of animal abuse. The campaign to disrupt the trade in ivory has brightened the future of the African elephant. Sweden has passed legislation outlawing many of the gruesome livestock- and poultry-raising practices of which most of us prefer to remain ignorant. The capture of killer whales for public display draws public censure; canners appeal to consumers by advertising tuna as dolphin-friendly; more and more cosmetics companies refine their products without blinding laboratory animals.

The legal and moral questions raised by Murray's fugitive odyssey—Was he justified in what he did? At what point does heavy-handed treatment of an animal constitute abuse? Who should own Tory and Dutchess?—grow out of more basic issues. When should human materialism be allowed to supersede the natural order? What rights of ownership should man be permitted to exercise over other sentient beings? How can we justify the chaining, caging, and disciplining of creatures whose natural entitlement is no less sacred than our own?

Such questions are of interest to a growing segment of the population, but they are questions our courts remain unequipped to deal with. Slavery was once broadly accepted, of course, and child labor used to be universal. The law gradually caught up with public understanding, and these practices were outlawed as barbaric. The same evolving morality has, in Murray's lifetime, made the animal-rights movement a social and political force. It has begun to change the way our institutions adjudicate the moral obligations of our standing in the animal kingdom. And it has made Murray Hill, and animal trainers of his generation, members of a dying breed.

The life Murray led as a young man has been legislated out of existence. No longer can you make your living by putting a caged chimp in the backseat and driving from nightclub to nightclub. You can't import elephants from Bangkok or gorillas from Nairobi. Some North American cities have banned live animal acts, and some traveling circuses attract as many protesters as paying customers.

Despite his extensive experience with exotic animals of all kinds, Murray today couldn't get a job as a zookeeper. The modern zoo is embarrassed by the old-time animal man, preferring to hire college-educated conservationists to project the image of a scientific and educational institution. The question of what Murray was going to do with the remainder of his life began weighing on him in Arizona, and Paul and Jo wondered how they could help. They offered him a job as a maintenance man at the Primate Foundation and were relieved when he declined. It wouldn't have been easy watching someone who'd been an equal reduced to menial servility—not that Murray was the servile type.

When he'd completed his community service near Phoenix, Murray visited his mother and his brother in Tucson. In spite of her financial support, Shirley Seidon couldn't understand why her son would willingly break the law; she disapproved of what he'd done and told friends that he'd broken her heart. She was in failing health, and their time together, though weighted with the knowledge that it was likely to be their last, did little to heal their differences.

Murray stayed with his brother for a while, and they talked at length about the future. Wally and his wife had started a salsa-manufacturing business, and Murray got sufficiently involved to see it wouldn't have been something he cared to pursue, even if the enterprise had grown to the point where it could have afforded an employee.

Meanwhile, he felt the old stirring in his blood. It was spring-time, and all the shows would be going out—the blacktop Bedouins gearing up for another nomadic trek through the shopping malls and fairgrounds of North America. He could have signed on with one of them, handling elephants, trucking through the night, setting up and tearing down, but he was sixty years old and in no shape to go on the road.

In the end, he took the bus back to Missouri, to the farm now owned by his brother and occupied by his estranged wife. Denise had put her life back together and adjusted to being on her own—Murray's return was the last thing she wanted. But he had to go somewhere, and there was nowhere else to go.

Dick's last bit of unfinished business with the elephants resulted from his cavalier attitude to permits. California Fish and Game was breathing down his neck and threatening to prosecute. Bringing the elephants into the state without a permit had been illegal. Summoned to a hearing in Municipal Court, he pled guilty to four charges connected to the unlawful entry of the elephants. He received three years' probation and an $11,000 fine, which was suspended indefinitely. His violation went virtually unpunished, in other words, and he was granted the necessary permit after the fact.

These days Dick has his hands full at Indian Hill Campground, where there are always a hundred jobs to be done. He and Doy are busier than ever with the powwow each summer. He has commitments at the Masonic Lodge, he gets involved in civic projects, and the members of a local New Age group seem to have decided, improbably, that Dick is one of them, if only he knew it. The group has chosen Tehachapi as the place from which to levitate when the apocalypse comes; in recent years they've bought up some prime real-estate in the area. Group members refer to him as Brother Dick; when they found out he had a tractor-trailer, they asked him to haul a load of books up from San Diego. Curious as to why they approached him, he was told the Lord had chosen him to make the run.

"I see," said Dick. "And did he say how much I was supposed to get paid?"

Eddie Drake, too, is busier than ever—five kids in six years will do that. In the decade since the Drakes bought the elephants, his life has changed in ways that make it impractical for him to work them. Going on the road isn't as simple as it used to be. Children cost money, and Eddie has to go where the work is. For a time he operated a crane on a military base near Riverside, California, while Julie and the kids stayed in Tehachapi.

That left Dick's and Doy's second son, Kenny, to care for the elephants. Kenny is a taciturn, gap-toothed young man who wears jeans and a peaked cap. "It's great having them back," he said, soon after Tory and Dutchess had been returned to Tehachapi. "We missed them after Murray Hill stole them. It's more than just money. Once you've spent time with elephants, it's like they're part of the family."

Eddie still felt a proprietary interest, however, and couldn't resist offering advice. Kenny figured so long as he was shoveling the shit, he got to do things his own way. The brothers have always had a testy relationship; their disputes about the handling of Tory and Dutchess led to shouting matches, sullen silences, and fistfights. When the work in Riverside ended, Eddie moved back to Tehachapi and found that the house at Cameron Canyon wasn't big enough for both their families. He ran Kenny, his girlfriend, and their daughter off the property, and took over the house and the elephants himself. And though he got some work for Tory and Dutchess—including a shoot for a Japanese video—the jobs seemed harder to come by than ever, and costs kept going up. Selling the elephants began to look like the only realistic option.

Somebody with a twenty-thousand-acre ranch in Hawaii expressed interest in buying them, but that didn't work out. Dick and his financial backer spoke to several circuses; they found a buyer in George Carden, who runs Carden-Johnson Circus out of Springfield, Missouri—not twenty miles from where Murray lives. The deal took some negotiating. It seems Carden wanted to buy the elephants on time; Dick, knowing that even the most well-meaning among us sometimes fail to meet our obligations, preferred cash.

So the girls, after all this, end up back in the circus ring, coerced into choreographed behavior? Maybe; then again, the tale may be unfinished. For a time it was rumored that Michael Jackson, the pop star, planned to buy the girls and add them to his menagerie. One of the movie studios was said to be kicking around the idea of acquiring them. Murray, though happy that the Drakes were getting rid of them, doesn't like the idea of their being put to work. Fact is, he's quietly determined to get the girls back and—as we've seen—he's a man whose determination is not to be taken lightly.

Perhaps one day he'll even recover Onyx, the bull who tried to kill him, from the Springfield zoo. His dream is to reunite the Mitie Mites—not to work them, to let them live out their lives with few restraints. He wants to create a place for all manner of unwanted elephants and has drawn up the specifications for giant, energy-efficient, subterranean barns. If it sounds improbable, well, how probable is it that a man could spend five years as a fugitive with two full-grown elephants?

Perhaps no ending could be altogether satisfying; perhaps it's enough that there have been blessings along the way. Murray's understanding of the girls changed radically during the years in hiding. A period of excruciating deprivation turned out to be a time of change and growth as well. Strangers went to bat for him. But for their unselfish concern—and the irony of Dick's unwitting role in the lesser theft charge—Murray would have wound up in prison. Eddie Drake is more responsible at the end of the story than he was at the beginning. Dick, the man who never finished what he started, saw something through. At several junctures the Drakes could have resorted to primitive means of recourse. By accidental injury or exposure to the elements, the girls could have been disabled. Out of spite, they could have been put down. Considering all the terrible things that could have happened, perhaps the ending—if it really is the ending—isn't so unhappy after all.

Not long ago Howell Phillips IV retired, ending his career as an investment banker. Several of his colleagues were touched by scandal and may go to jail; he himself was not implicated. Mostly he putters around his New Jersey estate. He used to show visitors the elephant trails and stripped trees on his property, but nature soon took over; today few traces remain of Tory and Dutchess except for the pond that began as a single footprint. Howell still sees Veronica on weekends, though he plans —as he has for four years—to break off the relationship.

Howell's old friend Skip found Buddhism on his dope-sponsored wanderings through Asia. In Nepal he met an American woman who'd been a Buddhist for years; now married, they lived on the West Coast before moving to the Caribbean.

Bunny and Leonard Brook sold Meadow Gate Farm to developers, who carved it up into estate homes. The Brooks bought a larger farm, north of New York, where they keep even more animals and work even harder to feed them.

Dick's sister, Dot Wilkie, still lives with her husband and grown children on the property near Far Hills. Alex Wilkie still teaches martial arts and now worries about how his arsenal will be affected by the bleeding-heart legislation restricting the trade in automatic weapons.

Judge Peter Thomas has been appointed to the Appellate Division of the Superior Court of New Jersey.

Gerry Martin left Rinaldo and Rinaldo to practice law on his own from an unadorned little office near Union, New Jersey.

Bunce Atkinson is prospering; his bankruptcy expertise has stood him in good stead during the recession. He still hasn't been paid by the Drakes.

Isabelle Strauss increasingly devotes her time to animal-rights cases and hopes one day to meet Tory and Dutchess.

Bucky Steele still takes his elephants on the road and looks forward to the day he won't have to. Each year he and Bonnie and the kids become more self-sufficient. In the wake of Murray's arrest, the local weekly ran an article of Bucky's on the front page, which rekindled his literary dreams.

The young fellow who tipped off the Drakes (they refuse to identify him) no longer sends them letters asking when he's going to see the reward money.

In Jefferson, Texas, the judge who presided over Murray's bond hearing has a gold-painted shit shovel, appropriately inscribed, collecting dust in his office.

And what of Tory and Dutchess? We'll leave them for the moment in the high desert, dusting themselves, browsing contentedly on the bamboo that grows near the house where Eddie Drake lives, turning the heads of motorists who happen along Cameron Canyon Road. If it's disquieting to see them back in Tehachapi, there's something appealing and restorative about the way they accept their circumstances. They seem as unchanging in their essence as the desert or the mountains. Whether in the custody of Murray Hill or the Drakes, whether in Missouri or California, whether in hundred-degree heat or subzero cold, riding children on their backs or racking in their chains, prodded with a hook or bribed with a lemon drop, whether playing in mud or goaded into awkward poses, whether at the center of a circus ring or the center of a bitter vendetta, they confer on their surroundings an inviolate and mesmerizing dignity.

Maybe it's simple perseverance that gives the girls this majestic air. Maybe it's their awesome union of power and grace. Maybe it's the unhurried, shuffling way they go about their lives, giving equal value to everything they do. Maybe it's the way they constantly touch and smell and caress each other.

Or maybe it's the way they sometimes, at the same instant, interrupt whatever they're doing and freeze for a moment—just long enough to cast a skeptical eye on the exalted frailty of man.

About the Author

GARY ROSS is the author of two novels as well as many prize-winning articles and short stories. A former editor of *Saturday Night* magazine, he is currently a partner in the publishing firm of Macfarlane, Walter & Ross. *At Large* is his second work of nonfiction; his first, *Stung: The Incredible Obsession of Brian Molony,* earned critical acclaim around the world and was a number one bestseller in Canada. Ross lives near White Rock, British Columbia.